JTL

Journal
of
Turkish Literature

Bilkent University Center for Turkish Literature
Issue 2 (2005)
Ankara

Distributed internationally by Syracuse University Press and domestically by Dünya Süper Dağıtım Tic. ve San. A.Ş. and the Bilkent University Center for Turkish Literature.

Bilkent Üniversitesi adına sahibi: A. Kürşat Aydoğan. Yayın yönetmeni ve sorumlu müdür: Talât S. Halman. Yönetim yeri: Bilkent Üniversitesi Türk Edebiyatı Merkezi, 06800 Bilkent, Ankara. Tel: +90 (312) 290 2317. Faks: +90 (312) 266 4059. E-mail: *jtl@bilkent.edu.tr*. Basıldığı yer: Meteksan A.Ş., Ankara.

Cover design by İdil Avcıoğlu Battal. Cover image courtesy of the Topkapı Palace Museum (image has been restructured for cover design). Photo of Annemarie Schimmel courtesy of the Manuscript Dept. of the University Library of Basel. Photo of James Stewart-Robinson courtesy of Yvette Stewart-Robinson.

Special thanks to: Günil Özlem Ayaydın-Cebe, Reyyan Ayfer, Orhan Aytür, Nedim Bakan, Şaban Bavuk, Ümit Berkman, Demet Güzelsoy Chafra, Erkan Erginci, Wolfhart Heinrichs, Doğan Hızlan, *Journal of the American Oriental Society*, Mehmet Kalpaklı, Murat Kaman, Anooshirvan Miandji, Emine Öcal, Gudrun Schubert, Göksen Sonat, Behçet Şensoy, Nuran Tezcan, Jayne L. Warner, Cemal Yalabık, Hilmi Yavuz.

JTL

Journal of Turkish Literature

The *Journal of Turkish Literature*, published annually by the Center for Turkish Literature at Bilkent University, Ankara, Turkey, is the first and only international scholarly journal in English devoted in its entirety to Turkish literatures from their outset to the present day.

The literature of the Turks is among the oldest of living literatures. In nearly twelve centuries, it has been alive in many continents and regions, expressing itself in a diversity of languages and scripts, and remaining receptive to external influences as well as maintaining its intrinsic impetus for renewal. From Central Asia to Anatolia and beyond, it has served as a faithful mirror of Turkish societies and cultures, often functioning as a vehicle for pioneering ideas and ideals. As such, Turkish literature is both a repository of time-honored values and a powerful catalyst for change. *JTL* aims to reflect these aspects while encompassing the literary output of the Turks in Asia, the Middle East, the Balkans, and elsewhere. Its main emphasis is on Seljuk, Ottoman, and modern Turkish literature as well as on Central Asian roots.

Our inaugural issue, published in 2004, featured a panoply of articles—among them Walter G. Andrews's essay on Ottoman literature in modern Turkey and Jale Parla's study of narrative time in Adalet Ağaoğlu's *Dar Zamanlar*, a trilogy of novels. The issue's special feature was a hitherto unpublished comprehensive analysis of Mihrî Hatun's poetry by Nicholas N. Martinovitch, with accompanying brief essays by Geoffrey Fox, Didem Havlioğlu, and David Selim Sayers. The "Memorabilia" special was "Modern Turkish Poetry" by Orhan Burian. Two book reviews also appeared in issue 1—Ayşe Lahur Kırtunç on Aziz Nesin's *Istanbul Boy* and Richard McKane on *Romantic Communist*, a Nazım Hikmet biography by Saime Göksu and Edward Timms.

This second issue of *JTL* is proud to present a momentous study by the distinguished scholar Halil İnalcık, the doyen of the Ottoman historians, who makes his impressive entry into the literary field. His authoritative treatise entitled "The Poet and the Patron" brings new insights into the dynamics of the relations between the patrimonial state and the poetic arts in the Ottoman experience.

Robert Dankoff, the leading expert on Evliya Çelebi as well as on early Turkish literature, graces this issue with his seminal article on the *Seyahatname* from a literary vantage point. Our "Memorabilia" special is also a piece on Evliya Çelebi—Albert Howe Lybyer's 1917 essay entitled "The Travels of Evliya Effendi".

Modern literature is represented by three stimulating articles—on Adalet Ağaoğlu's plays by Sevda Şener and on Erendiz Atasü's novel *The Other Side of the Mountain* by Yasemin Alptekin and Dilek Doltaş. The issue contains two fine book reviews—one by Hande Birkalan-Gedik on İlhan Başgöz's *I, Hoca Nasreddin, Never Shall I Die*, and another by Erdağ Göknar on *The Unreadable Shores of Love* by Victoria Rowe Holbrook.

The *Journal of Turkish Literature* is committed to the principles of objective scholarship and critical analysis. Submissions and solicited articles are evaluated by international peer referees through a blind review process.

JTL hopes to provide new dimensions of literary assessment to the growing corpus of Turkish cultural studies in the international academic sphere.

The *JTL* editors welcome suggestions and critical comments from readers and subscribers. We hope *JTL* will make significant contributions to a better understanding of Turkish literature and culture.

Talât Sait Halman
Editor-in-Chief

CONTENTS

The Poet and the Patron: A Sociological Treatise Upon the Patrimonial State and the Arts[1]

Halil İnalcık

Translated by Arif Nat Riley[2]

A mechanism of rivalry for court prestige from Istanbul to Samarkand and Delhi, patronage profoundly influenced the development of Ottoman poetry, prose, and other art forms. After introducing high court-culture and discussing the modes of poetry transmission, evaluation, and reward, this treatise focuses on the impact of patronage on the life and work of Fuzulî, guided by a thorough examination of *tezkire*s, *inam* registers, and Turkish and Persian divans.

I. THE PATRIMONIAL STATE AND THE ARTS[3]

Ma'rifet iltifâta tâbi'dir
Müşterîsiz metâ' zâyi'dir

Virtuosity depends on favor and praise
Goods without buyers go to waste[4]

Generally speaking, scholars and artists express their arts within the framework of a particular culture and a particular society's dominant social relationships. In a society of the patrimonial sort like that of the Ottomans, that is to say, in a society in which honor, status, and station are determined by an absolute monarch, this reality is all the more evident.[5]

Until the advent of the printing press, which empowered the broad masses to read, thereby allowing literary and scholarly works to secure the livelihood of their writers, the scholar and the artist depended upon the ruler and the elite class for support. The ruler, the "Keeper of Estates", was the scholar's and artist's leading benefactor or sponsor. As Max Weber pointed out, in monarchies of the Middle Ages, in both the East and the West, the state was structured patrimonially: sovereignty, property, and subjects alike were considered absolute possessions of the monarch's family, and only the recipients of that family's favor and benefaction made up society's noblest and richest class. Interdynastic rivalry and the race for ascendancy manifested themselves not only in magnificent courts, servants, and retinue, but also in the sponsorship of scholarship and art.[6]

High culture in the patrimonial state existed only as High Court-Culture. The royal court and dignitaries' residences were the sole source and preserve of honor and prestige, wealth and skill in society. Among the Ottomans, the top architect was the court's chief architect, the best jeweler was the court's chief jeweler, and the poet in highest esteem was the *sultanü'ş-şuara* (poet laureate, literally "sultan of poets"), who was deemed worthy of the sultan's attention and favor. Scholars and artists were agents regarded as de rigueur for the exaltation of the ruler's prestige and the court's renown. In order for the ruler, who was the custodian of knowledge and the arts, to be able to do justice to his function as arbiter, he himself had to be a man of scholarly and artistic cultivation. Had it not been for the Medicis, who possessed a high aesthetics and philosophy of art, the great masters of Florence would surely not have come into their own.[7] Had it not been for sultans who themselves composed poetry, the great geniuses of Turkish literature might well never have arisen. Most masterpieces of that period can, to a significant extent, be accounted for by the elite class's favor, its high culture and refined sensibility, and its penchant for taking artists under its wing. "Patronage of culture" was a long-standing tradition in medieval Iran and Central Asia. According to Professor Maria E. Subtelny, in this region such patronage subsequently became the mechanism whereby the military class within the Turco-Mongol states embraced a new civilization.[8] Thanks to the single High Court-Culture common to Samarkand, Herat, Tabriz, Istanbul, and Delhi in the fifteenth century, when an artist traveled from one land to another, he met with the same sponsorship, mindset, and warm, hearty welcome. The Ottoman sultan was prepared to make large sacrifices in order to attract secretaries skilled in *inşa* (ornate official prose), poets, and scholars versed in Turkish and Persian, especially those from Central Asia and Azerbaijan, to his capital.[9] Mehmed the Conqueror (1430-1481)[10] and Bayezid II (1447-1512) went to great lengths to bring Mullah Jāmī,[11] the great Iranian poet and mystic of the age, to Istanbul.

Herat, the capital of the Timurid state, which held Iran and Central Asia under its sway, rose to prominence as the hitherto unparalleled, illustrious civilization center of the Iranian-Turkish world in the years of the sultanates of Abū Saʿīd Mīrzā and Hüseyin

Baykara, both of whom were great patrons of the arts. During this period, two giants of literature and thought, 'Abd ul-Raḥmān Jāmī (1414-1492) and Ali Şîr Nevâyî (February 9, 1441-January 3, 1501), representing Iranian and Turkish culture respectively, were adopted as models for Ottoman literature. Mehmed the Conqueror and Bayezid II carried on a correspondence with Hüseyin Baykara. Bayezid II, in his letter to Hüseyin Baykara,[12] writes of "the long-standing communion" and indicates his wish for the correspondence's continuance. In his reply, Hüseyin Baykara addresses the Ottoman sultan as "God's caliph among men" and "ghazi in the way of God" and expresses his desire that the friendship deepen and the dialogue endure.[13]

The centers of fifteenth-century high culture were the seats of the rulers of Timurid lineage. Ottoman and Indian sultans took these rulers' courts as their models and would make any sacrifices to attract to their own courts scholars and artists raised, or "hailing from", there. The same one-upmanship that we saw among the cities of Renaissance Italy, and subsequently among the royal courts of Europe, played a role in the Islamic world as well, where it had a most profound influence upon the development and quality of refined high culture. In the Middle East, for a ruler to be able to lure the most renowned scholars and artists to his palace—if necessary seizing and bringing them by force—was commonplace. Tamerlane, in every land he overran, rounded up the most renowned scholars and artists and took them to Samarkand;[14] and Selim the Grim (1467-1520), upon taking Tabriz and Cairo, drove hundreds of artists to Istanbul.[15] Artists who were sent for or "exiled" with assurances of profit and promotion had a huge hand in the development of Ottoman patrimonial court culture,[16] in the fields of poetry, inşa, calligraphy, and miniature art, so much so that the native Ottoman Turkish artists had no qualms about openly voicing their objections to these privileges lavished upon "Arabs and Persians". Lealî says (Latifî 290):

> Acemin her biri kim Rûm'a gelir
> Ya vezâret ya sancak uma gelir

> When a Persian comes to settle in this Ottoman land,
> It is a vizier's or governor's job he hopes to land.

On the other hand, a scholar or artist who had made a name for himself in one locale would seek wider celebrity and prosperity at the courts, and in the favor and beneficence, of the great and rich rulers. Patronage, or sponsorship, was thus a reciprocal affair: both for the court and for the elite scholar or artist, it was accepted as the sole avenue for self-aggrandizement.

In the East and West alike, the wellspring of fame and fortune in patrimonial dynastic states, after the court, was landed gentry and dignitaries well-connected with the ruler. In the West, in Renaissance Italy, once commerce and industry superseded land and agriculture as the basis of affluence, the nouveau riche bourgeois class began to supplant the feudal-patrimonial lords. Obviously, in the East no such development could come about.[17] While the city states in Italy were undergoing such a development, in the East the state's centralistic, patrimonial structure grew steadily further fortified, and the scholar and artist became more dependent than ever upon the court and dignitaries.

One must add that the observation made concerning the disconnect between high court-culture and local folk culture should not be taken as some absolute fact of the Eastern cultural milieu. The first Ottoman rulers were attached to Babaî-Kalenderî dervishes as well as to religio-epic folk literature—in a word, to the Turkmen cultural milieu. In the centuries that followed, particularly in the reign of Mehmed the Conqueror, this Turkmen cultural tradition retained its influence even as the court inclined toward cosmopolitan Middle Eastern culture. Alongside ulema, scribe-poets, and mystics from Cairo and Tabriz, the Ottoman ruler would perpetuate his esteem for and devotion to the head of some popular dervish order.[18] Into the carpets to be woven in Uşak for the palaces and mosques of Istanbul were incorporated samples crafted by palace designers (nakkaş), some of whom were Iranian, as well as the designs and motifs of Iranian court carpets, so that, in imperial Uşak carpets, Iranian motifs and designs began to predominate in conjunction with Yörük-Turkmen geometrical motifs and arrangements, spawning a court style in carpet-weaving.[19] This fact should be noted as further evidence of royal patronage of the arts.

At the recreational gatherings of scholars and poets whom Ottoman sultans would assemble at certain times, sultans owed their competence in discharging their arbitral function to the high culture they received from select tutors during their princely years.[20] It is known that each sultan from Murad II (1404-1451) onward acquired poetic proficiency enough to compile a divan (collection of poems) of his own.[21]

In a nutshell, the artist, under the sponsorship of a patron possessed of a particular taste in and conception of art, would take pains to tailor his works accordingly. If Ottoman classical culture in the reign (1520-1566) of Süleyman the Magnificent (1494-1566) produced works of high art, the sultan's notion of high art had an important hand in this. Indeed, we can say that it was frequently the ruler who determined the quality of works of arts-and-letters and the eminence of artists. A work's status as "agreeable and seemly" was above all contingent upon the sultan's favor.[22] Under the Ottomans, it was no one's place to commission a palace or mosque more imposing or ostentatious than the sultan's. In order to be chosen "sultan of poets" and procure an "honorarium", one first had to get invited to a poetry party, present the sultan with a *kaside*, be acknowledged, and be deemed worthy of a gratuity. On the other hand, poets risen to high station (for instance Necati) would themselves assume the position of patron and surround themselves with numerous distinguished poets.

Those who captured the patron's personal attention secured good positions thanks to his "tutelage" and were counted among his "protégés", or trainees. In Ottoman patrimonial society—not only regarding artists but in general—tutelage, servitude, and well-connectedness became the foundation of social relations and formed a requisite social bond for patron and vassal alike. For the patron to elevate his reputation and station, and for the vassal to survive and advance, this interdependence was essential. This patrimonial principle, or patron-vassal relationship, was visible in the basic structure and origin of the Ottoman state. From its very inception, the Ottoman ("Osmanlı" in Turkish) state involved the groups of *nöker* (dependent companions) under Osman the Ghazi (1258?-1326?). The State was "Osman's" state, the "Osmanlı" state. In Ottoman patrimonial society, well-connectedness and patronage were the core principles underlying social relations and hierarchy in every segment of the elite class: in status groups, in bureaucracy, in the military, even in jurisprudence. In jurisprudence, the reaction of lower-level groups against high-ranking mullahs' favoritism of their kin and counselors in time reached vast proportions.[23] In bureaucracy, the apprentice-journeyman-master system, and hence patronage, governed the training of scribes. In the military-administrative system, appointments and promotions were possible only via the closest commander's petition and recommendation.[24] By no means did the artist fall outside of this general patrimonial system.

In the patrimonial state, since all manner of benefaction and station emanated exclusively from the ruler's favor, there reigned among aspirants fierce rivalry, jealousy, intrigue, and sycophancy, which accounted for society's morality—or rather immorality. Ottoman chronicles and *tezkiretü'ş-şuara*s (critical surveys of poets from a biographical perspective) are full of accounts of this merciless competition and strife. Fuzulî, unable to win a place at the side of the preeminent, finds solace in keeping his distance from the "clan of envy". The only way to draw near to the ruler, or to "enter into his sight" by way of his "good graces", was to secure the sponsorship and intercession of one of his inner circle. Fuzulî recognizes this:

Mā ghulāmān-i māhrūyānīm
Māhrūyān hamah ghulām-i shumā (*Farsça Divan* 641)

> We are the slaves of moon-faced beauties
> And all of those are in bondage to you.

Thus, between patron and individual stood personages of influence with whom one had to become well-connected. Supplication and networking manifested themselves in such institutionalized, art-friendly forms as the presentation of *kaside*s and the exaltation to the high heavens of the sultan and gentry in the most effusive, resplendent language. In this regard Fuzulî, with his *kaside*s to Süleyman the Magnificent and dignitaries, was no different from the rest. He addresses the patron thus:

> Ārzū-yi dawlat-i pābūs-i khuddām-i darat
> Mī rubāyad rūz u shab az dil qarār az dīdah khvāb (637)

> The servants at your palace-gate crave the bliss of kissing your feet;
> Night and day, that hope robs all calm from my heart and sleep from my eyes.

In order to remain in the patron's good graces, the poet, like the other vassals, had to exercise the utmost caution and refrain from things his patron would frown upon. Among those who thus incurred the Conqueror's wrath and were exiled, we can recall Mevlâna Abdülkadir, Nahifî, and (Veliyüddin's son) Ahmed Paşa.

II. THE DEVELOPMENT OF OTTOMAN COURT-CULTURE AND THE OTTOMAN DIVAN POETS

The Seljuk sultans of Konya, like all the courts of the Near East, were not to be outdone in sponsorship of distinguished poets. In the Seljuk state, the official language was Persian; however, one gathers that even at court Turkish was spoken. Around the end of the thirteenth century, Seljuk sultan Alâaddin III (1297-1302?) commissioned Hoca Dehhânî of Khorasan (second half of the thirteenth century) to compose a Seljuk *Book of Kings* in Persian, yet we know that Dehhanî was presenting the sultan with *kaside*s in Turkish during the same period.[25]

The renaissance[26] of advanced learning and the arts represented by the Timurids in the fifteenth-century Islamic world, Central Asia, and Iran served as a model for the Ottomans. The dazzling development of civilization during the Timurid period in Central Asia, as well as the peerless creativity and perfection achieved in branches of the arts, has led historians to compare this period with the Italian Renaissance. At the root of this, Subtelny sees the rise of rich patrons in that time.[27] Foremost among these patrons stands Ali Şîr Nevâyî, of Uygur extraction. Nevâyî (who himself became the companion, or close associate, of Hüseyin Baykara) was admitted to the ranks of the Supreme Council executives in a bureaucratic capacity and spent the immense wealth that had previously accrued to him and his family through rich land grants in *soyural* form (private property with complete immunity from taxation) in order to stimulate and fund scientific, literary, and architectural projects.[28] His generosity was legendary. His friend 'Abd ul-Raḥmān Jāmī, who was the last great representative of classical Iranian literature and thought, was the Islamic world's Voltaire. Numerous Muslim rulers competed to invite him. Mehmed the Conqueror, sending him a gift of five thousand gold pieces, summoned him to Istanbul, and Bayezid II went to great lengths to bring him to the Ottoman realm. In the letter he sent to Jāmī (Ferîdûn I, 361-62), Bayezid referred to him as "the divine radiance of truth" and "Nakşibend of the faith". Jāmī, in his reply, proclaimed "the sultan's generosity knows no bounds". The Ottoman sultan, acknowledging that he had received the works Jāmī had sent ("the collected works of a compiler of perfections"; perhaps the *Nafaḥât*), sent him one thousand gold florins (Ferîdûn I, 363). In his reply, Jāmī expressed his gratitude for the Ottoman sultan's favor:

> Jāmī kujā 'aṭā'-i Shah-i Rūm az kujā
> k'īn luṭf-i ghayb mī rasīdash az rah-i 'umūm

> Where Jāmī is, there is the Ottoman Sultan's munificence:
> Out of nowhere, his largesse has graced me through public ways and means.

Doubtless, the Ottoman sultan, by way of the letters and contributions he sent to Jāmī, the best-known representative of the shared high culture of Iran and Central Asia, wanted to demonstrate that he was one of the sponsors or patrons of this culture. The humble Iranian mystic, who was one of the founders of the Nakşibendî sect, greeted these gifts with the prayer "of all kinds of heartfelt sincerity of a dervish". As a result of the Ottomans' claim, starting with Mehmed the Conqueror, to being the foremost Islamic empire, scholars, artists, *inşa* stylists, and poets from distant regions were invited and received with high favor.[29] According to *Heşt Bihişt*, the *tezkiretü'ş-şuara* of Sehi, the Conqueror "would round up, from among the Arabs and Persians, those with talent to their names and put them on a pedestal" (97). In commissioning his New (Topkapı) Palace, the Conqueror "had skilled architects and engineers brought from Arabia, Persia, and Anatolia".[30] The scribe Lealî resided long in Iran, passed himself off as Persian (Iranian) upon his return, became companion to the Conqueror, and had his convent appointment revoked once the truth came out. Many Ottoman poets (for example, Halimî and Câmî-i Rumî) went to Iran and received a master's welcome upon their return.

Just as the Italian masters were adopted as models by European countries other than Italy during the Renaissance, so did the Central Asian and Iranian poets, especially Ḥāfeẓ, Sa'dī, Khāqānī, Neẓāmī, Nevâyî, and Jāmī, each serve as a model and source of inspiration for Ottoman poets.[31]   In other words, just as we speak of a French or German Renaissance, so too in the Islamic world did the common court-culture in Central Asia, the Ottoman Empire, and India take on a stylistic originality and a character all its own.   We can observe this pronouncedly in miniature painting.   Of Ahmed Paşa, who was well versed in Persian literature, Latifi says in his *tezkire* that he "clothed" the meanings he borrowed from Persian poems "in garments of Anatolian idiom" and so presented them as "conniving Turkish Beauties" (77).   Thus, according to some, Ahmed Paşa was merely an "interpreter".   Those unschooled in Persian were not considered true poets (Âşık Çelebi 277b).

In the *tezkire*s, the Ottoman poets were measured against Iranian poets.   The capacity of the former to simultaneously compose poems in Persian was pointed out as a hallmark of superiority.

Probably, classical Ottoman divan poetry ought always to be studied comparatively in conjunction with classical Iranian poetry.   Only by such a method can one establish to what extent Ottoman poets remained under influence and to what extent they possessed originality.[32]   Latifi partially did this (230); for instance, in Nihalî, who did not remain under the influence of the Iranian masters, he identified an "idiosyncratic style" and passed the judgment, "not in Anatolia, and maybe not in the languages of the Arabs, Persians, or Pahlavis either, is there a soul who has written in such an original style".

One must also point out that in the Ottoman state, which laid claim to primacy among the Islamic states during the reign of the Conqueror,[33] there appeared a tendency toward superiority over and rivalry with the Iranian poets.   Latifi (157) pronounces the poet Zatî superior to Jāmī and Nevâyî.   In fifteenth- and sixteenth-century Ottoman poetry, one sees conscious searches for a fresh, original style.   Poets of that period worked hard to create an original style by employing idioms and adages unique to Turkish (Latifi 300-01).   In fact, the great Ottoman poets who drew their topics, like Neẓāmī's *hamse* (set of five *mesnevî*s), from Persian literature sometimes came out with original works that overshadowed their Iranian prototypes; at this juncture, one should especially mention "the ancient" Şeyhî's *Hüsrev ü Şirin* and Fuzulî's *Leylâ ve Mecnun*.   In their *tezkire*s, Sehi, Latifi, and Âşık Çelebi constantly laud this original style as "a singular style", "an inimitable style", and "fresh".

In this regard, the first great Ottoman poet was undoubtedly Şeyhî, one of "the *kudemâ*" (ancients), who emerged around the beginning of the fifteenth century.[34]   In his youth, Şeyhî himself went to Iran and deepened in mysticism.   Latifi (215-16) lauds his

Hüsrev ü Şirin as a matchless work "on a level hitherto unattained by any" and says that he was the one who created the Turkish *mesnevî* genre.

Yet even Fuzulî is not terribly comfortable with Turkish poetic style; he says (*Türkçe Divan* 481, selected couplets section, no. X):

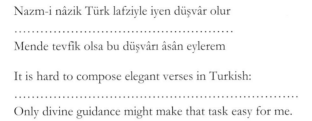

Nazm-i nâzik Türk lafziyle iyen düşvâr olur
....
Mende tevfîk olsa bu düşvârı âsân eylerem

It is hard to compose elegant verses in Turkish:
....
Only divine guidance might make that task easy for me.

Nonetheless, sixteenth-century Istanbul found Fuzulî's Turkish (Azeri-Turkmen) idioms "curious" (Latifî 265). In the years 1350-1450, "the *kudema*"[35] had been heavily using Turkish words and idioms; after 1450, Persian and Arabic vocabulary and lingo, considered "verbal adornment" in poetry, gradually grew widespread, and the Turkish of "the *kudema*" came to be seen by some as "Oğuz-ish and provincial" or "bizarre of tongue"; "Turkic phraseology" was considered unique to the villager and to the mountain tribes. Standing against these views, Latifî (216), who was a veritable literary critic, specified that every work of literature needed to be appraised within the context of its own period and observed that "whenever something new-fangled comes out, it gets admired and preferred, while those using the old style are forgotten". According to Latifî, in divan poetry a new style began to predominate with Nizamî-i Karamanî and especially Ahmed Paşa, who both imitated Persian literature; of Ahmed Paşa's divan, he says, "Like the divans of Ḥāfeẓ and Jāmī, no matter how much you read it, it is always fresh and refreshing". Latifî does not hesitate to point out that, from a certain standpoint, the freshness and originality in them and in Necati derive from uses of Turkish adages. "As for the above-mentioned, it is because", he says, "those of prior mention would pore over poetry from Persian divans. As for Necati, poetry grew steeped in parable, and everyone found in it adages pertaining to his venting".

Kaside Presentation and Banquets

In Eastern literature, the poet's quest for sponsorship and benefaction finds expression in the *kaside* genre, praise presented to the patron in a special arrangement and fixed form.[36] First and foremost, *kaside*s were written to secure the blessing of God and the intercession of prophets and saints in the next world, as well as to garner the sponsorship and favor of the wielders of patrimonial political power in this world.

The Ottoman sultans, each one of whom received instruction in "poetic technique" from select tutors and whose poems filled painstakingly assembled divans, were capable patrons who could appreciate good poetry with the enthusiasm of a connoisseur.[37]   Above and beyond listening to poems at poetry-party competitions, sultans would actively read poems in casual circulation and would award the originators with benefactions and tokens of appreciation. It is interesting what Sehi wrote about Sa'yî (77b-78a): Bayezid II "came across one of his ghazals that so delighted his noble sensibilities that he commanded, 'Locate the author!' " and bestowed upon him the post of *divitdar*ship in an official bureau. But it is worth noting that Sa'yî at first turned down this gesture, saying "I have no need of high office", and only in the reign of Selim I agreed to tutor the palace lads.

The highest compliment was to become the sultan's companion. The *musahip*, in other words conversational partner or intimate associate, was an adviser and confidant the ruler would share his private life with and keep constantly at his side like a bosom friend. The relationship between Mehmed the Conqueror and Mevlâna Abdülkadir, who had distinguished himself in music theory, makes an interesting case in point. The latter advertised his nearness to the sultan enough to draw upon himself the envy of Grand Vizier Mahmud Paşa. Although Nahifî (Mevlâna Şemseddin), who in Iran had been a professor of rhetorical exposition and especially of music, had been an inseparable companion of the Conqueror's; upon one wrong move he was thrown out of the palace, retreated into seclusion in Bursa, and in order to make ends meet began sending *kaside*s in Arabic, Persian, and Turkish to the notables. An excellent example of companionship is the life of Selim I's companion the scholar-poet Halimî Çelebi. Prince Selim (the Grim), while the governor of Trebizond, summoned Halimî, who had spent long years in Iran and Arabia, to his side "for religio-jurisprudential discourse and spiritual conversation" and, after acceding to the throne of the sultanate, kept him on at his side like a best friend. "He was made privy to the sultan's disposition, adjusted to his temperament, and was on the same wavelength. On campaign as well as back home he proved a kindred spirit and lightener of heavy hearts, and his privileged connection existed both in name and in fact" (Latifî 134). State dignitaries would handle their important business with the sultan through him. For the sultan, who had composed a divan in Persian, Halimî would solve everything in the way of "challenging Persian and Arabic couplets and conundrums". Halimî kept his own poems to himself.

A similar closeness was established between Süleyman the Magnificent and Baki of the ulema. After Baki, who faced hardship early in life, attained the favor of Süleyman, he became his companion and was promoted to the highest offices. When

Süleyman exceeded good measure in favor and favoritism by appointing him *kazasker* (a high Ottoman religious post, formerly written *kadıasker*), the ulema could put up with it no longer and opposed it. When in 1574 Murad III (1546-1595) at last acceded to the throne, those who envied Baki had him dismissed from the instructorship of the Süleymaniye mosque complex, which was the highest rank in the madrasa hierarchy.

The traditional banquets held "in seclusion" in the "private" palace gardens or in the pavilions (kiosks) constituted a competitive arena where artists like poets, musicians, and singers had an opportunity to prove themselves before the ruler. In the *Shāhnāmah* (Book of Kings, ca. 1000), Firdawsī at length depicts the banquets thrown by the ancient Iranian ruler Khusraw (IV: 194, 275-76, 299, 330, 332, 389-90). At these extravaganzas in the palace gardens and pavilions decked out to mark a victory or other occasion, which might last three days and three nights, sometimes a whole week, "decorative trees of tinsel would be planted, and fairy-faced servers would decant mature wine to guests to the accompaniment of melodious instruments and fragrant aromas". Everyone would get drunk; tales of triumph would be recounted, and poets would vie with one another in delivering their most beautiful poems. It is in such a gathering that Firdawsī wins Sultan Maḥmūd's appreciation in front of his opponent poets. Hoca Dehhanî, who presented a *kaside* to the Seljuk sultan Alâaddin, speaks of "the king-of-kings's lavish gatherings replete with drink and musical accompaniment".[38] At another banquet, for one *kaside*, the Anatolian Seljuk sultan awarded five handsome slaves to the poet Zahireddin, and İzzeddin Keykavus I (1210-1220) bestowed honoraria upon conversationalists and poets at a banquet on the occasion of the conquest of Sinop.[39] Ottoman sources indicate that poets at such functions usually met with the ruler's gracious acknowledgment and favor.[40] As social institutions that reinforced patrimonial relations among those in the service of the ruler, these parties and banquets, known variously as *işret meclisi*s, *şölen*s, and *toy*s, were endowed with a vital social function in the Eurasian Turco-Mongol states. According to Karl Jettmar, drinking parties organized down to the last detail constituted a sort of ritual performed in order for the ruler to elevate his renown and prestige (240). The sumptuous royal festivities known as *sur-i hümayun* (sultanic wedding or circumcision celebrations), which for the Ottomans sometimes lasted for weeks on end, were occurrences that proved how much importance was placed upon this tradition and that were sought to be preserved in the splendid *surname*s.[41] In Ibn Bībī's history, we see illustrated in detail what a vital place the banquets held in the life of the Seljukid ruler and court: "The banquet of Alâaddin Keykubad was arranged […] with ruby-red wines […] and they furnished and decorated with all sorts of tinsel trees, and the musicians kicked off the entertainment with rousing ballads like myriad epics, and they set to quaffing goblets of wine and listening to the strains of *barbut* and *rebab* [instruments]" (Yazıcızade translation, 170; for these frequently-held banquets also see 117, 140-51). He relates that at a banquet the sultan once, "along the lines of a test, instructed the fellows [artists] to incorporate the place names [Kayseri and Aksaray] into those couplets" and, since he quite liked what the *inşa* stylist Şemseddin came up with, awarded him a promotion.

At some sultans' courts, the banquet-attending circles would assemble frequently. It was probably at such a party that Murad II (1404-1451), whom all the sources agree was "an utter sot", drunkenly uttered the following quatrain reminiscent of Khayyām:

> Sâkî getür getür yine dünkü şarâbımı
> Söyle dile getür yine çeng ü rebâbımı
> Ben var iken gerek bana bu zevk bu safâ
> Bir gün gele ki görmiye kimse türâbımı (Sehi 95)

> Rush, cupbearer, bring me again my wine of yesterday.
> Recite and sing! With music let us while our time away:
> I must have this fun, all this joy now, while still alive;
> Nobody will see my dust when I turn to it someday.

Viziers and generals too would host banquets. The poetry parties of Mahmud Paşa, the Conqueror's grand vizier, were known far and wide. Fuzulî said of Baghdad governor Üveys Paşa, whose protégé he was and to whom he presented *kaside*s, that he "belonged to the reveling crowd". When in the *Sāqīnāmah* he says

> Biyā sāqī ān āb-i ātashmizāj
> k'azu jumlah-'i dard dārad 'ilāj (677)

> Cupbearer, bring me the chalice brimful of fire
> That provides the cure for all distress and desire.

he is probably not referring to mystical ecstasy. In the introductions to his divans, Fuzulî depicts such splendid court banquets and takes refuge in his own private "shack of sorrows" from these delights he cannot share with sultans and poets. Poets would carry on quite uninhibited, loose lives (see the lives of Halilî, Melihî, and Gazalî: Latifî 254, 315; about Latifî himself, 298). The ulema's attitude toward them was reflected in one of Ebussuud's fatwas (Âşık Çelebi 16a). Wine was permissible for poets, and hashish for sufis (see Fuzulî, *Beng ü Badè*).

The patron's benefaction would manifest itself in manifold ways to the author presenting a *kaside* or other work. The sultan would make appointments according to occupation: if an *inşa* stylist, to the secretariat; if a member of the ulema, to a religio-jurisprudential post like instructorship or judgeship, or to the service of some charitable foundation. If a soldier, his feudal land grant would be enlarged. Poets presenting *kasides* would be awarded *caizes* (prizes), usually in the form of silver *akçe* (on rare occasion gold *sikke*) coins and/or woolen or silk *hilats* (robes of honor). In divan parlance, the monetary contributions, *inams* (honoraria), *caizes*, and *hilats* bestowed upon scholars or poets were collectively known as *came* (literally, "apparel"). *Caizes* would generally range between 1,000 and 3,000 *akçes* (20-60 gold pieces). We gather that these donations came out of the general state treasury (see section VI, on *inam* registers). The funds disbursed into the sultan's pocket to cover all manner of his personal expenses reached 31,466,314 *akçes* in the 1567-1568 fiscal year. (Thirty million of this was the 500,000-gold-piece *irsaliye*, or payment, sent every year from Egypt, 850,000 *akçes* of it was the royal discretionary allowance disbursed daily from the treasury, and 616,314 *akçes* of it was the proceeds from the sale of produce from the palace vineyard and gardens.)[42]

From the Azeri-Turkmen Seyyid Lokman, author of the *Hünernâme*, we glean a detailed account of how possessors of talent, who spoke Turkish and Persian derived from Iran (mostly from Azerbaijan) and represented the high court-culture, would network with the Ottoman court. While Süleyman the Magnificent was spending the winter in Aleppo for his Iran campaign, Lokman, together with his father, had left his hometown and come to stay with his paternal uncle, who was a landed soldier at Hasankeyf in the Ottoman realm.[43] From there he went on to Aleppo and found Şemsi Paşa, who paid Lokman's father high compliments. Şemsi Paşa, himself an accomplished *inşa* stylist and poet, inspired Lokman "to join in the camaraderie among the ranks of poets and rhetoricians devoted to perfecting paragons"[44] and encouraged him to recite poems in Turkish at the poetry-party competition. One of Lokman's ghazals in praise of Süleyman struck the pasha as worthy of bringing to the sultan's attention. In his ghazal, Lokman requests a contribution thus:

> Çü bî-tâb oldı cûdundan zer ü sim ü güher şâhâ
> Sarardı zer bozardı akçe odlar düşdü mercâna

> O King, your largesse makes gold, silver, and gems lose force and flash;
> Gold turns sallow, silver grows pale, and flames engulf the corals.

In the spring of 956/1549, while the sultan was resting at Elmalu Yurdu after crossing to the Diyarbakır side, Şemsi Paşa delivered the ghazal to him. The sultan liked it very much, rewarded Lokman with a *caize* of one hundred gold pieces, and commanded that he be apportioned a salary ("some small measure of benefice")[45] from the operating surpluses of Diyarbakır's charitable foundations. Thanks to this income, the young

Lokman had the opportunity to devote himself to acquiring an elite education. At his Elmalu way station, the sultan sent the following opening couplet to the poets accompanying him on campaign:

> Âhumla nâle gulgulesin inleyen bilür
> Çeng ü çegâneyi lülesün dinleyen bilür

> Only those who moan know about the clamor of tears and sighs;
> Only those who listen to songs know what music signifies.

Şemsi, Haydar Remmal, Hayalî, Sehabî, Bidarî, and Lokman completed the ghazal by each contributing a couplet. Lokman's couplet was this:

> Eyyûb kıssasın dime her dinleyen bilür
> 'Âşık gibi belâya düşüp inleyen bilür

> Don't assume everyone who has heard it understands Job's story;
> It is known only to those who moan from love's woes and misery.

After this parallel patchwork ghazal was presented to the sultan, everyone received a *caize* of between 3,000 and 10,000 *akçe*s according to his share. When some "hagglers" from the team of poets voiced their consternation at not having received more, Lokman shut them up by affirming that the awarded sum was already sufficiently large. Şemsi Paşa congratulated Lokman and gave him a further *hilat* and *caize*. Lokman recalls this episode as the point of departure for his admittance to the service of the sultan. Later on, in the *Hünernâme*, he hints at his veiled desire to be appointed treasury secretary to Egypt.

The *nişancı* (head of the chancery) Celâlzade Mustafa, who like Şemsi Paşa was an accomplished *inşa* stylist and poet, was known for bringing many capable poets to the sultan's attention and assisting with their livelihoods. Celâlzade appears to have sponsored Fuzulî as well (see the section on the *Şikâyetname* below).

In order to enter into the patron's good graces, artists would struggle to come out with ever more excellent works than those of their peers; thus, from the standpoint of the arts, patronage truly played a positive role. But as we have pointed out above, this conclusion depends exclusively on the patron's own personal artistic taste and level of artistic understanding. On the other hand, the patron—be he the sultan or one of the state dignitaries—always had to take into account the populace's sensibilities when selecting his close companion, *nedim*, or *musahip*. In Ottoman history, when affairs went awry, it was usually not the sultan himself who was held responsible, but rather his companion, who kept close to him, influenced his lifestyle, and advised him on important decisions.[46] We know of many poets who served as companion to a sultan.

If the companion's lifestyle or outward religious convictions did not suit the mores and traditions of the state and society, gossip would spring up, and the patron's reputation and influence would suffer. Especially if the companion, chosen from among poets, sheiks, ulema, and veteran statesmen, was an adherent of the Sunni sect and a practicing devotee of the religious codes of conduct, he would meet with everyone's ready approval. If he was a drunkard, a holder of esoteric mystical views, a disregarder of religious obligations like prayer and fasting, or a scorner of mores, he would drag both himself and his patron into a vexatious predicament; the patron would distance him from his presence, terminate his salary, exile him, or order his imprisonment or execution. Quite a few poets met with this fate.

Here one may recall the case of Ahmed Paşa, the master poet who was homosexual, never married, and dared take the liberty of gazing upon the very "darlings" of the sultan's palace.[47] His *kaside* with the refrain "kerem" (big-hearted) beseeching the sultan for forgiveness both softened the Conqueror's heart and proved a masterpiece of Turkish literature. Prince Korkud (d. 1512), who was known as a fine artist and a "master in [every] technical and theoretical discipline",[48] was forced to distance from his side Mevlâna Gazalî, whose writings consisted of "smut".[49]

After colorfully characterizing the happy life, set in beautiful gardens, of companion poets who have captured the favor and ear of sultans, Fuzulî consoles himself with the words: "O troubled poet, your rubbing elbows with sultans would boot you naught but the jealousy of others; as for the joys of wine, they make for eternal torment in the next world; as for your constantly keeping the conversationalists company, it would keep you from inhabiting the world of your own imagination".[50] Falling from favor to a bitter end is a fate many Ottoman poets met with. The poet Sunʿî, one of Murad II's companions, was thrown into prison out of the other poets' jealousy, but he composed a *kaside* to Veliyüddin and was released (Sehi 185). On account of his weakness for strong drink, the poet Melihî, who had befriended ʿAbd ul-Raḥmān Jāmī in Iran and risen to the companionship of Mehmed the Conqueror, was summoned into the sultan's presence and dismissed; he lived out his last days in loneliness and destitution (Sehi 189; Mecdî, *Şakayık* translation, 232; Âşık Çelebi 126b). Poets who, for various reasons, could not find a real patron turned their backs on the arts (like Latifî, see *tezkire* 298, 374) or retreated into their own solitary little corners and in defiance, as did Ruhî of Baghdad, said to heck with the world:

Ey sâhib-i kudret kani insâf u mürüvvet
Rindân-i mey-âşâma niçün olmaya rağbet (189)
....

Çarhın ki ne sa'dinde ne mahsinde beka var
Dehrin ki ne hâssında ne 'âmında 'atâ var (190)
....
A'yân-i cihândan kerem umma anı sanma
Âsâr-i 'atâ ola ne paşada ne begde (195)
....
Yâ Rab bize bir er bulunub himmet eder mi
Yohsa günümüz böyle felâketle geçer mi (195)

That mighty person is not generous nor does he understand:
Why should epicureans who love drinking not be in demand?
....
In this world, neither happiness endures nor the throne through and through;
The common people lack fidelity, so do the select few.
....
Expect no generosity from people high up. Don't presume
That the sovereign and the notables perform beneficent deeds.
....
O God, is there no brave man to help us?
Or will all our days go by in distress?

Ultimately, in despair, he says to heck with the entire universe:

Çarh-i felekin sa'dına vü nahsına la'net
Kevkeblerinin sâbit ü seyyârına hem yûf (194)

Cursed be the firmament's happiness and misfortune;
To hell with the fixed and moving stars in its constellations.

Fed up with the world just like Ruhî, Fuzulî later expanded the couplets of Ruhî's ghazals into five-line stanzas. Fuzulî, who in 1534 suddenly found himself a subject of the Sunni Ottoman sultan after twenty-six years of adherence to Shiism in the service of the Safavids, could not find a patron among the Ottoman notables during these fiercest years of the struggle against the Kızılbaş "heretics". He sequestered himself in Karbala, "this desert kneaded with the blood of downtrodden martyrs of prophetic lineage", this ground "nourished by the milk of hardship in the cradle of trauma" (*Farsça Divan* 8), and like his countryman Ruhî defiantly rained down curses upon fate and sultans alike:

Eyleyüb nâ-dâna 'arz-i fazl ü izhâr-i hüner
Şermsâr etmek 'atâ ummak nedür zulm-i sarîh (*Türkçe Divan* 479)

Clearly it is wrong to ascribe grace and art to the vulgar
And to embarrass him by expecting generosity.

Feth-i kişver kılmağa eyler müheyyâ leşkeri
Yüz fesâd ü fitne tahrîkiyle bir kişver alır
Ol dahi âsâr-i emn ü istikametten berî (496)

The sultan assembles his standing armies to conquer lands,
Seizes one with a myriad insurgencies and intrigue:
That land has safety and direction taken out of its hands.

Zulm ile akçalar alub zâlim
Eyler in'âm halka minnet ile
....
Cenneti almak olmaz akça ile
Girmek olmaz bihişte rüşvet ile (493)

Taxing by cruel means, the tyrant seizes coins;
To some, for their gratitude, he makes donations.
....
For Paradise, money will secure no entry:
You cannot enter Heaven through bribery.

He curses the grand vizier as well:

Ey vezîr-i mülk-perver kim nizâm-ı mülk için
İntihâb etmiş cemî'-i halktan sultân seni
....
İtmiş iken efdal-i halk-i cihân ikbâl ile
Erzel-i ehl-i cehennem eyleye sübhân seni (495)

O vizier, for warding over the land's law and order,
The sultan selected you from among the populace;
....
Though you were made supreme among the people of the world.
May God brand you the vilest and send you to Hell's worst place.

Despite according master status to the poets of Iran, the "resourceful" (creative) poet Mesihî of Pristina, who is accepted as having invented a colorful, original style by frequently incorporating beautiful Turkish[51] idioms and adages, was among those who found superfluous the excessive praise lavished in Ottoman lands upon those arriving from Persia (most of them via Azerbaijan).

Mesîhî gökten insen sana yer yok
Yürü gel var Arab'dan ya Acem'den (*Mesîhî Dîvânı* 231)

There is no place for you, Mesihî, even if you descend from heaven;
You would be better off coming from the Arab lands or from Persia.

Himself possessed of sufficient command of Arabic and Persian to compose poetry in those languages, he served as a master *inşa* stylist in the divan secretariat of Grand Vizier Hadım Ali Paşa, upon whose death (917/1511) he sought to hook up with Yunus Paşa and Nişancı Cafer Çelebi but, unable to line up a genuine patron, ended his days in dire straits. In the following couplet to Cafer Çelebi, he bemoans the paucity of donations:

> Ben senin bendelerin defterine geçmiş iken
> Ne revâdır bana pâ-bend ola bir cüz'i timâr (45)

> I was listed among subjects worthy of your largesse;
> How did I deserve getting tied down with a minor fief?

If, in his quest for a patron, he presented *kaside*s to sultans Bayezid II and Selim the Grim, especially to Nişancı Cafer Çelebi (five *kaside*s, nos. 6-10), who was the head of the divan secretariat, and to treasury secretaries (Ahmed Çelebi and Bedreddin Bey), he nonetheless could not reclaim his former lofty esteem, and like Fuzulî he poured out his troubles into couplets (his *Şitaiye* for Hasan Paşa, 51-54):

> Kâinâtı hâli sanma ehl-i 'irfândan ki ben
> Âlemin Selmânı olurdum olaydın sen Zahîr (53)

> Don't presume the world is devoid of men of learning and gnosis:
> I could be the Selmân of the age if you were my supporter.

In the following couplet, Mesihî's poetry unifies "artifice" and "imagination", the two components that according to *tezkire* authors constituted the soul of divan poetry:

> Sûsen gibi çün kim uzadam medhüne ben dil
> Ağzını yumar gonca gibi bülbül-i gûyâ (65)

> If, like the iris, I were to protrude my tongue to praise you,
> The singing nightingale would close its mouth like a rosebud.

Naturally, this lovely *kaside* concludes with the following couplet soliciting a contribution from the patron:

> Olmaya 'imâret ebedî hâne-i kalbim
> Ger lûtfun ile cûdun ana olmaya bennâ (66)

> If your grace and largesse were not its architect,
> My heart's edifice could not flourish forever.

When Hadım Ali Paşa fell on the field of battle, Mesihî made the devoted gesture of composing a hauntingly beautiful elegy for his late generous sponsor.

III. THE PATRON AND THE CONCEPTION OF ART IN CLASSICAL POETRY

It is crucial to note that in divan poetry it was artifice, not natural enthusiasm or lyricism, that was fundamental. Showy artwork, in which various "formulae" were applied, addressed the rulers and state dignitaries versed in court-culture. These sorts of works were products of artifice and demanded subtle symbolic and intellectual insight. In contrast to this, poetry with realistic-naturalistic features that, like the poetry of Karacaoğlan, appealed to the masses, did not count as art.[52] The dexterous poet who, like Zatî, could best incorporate the mechanical flourishes of wordplay known as *sanayi-i şiiriye* (the particular artistic conventions of poetry) was held to be the best poet. Âşık Çelebi (278a) rated Zatî as the "trendsetter among poets": he "is solid and steadfast in poems with language that is sound, sturdy, and witty", and in his poetry he draws together "so many delicate meanings, bizarrely unique visions, and aesthetic feats". While my late professors Fuad Köprülü and Abdülbaki Gölpınarlı admired Fuzulî's lyricism, they ascribed somewhat less significance to his artifice-embellished poems. Gölpınarlı did not consider Zatî a poet at all. According to the *tezkire* authors, those who acquired elite status in divan poetry, including Fuzulî, were poets who, whilst practicing artifice, simultaneously managed to innovate in delicacy and imagination.

Those literary historians who study divan poetry must of necessity appraise this style of poetry not by today's criteria or conception of conventional aesthetics, but from the standpoint of *sanayi-i şiiriye*,[53] which developed within the framework of Islamic civilization—just as it would be meaningless to study or appraise Eastern miniature painting according to the principles of Western naturalistic-realistic painting.

According to the *tezkire* authors, the genuine divan poets were those creative poets who assimilated "the disciplines", such as semantics, rhetoric, aesthetics, exposition, prosody, and poetic technique, and achieved synergy between artifice and imagination in their poems. As the *tezkire* authors pointed out, the sought-after poems were the "artificial" ones in which linguistic stunts were pulled off with finesse. Yet artifice should not confine itself to artifice: it should be pleasing, charming, delicate, and artistic; it should steer clear of awkwardness; it should be "fresh" (original) with novel insights arrived at through exercise of the imagination; and it should not smack of imitation. Latifî lauds Lamiî's command of artifice but says that "his verse and official prose are drab and insipid" (292). Let us provide an example of poetry that successfully blends imagery and artifice, by Cem Sultan (d. 1495):

> Dilde gamzen oku var iken gamun gönderme kim
> Konmağ olmaz ey sanem mihmân mihmân üstüne (210)

> Don't torment me while the arrow of your glance is stuck in my breast;
> Darling, it's wrong if a guest turns up on top of another guest.

Here, the pun on *gamze* (furtive glance) and *gam* (anguish) and the allusion to the adage "misafir üstüne misafir olmaz" ("never guest upon guest": since a guest deserves a host's undivided attention, no new guest should impose on the host before the old one has left) are perceived as the poem's artistic worth. Allusion to adages was a feature sought in Ottoman poetry of the early period. "Among Anatolian poets, the practice of incorporating adages began with Safi [Cezerî Kasım Paşa] and matured to perfection in Necati" (Latifî 219). The following couplet is by Ahmed Paşa:

> Çîn-i zülfün miske benzettim hatâsın bilmedim
> K'ey perîşân söyledim bu yüz karasın bilmedim

> I likened her lovelock to musk, never knew the error;
> I talked helter skelter, knew nothing of the dishonor.

Here, such artifices as the reminiscence between the expressions *misk* (musk), which comes from the land called *Çin* (Hatay), and *çîn-i zülf* (the curliness of hair); the pun between *hata* (mistake) and Hatay (implicit from *Çin*); the motif of distressed dishevelment in the black curly locks (*zülf*), the figurative shamefacedness or embarrassment of someone making a mistake (*yüz karası*, literally "darkfacedness", is Turkish for "shamefacedness"), and the parallel disarray of hair and language; and lastly the feigned ignorance have all been expressed with such finesse and facility within a single couplet that Sehi (114) includes this example in his *tezkire* as a matchless specimen of the poetic art. Here, according to Sehi, artifice and imagination have become one; the hidden artistry whets the reader's appetite for discovering the same harmonious forms, colors, and meanings he finds in a miniature painting or arabesque. What qualifies this verse as poetry is not so much the enthusiastic natural expression of apparently sincere emotions, as rather a subtle artistic mastery.

This is the sort of artwork sought by the patron whose upbringing has inculcated such taste in art; it has been called "artifice steeped in imagery". The patron seeks not bare human feelings and depictions naturally and plainly expressed, as in Western naturalism and realism, but rather subtle beauty concealed beneath vestments of vision and symbolism, mastery and delicacy.

The poet should be refined as well as articulate and eloquent. Fuzulî speaks of the Ottoman poets as "the polite society of Anatolia" and "the Turks of finesse". In the introductions he wrote for his Persian and Turkish divans, Fuzulî relates how he abandoned the "mushy poems" and "ghazals" of his youth, how he gave up getting "intoxicated like an infatuated nightingale" in favor of "the trappings of cultivation", how he tried to acquire "the jewels of knowledge", how he toiled in order to learn "the innovations in the techniques of verse" and "the artistic contrivances", and ultimately how he conquered the "systematic kingdoms of verse and prose" (which would please his patrons in high places). Fuzulî apologizes for his inevitable ignorance of the idioms and adages commonplace in the Ottoman realm. He finds consolation in thinking to himself: I may not have managed to get to the Ottoman realm for edification, but I still get to live in a sacred spot like Karbala.[54]

In the introduction to his Persian divan, he says, "know that poetry is a field all its own, a field venerated among the illustrious genres". Also, "the practice of poetry relies on a plethora of techniques and devices, without which the pursuit of art would be difficult". As for himself, he adds, in poetic technique "my pen has always inclined towards the *muamma* [versified riddle] and *kaside* forms" (*Farsça Divan* 6-9), because his knack for *sanayi-i şiiriye* is best displayed in these forms of poetry. While working with imagery and artifice, "elegance" must not be forgotten. In Fuzulî we find a couplet that the *tezkire* authors rejected as *kerih* (ugly):

> Dar shabistān tamannā-yi khatat ḥāṣil-i man
> Bar sar-i har muzhah sad qaṭrah zi khūn-i jigar ast (*Farsça Divan* 223)

> In the bedroom at night, I yearned to kiss the down covering your face,
> That's why drops of blood from my heart stand on each one of your eyelashes.

Doubtless, in order to become a perfect divan poet, one needed to learn well the *sanayi-i şiiriye*. The lyric ghazals of Fuzulî's that today we so admire were, by his reckoning, works of youthful folly; the real poet was the Fuzulî capable of learning and applying the poetic artifices. It is here that we encounter the classical divan poet attempting to rise to the challenge of the patron's high court-culture. The poetic form he held supreme was the *kaside*.

Beyond the patronage by the sultan and the state dignitaries in Istanbul, powerful and rich warlords in the "outlying" (frontier) regions of Rumeli, such as the Sons-of-Mihal and the Sons-of-Malkoç, formed a second category of patron, which sponsored popular Sufi poets and the heads of dervish orders. Fuzulî's bosom friend[55] Abdal Hayretî, a fellow Shiite, appears to have been well-connected with the governor of Bosnia. From his divan (13):

> Küfr ile îmânı yeksân eden abdallardanız
> Gâh mescitte gehî gebrin kilîsâsındayız[56]

> We are dervishes who equate sacrilege and faith:
> Sometimes we go to mosque, sometimes to the infidel's church.

IV. THE POET AND THE PATRON IN THE *TEZKİRE*S

Sehi

Our most fundamental sources on the subjects of patronage and the elite class's conception of art are the *tezkiretü'ş-şuara*s. The *tezkire* of Sehi,[57] who is accepted to be the author of the first Ottoman *tezkire* about poets (finished in 1538), provides interesting details on patronage's vital importance to the Ottomans. Sehi, who expects "favor and benefaction" upon presenting his work to Süleyman the Magnificent in person, expresses the patron-vassal relationship thus:

> Kul olana çoğ etti Şâh himmet
> N'ola etse Sehî'ye dahi şefkat
> ....
> Günahım n'oldu bilsem dirliğümde
> Sürüldüm Kapu'dan ben pîrliğimde
> Ne var bir himmet etse yine Sultan
> Koca kul Kapu'sunda olsa derbân (84)

> On all his slaves he lavishes his generosity;
> On Sehî, too, I wish our Emperor would take pity.
> ....
> In what way did I falter, what was my sin, I wonder?
> In old age, I've been banished from the Court, torn asunder.
> If only I could be blessed once again with my Sultan's support
> To be enabled to serve as a porter at his sublime porte.

In the *kaside* he composed for Süleyman:

> Ganî eyler 'atâsı her fakîri
> Olur her bir za'îfin dest-gîri
> Kime kim bir kez etse medh ü tahsîn
> Bağışlar ana hep dünyâ harâcın (82)

> Destitute men are enriched by his generosity;
> His hand reaches out to those languishing in poverty.
> It is a world of gifts that the Emperor contributes
> To the person who praises him and offers him tributes.

It was important for the patron to personally listen to and acknowledge the poet. According to Sehi, Süleyman was such a patron of poets (86).

In the concluding section of his book, Sehi reiterates his expectations:

> Sözün cehd eyle irgür Pâdişâha
> Ki Sultân-i cihân sâhib-nazardır
> Hüner kadrin bilüp sâhib-hünerdir
> Bilür her nakd-i kalbin ol a'yârın
> Ona göre eder hem i'tibârın (313)

> Try as hard as you can and send word to the Emperor
> That the Sultan of the world can create miracles at one glance.
> As a creative artist, he knows the value of art;
> He is capable of assessing the worth of each heart
> And responding in kind to prestige and significance.

Sehi, who clerked for the Royal Council in the reign (1481-1512) of Bayezid II and subsequently in old age was distanced from this office in the reign of Süleyman, is expecting "favor", "compassion", "support", "contributions", "cash", and "respect" from the sultan and from his mighty grand vizier İbrahim Paşa. The people for whom he composed *kaside*s were: the *kazasker* Fenarî Muhyiddin Çelebi, the "second vizier" Cezerî Kasım Paşa (Safi), the treasury secretary İskender Çelebi, and the grand viziers İbrahim Paşa, Hersekzade Ahmed Paşa, Lütfi Paşa, Pirî Paşa, and Ferhad Paşa.

While eulogizing the sultans, Sehi points out Mehmed the Conqueror's unparalleled stature in art patronage: "No sultan showed such respect for, or so spread the fame of, the poet population as did he [….] He would arrange grand regular income for each one of them and was always summoning them into His Majesty's presence for poetry competitions." According to Sehi (99), Bayezid II "was a benevolent sultan beyond compare in munificence". "He brought İdris-i Bidlisî from Persia and showered him with lavish assistance and further compliments so that, beyond the regular income which the sultan had apportioned to him, he received bonuses of the sultan's discretionary *inam*, which made him well-off. In this manner the sultan commissioned him to write the *Tevarih-i Âl-i Osman* [History of the Ottoman Dynasty]." (For the extraordinary donations İdrîs received, see section VI, on *inam* registers.)

We know that sultans and princes would retain the *inşa* stylists and poets they liked as close companions at their sides. Ahmedî, Safi, and Şeyhî served as companions to Süleyman Çelebi (1402-1411); Atâyî and Şemsi to Murad II (Sehi 169); Ahmed Paşa, Melihî, Aşkî, and Lealî to Mehmed the Conqueror; and Necati to Bayezid II. Nihanî was Grand Vizier Hadım Ali Paşa's companion (238). In their poetry-party competitions, in which poems would be recited at turns, sultans would reward an artifice-laden couplet with generous contributions. Through the biography of Mevlâna Abdülkadir (*Şakayık* translation, 198-99), who served as tutor and companion to Mehmed the Conqueror, it has been related that the Conqueror and dignitaries would assemble the "polite society" in gardens and keep company with them. *Tezkire* records of the various parties attended by scribes, historians, and poets indicate that the basic function of these get-togethers was to spread the patron's fame as much as to stimulate the arts. Cem Sultan "had an uncommon appetite for, and would pay extraordinary compliments to, the fraternity of poets, that exemplary assemblage of skillful folk [....] He would keep several members of this fraternity ever at his side [...] himself a matchless poet". We know the names of the poets and *inşa* stylists who shared his suffering abroad: Türabî, La'lî, Haydar, and Kandî. Bayezid II, too, constantly maintained close relations with the "poets and men of refinement" and would engage in "companionship and bonding" with them. In this period, not just members of the Ottoman dynasty, but most of the grand viziers as well, were generous patrons who, "capable of writing verses and able reciters of poems", would host poetry-party competitions.

What kind of a person should the court companion be? Yazıcızade Ali relates this as follows in the *Tevarih-i Âl-i Selçuk* (116b): "Since they even sit around with the sultan for long stretches, sultans' friends and close companions should be such personages as have proven themselves to be sensible, clever, comely, of noble birth, of good repute, of pure and unblemished character, good-natured, silver-tongued, worldly-wise, well-traveled, and downright tough".

At poetry parties, the poet who awed everyone, whose poetic power overshadowed the others, and who attracted the sultan's special appreciation would be celebrated with titles like "the preeminent", "the emir of verse", "the king of poets", or "the sultan of poets". "Darling youths of strapping build and baby-faced complexion" would also attend these poetry parties, where all night long wine would be quaffed, instruments played, and fortune celebrated.

Poets would also organize such get-togethers among themselves: "In tandem with each new recitation at the meetings of congregations of detached free spirits and circles of mystical insight, the cries of overcome lovers would make the entire dome of the sky, from horizon to horizon, resound with the murmur of moaning" (Sehi 211). Listing the functions of patronage, Sehi says that one of its "miracles" is making people generous (18a). Also, "it makes a person upright, and perhaps big-hearted as well"; it "recycles acts of favor so that countless ailing poor folk benefit and your heart of hearts is uplifted by those kind deeds; it becomes a polished mirror in the hands of eulogizers; it is the conversation mate of sultans who embody the scripture; the ancient beloved of beggars;

the ulema's candle for nighttime study; and the breathtakingness of the glow of the pre-dawn twilight in the devotional chambers in which the righteous sequester themselves".

Latifî

Unrivaled in literary criticism and appraisal, Latifî of Kastamonu, like many who entered the career path of Islamic jurisprudence, dropped out halfway into his madrasa education and attempted to become an expert in the scribal arts and accounting. At the same time, he grew expert in verse and *inşa*, two undifferentiated literary genres.[58] At appropriate places in the *tezkire* he wrote (first version: 953/1546), Latifî incorporated masterful couplets and expanded some poets' couplets into stanzas. Sehi includes him in his list of poets. Of course he, too, like his peers, spent his whole life on a quest for a patron/sponsor who would secure for him a comfortable and admirable standard of living.[59] In the concluding section of his *tezkire*, he complains that time has not been on his side in composing works or getting compensated for them, and that he has not been able to find a patron to appreciate his work: "No eloquent, ostentatious benefactor of the talented or champion of men of aptitude was to be found among the notables of the age [....] It closed the book on verse and *inşa*". Everyone had become obsessed by worldly ambition and appearances, had turned their backs on values like the arts and sciences, and "what was dearest to everybody's hearts were the dirhams and dinars, and to get worldly items had become the sole desire of a merciless world". Nobody was left who possessed the prerequisite attributes of "connoisseurship, compassion, and goodwill" for sponsorship (patronage) of the arts. In resentful desperation at this state of affairs, Latifî says: "I even swore an oath that thenceforth I would not utter a single anecdote or line of verse, nor recite for the bigwigs of the age any treatise or *kaside*, lest I suffer the disappointment of kickbacks and falling short of high office". "For this reason my heart suffered disillusionment, and I could not do my best or put forth a commendable effort"; "I could not proceed in the style or demeanor I had envisioned". He adds that he hopes that those of his friends possessed of insight will appreciate this book, the *Tezkire*, which he has written at the behest of his friends, and remember with compassion "this feeble slave a.k.a. Abdüllatifî" as "noblesse oblige" demands. These words of Latifî's (372-73) once again establish the decisive importance of patronage to Ottoman literature.

Latifî looked for a patron by presenting treatises and *kaside*s to Head Treasury-Secretary (*defterdar*) İskender Çelebi (d. 1534) and Grand Vizier İbrahim Paşa (d. 1536), who were the period's two most influential statesmen and arch rivals. Both of these statesmen were in fierce competition to show special consideration to poets and scholars, thereby to win allies and spread their own fame. Ultimately, İbrahim managed to arrange for İskender's death warrant; not long after, however, İskender Çelebi's allies started a bunch of vicious rumors against İbrahim, claiming that he had set his sights on the sultanate, which brought about his execution as well. Like Sehi, Latifi too seems to have gotten stuck between these two born rivals.

Latifi relates at length (104-06) that İbrahim Paşa (1523-1536) was a great sponsor and very generous patron of poets. When Şükrî delivered his *Selimname*, the book he had written on Selim the Grim, to the sultan by way of İbrahim Paşa, he received 20,000 *akçe*s (233 gold pieces) in *caize*. Moreover, the grand vizier rewarded him with a considerable *tımar* (land benefice). To everyone, great and small, İbrahim would supply "royal support and kingly funding" and "donate rubies and pearls like the rulers of old [....] He would seek out gentlemen of talent and support those of cultivation [....] Under his auspicious era this group of literary men flourished in numbers".

Latifi at first landed a clerkship appointment on the Belgrade side of Rumeli under the wing of his patron İskender Çelebi, and stayed there awhile; in the year 950/1543 he came to Istanbul, and Sehi's *tezkiretü'ş-şuara*, *Heşt Bihişt* (finished in 1538), which was gaining fame around that time, aroused in Latifî and Âşık Çelebi a desire to collect material for writing a work in the same vein; each embarked on the task and, if Âşık Çelebi's hearsay must be believed (107a), when Latifi attempted to imitate his system of categorization, Âşık Çelebi took offense, left his work half finished, and took it up again only fifteen years afterwards. According to Âşık Çelebi, Latifi did this since "comrades had designs on the morsel". Meanwhile, Latifi completed his work and, while at first trying to make ends meet with the salary he received in return for some trifling religious services, eventually became a foundation clerk of Yahya Bey, who was the director of the rich Eyüp foundation of Mehmed the Conqueror, then was dismissed and served as scribe to the *sultan imareti* (royal charities) on Rhodes, which was a locale of exile. This biographical note is reminiscent of the lives of quite a few poets and *inşa* stylists.

A master literary critic in the divan tradition categorizes poets by profession and lifestyle and points to the tie between their poems and their lifestyles.[60] He identifies with the following characteristics those who are recognized for their poetry, *inşa*, and witty conversation and who have entered the class of elites: articulate, communicative, matchless in fluency and finesse, refined, good-natured, polite, and adage-quoting. In his account, the liberal-minded, the self-indulgent, the big-hearted, the drunkards, the dervishes, and those of a detached-yet-free-spirited nature, such as Divane Gazalî, Meşrebî, and Melihî, make up a separate category.

When the poet hailed from the ulema, adjectives like "virtuous" and "impeccable" would be used, though former ulema who strayed from the way, like Mevlâna Hevesî,

Mevlânâ Sa'yî, and Mevlânâ Gazalî, were by no means nonexistent. Meanwhile, the poems of those coming from the military class, and sultans' poems too, would be found "valiant" or "daring". When characterizing a sultan's poems, Latifî would express stylistic properties by employing attributes like "artistic", "imaginative", "adage-steeped", "moving", and "tidy". He would qualify as "idiosyncratic of style" (original) those like Mesihî who introduced novelties and possessed special styles. Similarly, Sehi (214) admiringly expressed Necati's inimitability, saying "with his graceful style he was able to elevate poetry and prose to their highest charm". (Necati was Sehi's patron.)

Âşık Çelebi

Âşık Çelebi (Kadı Pir Mehemmed, d. 1572)[61] was himself a poet and *inşa* stylist who presented to Süleyman the Magnificent, and expected compensation for, his *tezkiretü'ş-şuara*, the *Meşairü'ş-Şuara*. According to Âşık Çelebi, a work's worth is determined by the worth of the patron: "the praisee determines the value of the praise" (34a). Thank God, he says, the person I praise is a "protector of the twin Holy Shrines" like Süleyman, so why shouldn't this work garner me contributions on par with the contributions of the idolatrous Mongol khans of Iran? In his book, Âşık Çelebi points out over and over again the fact that artistic and technical works depend on patronage. As he notes "the grand *caize*s bestowed upon the poets and the goodly gratuities afforded the gentleman verse-mongers" by the Abbasid caliphs (14b), he indicates that even the great imams "would grant the poet a *caize*" (15a).

Poets in the reigns of Ottoman sultans until Süleyman Çelebi "were known for their funding of endowments, and the *kaside*s in their names would be inscribed in anthologies" (20a). The sponsor of poets of his period was Ahmedî, the companion of Süleyman Çelebi, who had a weakness for banquets.[62] Poets were especially complimented by Murad II, who ordered one thousand *akçe*s per month to be given to poets who lacked a salaried position; "this donation was that sultan's innovation. Posterity followed in his footsteps by making the same donation to some worthy recipients". Also, a divan compiling this sultan's poems is famous (21a). Sehi (94) has this to say about the besottedness of Murad II, who spent most of his life at banquets: he was "an utter sot and extremely jovial character".[63]

Bayezid II, who was worrying about Cem Sultan, vied with his rival in lavishing attention on poets. In his time, according to Âşık Çelebi, most of the ulema and dignitaries busied themselves with poetry and thoroughly rewarded poets. "In donation season, so much cash was scattered about that the ulema, the righteous, the lofty, and the poets would all, out of the special treatment accorded them, come out with prayer-missives and inscribed writings in praise of the sultan". Bayezid II, who went by the pen name Adlî, was himself a good poet. An *inam* register pertaining to the donations Bayezid II distributed among scholars, dignitaries, and poets is extant among his archival documents.[64] The reign (1512-1520) of Selim the Grim was a turning point. During his conquest of Arab and Persian lands, Arab and Persian literati presented him with *kaside*s and books. Those in Anatolia who were able rose to the challenge and adopted these as models; in this period the art of poetry underwent an unprecedented development. "The sultan was a personage of insight and a cultivator of the refined; he recognized the impeccable according to their desires, and the capable according to their abilities, with assorted funds and funding as well as by opening the gate of favor and contribution [....] That said, by virtue of his being a Turk himself, he dwelled upon the vernacular Turkish poetry and at the same time studied the Persian style, for which reason his Persian poems are more plentiful than the Turkish ones and well known to the commoners" (Âşık Çelebi 22a).

In a Ledger of Revenues and Expenditures[65] from the reign of Süleyman dated 954-955/1547-1548, the donations made to ulema, treasury clerks, needy folk, etc. identified in the list of alms-giving and *inam* amounted to 2,653,874 *akçe*s. In this we come across not a single poet. Murad II's annuity apportioned to unemployed writers was in this period revoked.[66] One should not be surprised that the grand vizier Rüstem Paşa (1544-1553), the one responsible for this, went down in history as an avaricious and venal fellow. (The fact is, the Ottoman treasury reached its richest level during his period in office.) At that time, the *inam*s given to poets must have come out of the royal discretionary allowance or out of the operating surpluses of charitable foundations. It has been said that during the reign of Süleyman the Magnificent, the *inam*s given to the *nişancı* Celâlzade Mustafa for his *kaside*s alone amounted to 45,000 gold pieces. Âşık Çelebi (24a) commemorates Süleyman among Ottoman sultans as one of the rulers who most compensated the talented: "The Arab and Persian poets, as well as immaculate and impeccable personages everywhere, petitioned for asylum at the empire's doorstep [....] They sent *kaside*s [....] They were anxious to praise the sultan in their *kaside*s, hoping to be included among the eulogizers and receive regular salaries"; "He showed his favor by appointing to a position, granting a donation, or just graciously complimenting everyone according to his aptitude and the established rules". As a result of this, the country's capable people "made progress, some acquiring a mastery in his art and some complementing his ability [...] and others, being in his company, developed their skills. In sum, he helped all with his favors. He granted the position of *kadı* or *müderris* or any salaried status. Many times it happened that he personally gave one gold piece for each couplet in a love poem read" (Âşık Çelebi 24b).

Kınalızade Hasan Çelebi

Kınalızade Hasan Çelebi, who completed his *Tezkiretü'ş-Şu'arâ* in 1586 and presented it to Hoca Sa'deddin Efendi, the great *inşa* writer of the age, complained about patrons. He says: "The bigwigs of the age and big shots of the universe have no taste for these kinds of gems [....] They won't even stop to take a look at couplets or *kaside*s, which ironically strike them as good-for-nothing, on the view that specimens of trite tribute and eulogy do not bring out any material benefit; they won't pick up and read any *kaside* unless it has a refrain like "silver" or "gold" [....] They believe that a *tezkiretü'ş-şuara* is a *tezkire* (table) for counting coins; they've got no idea what a real *tezkiretü'ş-şuara* is [....] How ironic that, while they feel not a whit of proclivity or fondness for men of cultivation, they rain down arrows of rebuke and stones of censure on all sides" (199-209).

The Poets According to their Professions

If we categorize the poets included in *tezkiretü'ş-şuara*s according to their professions, poets who dropped out of the madrasa half way, as opposed to those who studied the Islamic sciences at the madrasa "all the way to polished completion", were in the majority. Most of these, since they aimed to fill positions in the state bureaucracy, placed their emphasis on poetry and *inşa*, and their madrasa training secured for them a general background in language and literature.[67] Alongside career scribes, scribes coming from the apprentice-journeyman-master system (Kâtip Şevkî, Kâtibî, Mesihî, Refikî, Kâtip Hasan, Sun'î, Cahdî, Rumî, Sihrî, Serirî, Arifî, Latifî), artisans from the class of tradesmen (Likayî the secondhand book dealer, Resmî the weaver of variegated fabric, Garibî the violin-maker, Şeyhî the trouser-tailor, Sefayî the surgeon, Zincirî the horse-trader, and Subutî the pharmacist), heads of dervish orders (Ruşenî, Hayalî, Meşrebî), classical singers and musicians (Makamî, Razî the tamboura-player, Vas'î), and lastly one landed cavalryman (*tımar sipahi*), Hayretî, and one janissary, Aşkî, were included in the *tezkire*s. Sehi included two women, Zeyneb Hatun and Mihri Hatun, as poets who had been schooled in the religious disciplines, music, and poetry and whose poems had garnered fame among the populace. The *tezkire* authors left out a vast number of folk poets, who were uninitiated in *sanayi-i şiiriye* and most of whom composed in syllabic meters; they only considered the divan poets to be true poets.

The Turkmen folk poet Cemilî was recommended to Sehi. Sehi says that Cemilî is ignorant of theory but recites poems "extemporaneously". If we leave aside the composers of poetry who occupied high offices like vizier, governor, treasury secretary, *nişancı*, teacher, judge, and high-council clerk, the patron's rewarding of the poet would usually take place by way of appointment to a service like charitable-foundation director or secretary. Besides the salaries attached to religious offices, which were referred to variously as *cihet*, *idrar*, or *ratibe*, poets would be apportioned income from the operating surplus left over after charitable-foundation expenditures (for Fuzulî such an appointment was made, which he came out against in the *Şikâyetname*). These surpluses were ordinarily appropriated by the state treasury to cover extraordinary state expenses such as accrued in wartime. As of the date Shawwal 8, 896/August 14, 1491, "it is hereby decreed that the sultan's institutions will henceforth award all such surplus to absolutely no one" (Gökbilgin, *Edirne ve Paşa Livası* 302).

V. FUZULÎ AND PATRONAGE

In Fuzulî's *kaside* entitled "Enisü'l-Kalb" (Intimate Friend of Heart), one observes that no reference is made to any patron, and the idea was put forward by Ahmed Hamdi Tanpınar that Fuzulî was not on a quest for a sponsor.[68] In particular in "Enisü'l-Kalb", which was a parallel on Khāqānī's famous prophet-tribute, and in general in the *kaside*s Fuzulî composed for the Prophet's Family and the Holy Sites (the Sacred Shrines of Shiism), it was natural enough for him not to be seeking a sponsor.

During the period (1508-1534) in which he lived as a Safavid poet who had taken to the Shii sect of the twelve imams, Fuzulî labeled the Ottomans "apostates" and the Ottoman realm as "the land of apostates".[69] It was understandable when, unable to gain the esteem he expected upon suddenly finding himself an Ottoman subject in 1534, he turned away from the sultans and dignitaries and retreated into solitude. Of associating with sultans, Fuzulî says:

> Bimulk u māl kih hastand zāyil u ẕāhib
> Asās-i bunyah-'i ummīd ustuvār makun
> Agar turāst havā-yi faẕīlat-i bāqī
> Bi'ilm gūsh va'z taḥṣīl-i 'ilm 'ār makun (*Farsça Divan* 617)

> To fortify the foundation of hope with false structures,
> Illusory goods and transient assets—don't even try.
> If you desire to make the air of virtue permanent,
> Listen to learned lectures, acquire science—don't be shy.

Nevertheless, the letters and *kaside*s he wrote to Sultan Süleyman, Prince Bayezid, and Ottoman dignitaries and governors during the Ottoman period of his relatively long life (d. 968/1561) demonstrate that he had constantly been on a quest for a patron/sponsor.

(In his *kaside*s, the patron is expressed as *hami* or *velinimet*, and the expected donation as *inam*, *lütuf*, *kerem*, or *cud*.)

Here we shall analyze Fuzulî's famous *Şikâyetname* from the standpoint of his quest for a patron.[70]

At the opening of his letter, in the sense that the donations you make belong not actually to you but to God, Fuzulî affirms that God has created worldly sustenance as a charitable trust and delegated its stewardship and administration to rulers, and he indicates that how much sustenance is to be bestowed upon its rightful owners is up to the pens of the authorities charged with this task, stating:

> Sâkin-i gûşe-i kanâ'at iken,
> Başıma düştü câh sevdâsı
> Zevk-i ehl-i tamâ' temennâsı
> İstedim kim uluvv-i kadr bulam
> Mazhar-i lûtf-i Pâdişâh olam
> Bilmedim kim şikeste-hâl olurum
> Hased ehline pâyimâl olurum

> I was leading a spare life, contented, at my retreat;
> Suddenly, ambition for high office took hold of me,
> Craving to enjoy the pleasures of the rich and mighty;
> I yearned to acquire power and prestige through high station,
> To be graced by the generosity of the Sultan.
> I never realized, though, that this might result in defeat,
> That those jealous of me could trample me under their feet.

Here Fuzulî admits that he has approached the sultan with the aim of attaining some station, for no patron has materialized in a long time. Fuzulî accepts that reaching favor will be possible exclusively by attending the ruler of the day. For this very reason, he says, it would be wrong *not* to apply to the sultan. For Fuzulî, in a patrimonial society, the situation—notwithstanding all his dignity and pride—could not have been otherwise.

> Her ne kim 'âlem ana muhtâc ol andan ganî (*Türkçe Divan* 48)

> All the world is in need of him, he is rich enough to need none.

> Fuzulî hüsn-i etvâriyle olmuş kurbuna mâ'il
> Budur te'sîri 'âlemde hemîşe hüsn-i etvârın (53)

> With gracious style, Fuzulî leans toward proximity;
> In this world, that is always the effect of gracious style.

"Swallowing my pride toward the nine heavenly wheels of destiny, I contented myself with a salary of nine *akçes*[71] from the charitable foundations, for which I received an *arz* (petition of recommendation); for the award's conferral, I sent the *arz* for a *berat* (sultanic order) to the royal court, unto which the whole world applies for asylum, and observed the award's delivery [....] They brought me an imperial decree from the sultan [....] A wave of elation swept over my languid soul."

According to Ottoman bureaucratic procedure, every appointment began with an *arz*.[72] Generally speaking, the *arz* was a written recommendation presented to the sultan by an officer personally close to the petitioner. At the grand vizier's residence, after review by the relevant departments and approval by the department chiefs, the result would be submitted for the grand vizier's approval. Foremost among the appointment departments stood the *reisü'l-küttab* (head of the scribes). Following the grand vizier's "validation" (approval), the motion would go to the *nişancı* for the dispensing of the *berat*. After the *tuğra* (sultan's emblem) had been affixed by the *nişancı*, the *berat* would be handed over to the petitioner.

We gather from Fuzulî's "I received an *arz*" statement that someone (in all likelihood the director charged with overseeing the charitable foundations of Karbala) had set in motion a petition for his retirement pension. Upon receiving the retirement-pension *berat*, Fuzulî does not hesitate to express his great pleasure. His gushy and lengthy depiction of the sultan's *berat* is written in order to convey his gratitude to the sultan.

He receives the award decree, which he calls "a wonderful key to treasures of mercies and contributions", and goes to the director of charitable foundations.[73] At first, he can find no opportunity to enter into his presence. Through stubborn insistence, he eventually appears before the director. The director is probably in the middle of a staff meeting. Neither does Fuzulî like the director and his staff, nor they Fuzulî (they were probably aware that he had once been among the *rafizî* [Shiites attached to Shah Ismail]). "I greeted them, but since my business was not to bribe them, they didn't take it up; I showed them the award judgment, but they said it was of no use anyway and were not complimentary." "I said that the sultan felt it incumbent upon them to recognize me, and he delivered me this pension award decree so that I might become a perpetual beneficiary of these charitable foundations, so let me offer up an all-out prayer for the sultan." In reply, the attendees at the meeting said, "you're talking about the surpluses, which can't be left over [....] If any surplus were left over after covering operational imperatives, do you think any would be left over after we got our hands on it?".

In a charitable foundation, the surplus left over after the director's share, the salaries, the renovation expenses, the repair expenses, and the revenue collectors' commissions was called the *ziyade* (foundational surplus). This surplus would occasionally be reinvested for growth on behalf of the foundation in partnership with a merchant, and it would usually be appropriated by the sultan's treasury to spend on a campaign; or it would be apportioned as a salary for the clergy responsible for reciting prayers in mausoleums and mosques for the sultan, the army, or the souls of the deceased. There was generally no money left over for surpluses, and allotments from this source could generally not be carried out.

Above all, it was improper treatment for this allotment to have been apportioned to Fuzulî from the surpluses. Fuzulî himself points out that in the original *arz* there was no mention of deriving this salary specifically from the surpluses. The director and his assistants explained to Fuzulî the difficulties inherent in drawing a salary from the surpluses, but Fuzulî attributed their stance to bad intentions. The funds of charitable foundations would be accounted for and checked under the supervision of the local magistrate. It is true that bribery, which grew widespread under Ottoman rule, gave administrators an opportunity to internally retain the surpluses.[74] He says, "Helpless, I gave up the struggle and, disconsolate and deprived, I retreated into my corner of sequestration". For "the fateful sun of generosity" he pens this letter to Nişancı Celâlzade and does not give up hope that Süleyman will intercede:

Hâşe lillâh kim ferâgat küncünün sükkânına
Matrah-i mekr ola dergâh-i hilâfet-dest-gâh
Hâşe lillâh kim kanâ'at gencinün muştâkına
Ejder-i bî-dâd ola tuğrâ-yi hükm-i Pâdişâh

God forbid how could those who live in the hermits' dungeon
Use deceit to enter the court of the holder of the caliphate?
God forbid how could the Sovereign's signature be a merciless dragon
To those who aspire to nothing other than the treasure of contentment?

(How elegant for the sultanic curved monogram to be compared here to a vicious dragon!)

In any event, he says, in the original *arz* no mention was made of surpluses. But if "surpluses" means the leftovers after the salaries of foundation employees, the allotments to be distributed to retirees, the feed to be supplied to the animals, etc., then this command in the sultan's name is tantamount in the director's interpretation to: "I [the Sultan] have conferred this award decree proving my generosity, and I hereby pronounce that your level of power and share of prestige shall henceforth be lower than common foodstuffs, perhaps lower even than beasts, stones, and dirt; be advised of your station." Whereas I, says Fuzulî, had known myself to be "superior to even the most deserving". I'm not in fact writing this due to the damages I've sustained and suffering I've endured; it's that your (Celâlzade's) efforts have gone to waste, that's why I'm writing. He puts up with it, saying "Oh well, God will surely make amends".

> Gerçi endûh u mihnetim çokdur
> Hiç kimseden şikâyetim yokdur
> Tâli'ümdür bana cefâ yetüren
> Her bir ânında belâ getüren
> Yoksa dergâh-i Pâdişâh-i zemân
> Lûtfda menba' dürür mürüvvetde kân

> It is true I have suffered much distress and pain
> But no one is to be blamed, I will not complain.
> It is my own misfortune that brought me torment
> And a myriad afflictions every moment—
> And yet, in this age, the Court of our majesty
> Is a source of kindness and a mine of bounty.

The *Şikâyetname* summarizes the tragic life of every poet with hands outstretched in hopes of the patron's favor and generosity. Here, the voice is of a noble human being's or great artist's feeling of disillusionment at, revolt against, and ridicule toward the pettiness of the world. Here is the interminable encounter between patrons, who occupy powerful stations, and rich-spirited poor people struggling to survive in low places. The helplessness of the poet forced to beg from his lord in such a society is articulated here. The *Şikâyetname* is a document that reflects most accurately the real face of patronage and the psychology of the poet of that era.

Nevertheless, in a *kaside* he composed for the fourth caliph 'Alī, one gathers from the following two couplets that Fuzulî received a "reliable income" (staff salary for religious functions):

> Yā Amīr al-Mu'minīn shud muddat-i panjāh sāl
> K'az janāb-i ḥaqq bamadḥ-i tū Fuẕūlī mulham ast (*Farsça Divan* 145)
> ....
> Dāyim az khvān-i tū idrār-i muqarrar mī burad
> Rūz u shab bā chākarān-i āsitānat hamdam ast (146)

> So that he can praise you, O Commander of the Faithful,
> For fifty years, to Fuzûlî God gave inspiration:
> ....
> Together with the attendants at your mausoleum,
> He kept receiving a salary from your foundation.

One infers from these couplets that he drew a salary in return for the duty of eulogizing 'Alī at his mausoleum in Najaf for fifty years ("Sāqīnāmah", *Farsça Divan* 695: "Maddāḥ-i Payghambaram"). In describing himself, he uses the expressions "eulogizer of the prophet" and "paeanist". This function undoubtedly involved reciting "condolences" and "elegy"-*kaside*s on behalf of "pilgrims" visiting the holy shrines.[75]

His famous Persian *kaside* that opens with "As-Salām ay sākin-i miḥnat sarāy-i Karbalā" may be one example of this type of *kaside*. Parts of it read:

> Yā shahīd-i Karbalā kardam bigird-i ṭawf-i tū
> Raghbat-i sayr-i faẓā-yi gham-faẓā-yi Karbalā (*Farsça Divan* 204)
> ....
> Har kih andar Karbalā az dīdah khūn-i dil narīkht
> Ghālibā āgah nashud az mācarā-yi Karbalā (205)
> ....
> Karbalā khvān-i 'aṭā-yi tust gardūn dam bidam
> Mī rasānad bar hamah 'ālam ṣalā-yi Karbalā
> Har kih mī āyad biqadr-i sa'y u isti'dād-i khvud
> Bahrah-'i mī gīrad az baḥr-i 'aṭā-yi Karbalā (205)

> O martyr of Karbala, at your tomb round and round I go:
> Visiting its woeful space that adds suffering to sorrow.
> ....
> If someone in Karbala does not shed heartfelt bloody tears,
> He does not know the events that took place there over the years.
> ....
> For the generous gifts you donate, Karbala is the source:
> It sends to all people throughout the world its prayers in due course.
> If, with his own means and efforts, someone pays a visit there,
> From Karbala's ocean-like largesse, he shall receive his share.

The person Fuzulî was directly subject to was the director in charge of overseeing the charitable foundations of the "Sacred Shrines of Shiism", that is, Karbala, Najaf, and the region's other holy sites.[76] Fuzulî clearly states that from these foundations he received a lifelong "reliable salary", that is, allotments in perpetuity:

> Mā rātibah khvārān-i dar-i Āl-i Rasūlīm
> 'Umrīst kih īn rātibah dārīm muqarrar
> Masdūd nagashtah dar īn rātibah bar mā
> Z'an rūy kih hastīm bidīn rātibah dar khvur (*Farsça Divan* 612)

> Serving the Prophet's family, we receive salaries;
> For the whole length of our lives, we have been receiving these;
> The gate of such an income has never been closed on us,
> If we get paid, it is because we merit these wages.

In 1534 in Baghdad, Fuzulî had met Nişancı Celâlzade Mustafa, distinguished in his style of *inşa* and poet in charge of the department that processed Fuzulî's *berat*, and an amiable relationship had probably been struck up between them. Two of the *kaside*s Fuzulî composed for Celâlzade have survived to our day (*Farsça Divan* 710-712, *kaside* no. 49, and *Türkçe Divan* 101-04, no. 33).[77] The Turkish *kaside* coincides with the time of Celâlzade's appointment to the chancery; Fuzulî penned it in congratulation. Celâlzade was promoted to this office upon the decease of Nişancı Seydî Bey (10 November 1534) in the course of the Irakeyn Seferi (Twin Iraqs Campaign). Celâlzade Mustafa Çelebi (he came to be known by the title Paşa), who remained in this position for an unbroken stretch of 23 years until the year 1557, stands among the most famous *nişancı*s.[78] Süleyman, who appreciated the great service of Celâlzade, who had played a definitive role in the arrangement of the laws in Süleyman the Magnificent's reign and in the development of the courtly *inşa* style, left Celâlzade's *nişancı* income stream (300,000 *akçe*s or 5,000 gold pieces) untouched during the latter's retirement. After Celâlzade retired, he was once again appointed *nişancı* in 1566 (his death was in October 1567). Just as he possessed great renown for *inşa*, the official writing style, Celâlzade, who knew both Arabic and Persian well, was also a well-known poet; the large donations he received in return for the *kaside*s he delivered to the sultan (according to hearsay, some 45,000 gold pieces) are proof of how wealthy could become those who captured the patron's appreciation (contrast this with the daily allowance of 9 *akçe*s that befell Fuzulî). (Here let us also note that Celâlzade had a brother, Sâlih Çelebi, serving in the educational and judicial systems, who had composed a verse rendering of *Leylâ ve Mecnun*.)

In the commemorative *kaside* for Celâlzade, Fuzulî exalts him to the high heavens:

> Gül-i hadîka-i ikbâl Mustafa Çelebi
> Kim oldu devleti kurbiyle kâmkâr kalem (*Türkçe Divan* 102)

> Mustafa Çelebi, the rose of the garden of bliss,
> Nearness to whose opulence gave this pen prosperity.

and requests sponsorship from him:

> Arayub ehl-i hüner varını yetince sana
> Cihân içinde besi çekdi intizâr kalem (103)
> ………………………………………………

Sipihr-menziletâ, ol Fuzûli-i zârem
Ki hâl-i zârumı yazınca oldı zâr kalem (103)
....
Sen olsan ol kaleme i'tibâr içün hâmî
Sana hükûmet içün ola dest-yâr kalem (104)

The pen, searching for a great figure of art in the world,
Waited to find you for many years.
....
O great artist, whose station is high in the firmament,
When tearful Fuzulî wrote about his plight, the pen shed tears.
....
If you would become the pen's protector to give it prestige,
The pen will support you with your political powers.

In the Persian divan, *kaside* 11, which lacks a heading inscription, was probably composed for Celâlzade:

Tūyī muḥarrir-i aḥkām-i kārkhānah-'i 'aql
Tūyī muṣavvir-i ashkāl-i kārgāh-i khayāl (*Farsça Divan* 72)
....
Bilutf-i ṭab' mansūb ḥifẓ-i har qānūn
Biḥusn-i sa'y-i tū marbūṭ ḥall-i har ashkāl (73)

You are the author of decrees at the council of intellect,
The creative artist at the workshop of imagination;
....
You, as the appointed overseer of the pledge of the laws,
Do your best to send each problem to its happy destination.

Fuzulî subsequently expects favor and contributions from him:

Tūyī ki mī bari az luḥ-i dil ghubār-i alam
Tūyī ki mī kuni az ahl-i dard daf'-i malāl (73; see also 75, couplets 34-35)

You are the one who wipes off the dust of grief from the heart,
Who drives away the gloom from those living in tribulation.

In this *kaside*, Fuzulî clearly names (Celâlzade) Mustafa Çelebi; he sends this *kaside* to him in care of a friend. He attests that he was together with this friend for several years, himself in Baghdad while the friend was in Vâsit. He attests that the fellow proved ever helpful and a close friend to him. Ultimately, announcing that he is setting out for Turkey, he requests Celâlzade's assistance:

> Chū ham diyār-i manī ḥāl-i man tū mī dānī
> Niyāzmandi-'i khvud bā tū mī kunam irsāl (74)

> Because you know my country intimately and me, too,
> I am dispatching my letter of entreaty to you.

It was natural enough for Fuzulî to seek Celâlzade's sponsorship. No one was better qualified to evaluate his command of ornate prose than the great *inşa* stylist of the age Nişancı Celâlzade.[79] In the *Şikâyetname*, Fuzulî took pains to show off his command of the art of *inşa*, and this work was copied for centuries in documents.

Fuzulî and Süleyman the Magnificent

It appears that Süleyman, while touring the sacred gravesites during the conquest of Iraq[80] (18-23 March 1534), visited Hilla, and Fuzulî saw him there.[81] Addressing the sultan in various works of his, Fuzulî sought his sponsorship and favor. In his preface to *Leylâ ve Mecnun*, Fuzulî thus emphasizes how indispensable patronage has been throughout the ages:

> Rahm et ki garîb u hâk-sârım
> Bî-mûnis u yâr u gam-güsârım
> Ol bir nice hemdem-i muvâfik
> Ya'nî şu'arâ-yi devr-i sâbık
> Tedrîcile geldiler cihâna
> Ta'zîmile oldular revâne
> Devrân oları mu'azzam etti
> Her devr birini mükerrem etti
> Her birine hâmi oldu bir şâh
> Zevk-i suhanından oldu agâh
> Türk ü Arab u Acem'de eyyâm
> Her şâ'ire vermiş idi bir kâm (80)
> ....
> Söz gevherine nazar salanlar
> Gencîne verüp güher alanlar (82)
> ....
> Sarf eyle ri'âyetimde eltâf
> Tenhâlığımı gör eyle insâf
> ....
> Tutsan elini ben fakîrin
> Hak ola hemîşe destgîrin (86)
> ....

Mustevcib-i ʻizz u câh olurdum
Şâyeste-i bârgâh olurdum
Makbûl düşerdim âsitâna
Manzûr-i şehinşah-i zamâna (88)
…………………………………………
Var ümidim kim hemîşe irtifâʻ-i kadr ile
Ola ihsânun neşât-engîz-i her kalb-i hazîn

Pity me, I stand lonesome and sorrowful,
With no friends or confidants, I am woeful.
In former times, poets were supportive mates,
They banded together, they were intimates;
Joining the circles of poets, one by one,
They steadily rose to the highest station.
Every new era managed to elevate
One to a lofty place with the aid of fate:
He would become the bosom friend of a king
By excelling in the art of conversing.
Among Turks, Arabs, and Persians, the poet
Enjoyed the best life that anyone could get.
…………………………………………
Those who fix their eyes on verbal gems
Those who give a treasure for a pearl.
…………………………………………
Lavish on me your generosity:
See how lonely I am and take pity.
…………………………………………
If you care to hold the hand of poor me,
Your hand would be held by God Almighty.
…………………………………………
Thanks to your grace, I would rise to power and high station,
Perhaps worthy of life at the Palace of the Sultan.
I would earn a great deal of honor and esteem, for sure
If I were to become the world emperor's cynosure.
…………………………………………………………
I cherish the hope that my value will increase all the time,
That, thanks to your largesse, each sad heart will be engulfed in joy.

He exalts the Ottoman sultan to the high heavens and takes pains especially to point out his status as caliph and imam:

"Our sultan, whose sultanate is spiritually on par with the caliphate and upon whose sovereign throne the imamate rests" (X-99)

> Pādshāh-i baḥr u bar Sulṭān Suleymān kih hast
> Dar khilāfat jā nishīnhāy-i Nabī-rā jā nishīn

> Sultan Süleyman, Emperor of lands and seas, ranks
> With those ensconced in the caliphate of our Prophet.

In another place, he makes a point of Süleyman's shah-like status of imamhood and *velayet* (sainthood):

> Pâdişâh-i bahr u ber Sultan Süleyman-i Velî
> Hâli ondan olmasun yâ Rab velâyet tâ-ebed

> Sultan Süleyman, Emperor of lands and seas,
> Is a saint, my God, make his sainthood eternal.

Prior to 1534, he had used these same words for the Shah of Iran. Fuzulî articulated his expectation of favor and contributions in the introductory and concluding sections of his *Hadikatü's-Süeda* in language full of praise for Süleyman.

Fuzulî and Prince Bayezid

Bayezid, among Süleyman the Magnificent's sons who were the legitimate heirs to the Ottoman throne, was known to his contemporaries as a "virtuous, poetic, upright, humble, and benevolent" prince. He wrote under the pen name Şahî. He was known to be quite generous toward those in his retinue.[82] The letter Fuzulî wrote to Bayezid, who had been sent off to a province to serve as its governor, is a document that clearly proves he was on the lookout for a patron.[83]

This letter, which was published by Hasibe Mazıoğlu,[84] demonstrates that Fuzulî had been corresponding with Bayezid for a long time. In the letter, explaining that he was desirous of attending the prince, Fuzulî says: "By God Most High, I aspire to naught but honorable service. But numerous are the obstacles arising from the meagerness of sustenance". From his statement that "one desires discharge and deliverance from this dungeon of torment and its fetters of treachery", where he hopes for the material assistance requisite for setting out, it is obvious how badly he wants to quit Karbala. He had bound himself to Karbala on account of "men of worshipful indoctrination [...] and an aversion to traveling the climes" (*Farsça Divan* 9). Travel to the realm of Anatolia never materializes, and our poet retreats into solitude and dedicates himself to poetry: " 'Uzlatam shud mūjib-i mashghūl va kasb-i hunar" (In seclusion I live immersed in adoration and art).

The *Tezkire* Authors on Fuzulî

As for the opinions the *tezkire* authors held of Fuzulî as a poet, in Sehi (945/1538) there is no mention of Fuzulî. Baghdad was annexed to the Ottoman realm in 1534, four years before the completion of Sehi's work. Latifî (953/1546) rates Fuzulî as original but, by reason of the dialect he used, "curious". Âşık Çelebi (976/1569) provides more comprehensive information about Fuzulî and envisions him among the great poets, as masterful in his *kaside*s and lyric in his ghazals. As for Kınalızade (994/1586), he hails Fuzulî as accomplished in the art of poetry and a renowned poet famous in his own lifetime. These records show that it took time for Fuzulî's reputation to spread through the Ottoman realm.

From Âşık Çelebi, who understood Fuzulî the best, we can establish the following points based on what he wrote about him:[85]

I. Fuzulî was recognized as a master among the denizens of the Iraq and Diyarbakır regions, that is to say, among Turkmen poets (in my view, the epithet "Azeri", which derives from Iranian roots, is misleading).

II. He was a lyric poet whose heart had been consumed by the blaze of ecstasy, who therefore cast himself into the void, and who composed sincere poems from the heart.

III. During Süleyman's stay in Baghdad, Fuzulî presented *kaside*s to Grand Vizier İbrahim Paşa and *Kazasker* Kadirî (Kadrî) Efendi; Kadirî Efendi recommended him to the sultan and İbrahim Paşa and, for his livelihood, apportioned to him a regular staff salary from the funds earmarked for clergymen.

IV. From that time on, he lived on this income. He passed his time in solitude composing lyric poems. His verse is structurally sound, his ghazals are lyrical, and his *kaside*s, strong from the standpoints of both imagery and artifice, furthermore recount his troubles.

V. His works in the *mesnevi* genre, especially his *Leylâ ve Mecnun*, deserve mention; every word of them is a radiant candle, every punctuation mark a spark-flinging bit of flame. In particular, the *kaside* he composed for the Prophet Muhammad is a model of high rhetoric, flawless from the standpoints of artifice and imagery. It is unknown whether he was still living or had already died (Âşık Çelebi completed his work in 1569).

VI. His inscription, dated 1556 upon the fountain constructed at Karbala in Süleyman's honor, is a fluent and dazzling work.

The Ottoman *tezkire* author, in the following couplet he quoted from *Leylâ ve Mecnun* (*Türkçe Divan* 179),

> Fuzûlî el seni Mecnûn'dan artuk der melâmette
> Buna münkir değil Mecnûn dahî ma'kule kâ'ildir

> Fuzûlî, strangers claim you are more reproachable than Mecnun:
> This nobody would deny, Mecnun himself accedes to reason.

would have preferred the Persian word *efzun* instead of *artuk*. The *tezkire* authors assess the style of the Turkmen poet Fuzulî, who preferred Turkish words and expressions, as strange and crude. In the *tezkire* of Kınalızade Hasan Çelebi,[86] even if he repeats Latifî and Âşık Çelebi, he pronounces Fuzulî a "a poet of high character". He accepts him as a sui generis ("singular", "unique") master from the standpoints of the aesthetics and rhetoric (stylistic innovation, exposition, and eloquence) in his works. He is "a famous poet possessed of a command of every aspect, as" his poems "are solid, sound, delicate, and colorful". Hasan Çelebi's words, far more glowing than the rest, may be taken as evidence that Fuzulî attained his true renown in Ottoman Turkey after his death. His *Leylâ ve Mecnun* especially garnered him more fame than any of his other works. Even if his work *Hadikatü's-Süeda*, which he composed in Turkish for visitors to the Sacred Shrines of Shiism like Süleyman and which spread widely across the Turkish world, was actually a translation from the Iranian Ḥusayn Vā'iẓ, the *tezkire* authors accept that it manifoldly exceeded Vā'iẓ's work in rhetoric and eloquence.

Fuzulî and *İnşa*

The Ottoman "prose" that researchers of literary history find in Fuzulî and the other poets is actually the official *inşa* style[87] that scribes attached to the Ottoman bureaucracy would learn via an exclusive training program. This was an official style created by a bureaucracy that developed in Baghdad and parts of Iran, and it subsequently formed a model de rigueur for imperial regimes.[88] The language of *inşa*, which the scribes would employ in official correspondence, became a part of high court-culture and was a lingua franca among Iran, the Central Asian Timurid and Çağatay states, and the Indian Timurids from the standpoints of vocabulary, idiom, and style. This language was distinct from spoken Turkish. We find spoken Turkish in the epics, stories, and catechism books written for hoi polloi. The *inşa* language, modeled after Timurid-era Persian *inşa*, arose among the Ottomans according to these prototypes in the first half of the fifteenth century; [89] was further developed by Cafer Çelebi and Cezerî Kasım Paşa (pen name Safî),[90] who immigrated to the Ottoman realm from Shiraz during the reign of the

Conqueror; and attained its classic form under Nişancı Celâlzade Mustafa. Fuzulî penned his Turkish prose compositions in this style. He emphasized his proficiency in *inşa* and that others had been edified by his works of this genre (*Türkçe Divan* 5). That said, he apologizes for not having personally been able to sojourn in Turkey or Central Asia so as to pick up the "anecdotes and adages" used by the masters of rhetoric there (*Türkçe Divan* 7-9) and clarifies that he shrinks from the critiques of "the incompetent pencil-pushers".

We know that a certain group of Akkoyunlu bureaucrats (one of these being İdris-i Bidlisî, whose dialect was the Azeri-Turkmen dialect) occupied a select position among the Ottoman scribes.[91] These Akkoyunlu had taken refuge from Shah Ismail in the Ottoman realm, spoke Azeri-Turkmen Turkish, and were so well versed in Persian *inşa* that they could do it justice.

Bayezid II asked İdris to write an Ottoman history in Persian and yet commissioned İbn Kemal to write the Turkish version. Once the Ottomans had settled in Iraq, Fuzulî expressed his desire to go to Rum, in other words, to the Ottoman realm, and further develop his style there. As an Ottoman *inşa* stylist, he was eager to enter the scribal class and was upset that he was unable to acquire the privileges they enjoyed.

> Fuzûli ister isen izdiyâd-i rütbe-i fazl
> Diyâr-i Rûm'u gözet terk-i hâk-i Bağdâd et (*Türkçe Divan* 165)

> If you desire to raise your rank and status, Fuzûlî,
> Set your sights on the Ottoman lands, abandon Baghdad.

> Fuzûli eyledi âheng-i 'ayş-hâne-i Rûm
> Esîr-i mihnet-i Bağdâd gördüğün gönlüm (327)

> This heart of mine you saw in bondage to misery in Baghdad,
> Fuzûlî, is now set to enter the Ottoman house of joy.

But he could never realize this ambition of his. At the beginning of his Turkish divan, he regards himself as a master of both poetry and prose; supposedly one of his admirers has told him that God "has rendered your conquest of the provinces of the disciplines of verse and prose easy for you [….] There exists no assimilator of the disciplines of verse and prose as proficient in all three languages as you [….] Some worldly folk have been edified by your pearls of prose and conundrums" (*Türkçe Divan* 7; of course the quoted speaker is none other than Fuzulî himself). In his prose writings, Fuzulî demonstrated his thorough command of the overwrought *inşa* style. In the *Şikâyetname* he sent to Nişancı Celâlzade, the well-known *inşa* stylist of his time, he attempted to prove himself an *inşa* stylist in his own right, just as his mentor Habîbî had quit the service of the Akkoyunlu Sultan Yakub and gone from Tabriz to Istanbul. As expressed in his letter to Prince Bayezid, the "noble service" into which he sought to enter was probably the imperial secretariat.

In spite of all this, the prose works that Fuzulî wrote in the *inşa* style probably met with high appraisal in Istanbul. Couplets 3-6 of the *kaside* he placed at the head of the official reply he sent to Mosul governor Ahmed Bey were recycled into the epistle sent by Süleyman to the Iranian Shah concerning Prince Bayezid, who had fled to Iran.[92]

VI. THE PROVENANCES AND PROFESSIONS OF POETS LISTED IN THE *İNAM* REGISTER AS RECEIVING DONATIONS IN THE YEARS 909-917 A.H.[93]

WRITER	PROFESSION AND/OR PROVENANCE
Alâaddin (Şehdî)	tailor (Âşık Çelebi 227b, Latifî 213)
Ali Çelebi	from among the *müşaherehoran* (Âşık Çelebi 93a)
Ali	son of Seyyid Ömer
Ali	son of Karamanî Mehmed Paşa
Ahmed Çelebi	teacher
Azizî	poet (Âşık Çelebi 170a)
Basirî	poet
Bayezid Çelebi	nephew of Akşemseddin
Cevherî (Mehmed Çelebi)	poet
Derviş Mehmed	author
Dilirî	poet
Edibî	Persian, poet
Firdevsî	poet, *inşa* stylist, author of the *Süleymanname*
Hadidî	poet, historian
Haydar	scribe, *nöker* to a prince
İdris-i Bidlisî	*inşa* stylist
'Iyanî	poet (Âşık Çelebi 184b)
Kâtibî	poet, from among the *müşaherehoran*
Keşfî	poet
Lâlî, Mevlâna	poet, from among the legal scholars (Âşık Çelebi 105a)
Mailî	poet, of ulema lineage (Âşık Çelebi 111b)
Mehmed	poet, son of the *nişancı* Mehmed Paşa
Mehmed Çelebi	poet, son of a *kazasker*
Mehmed	one of the men of the viceroy of Egypt
Mihri	poetess
Muzaffer, Mevlâna	teacher, wrote a book
Müşteri	poet, wrote a book
Natıkî	poet
Necati, Mevlâna	poet, *nişancı* to Prince Mahmud (Âşık Çelebi 130)
Nişanî	*nişancı* to Prince Mahmud
Ömer Çelebi	poet, from among the *nişancı* scribes

Refikî	poet (Âşık Çelebi 238a)
Revanî	poet, court cavalryman (Âşık Çelebi 240a)
Ruhî	poet
Sabayî	poet
Sailî	poet (Âşık Çelebi 148b)
Sa'dî, Mevlâna	poet, from among the legal scholars (Âşık Çelebi 156a)
Sa'yî	poet
Sefayî	poet
Sucudî	poet (Âşık Çelebi 149a)
Süleyman Çelebi	*defterdar*
Şefiî	poet
Şerifî	poet
Şehdî	see Alâaddin
Şehrî	poet, author of the *Tevarih-i Âl-i Osman*
Taliî	poet, one of Prince Mahmud's men (Âşık Çelebi 91b)
Visalî	poet
Vasfî	poet
Zamirî, Mevlâna	poet, from among the legal scholars
Mevlâna Yarhisarî's son (?)	poet

Prince Mahmud, who was relegated to the governorship of Manisa, was one of the age's leading patrons, assembling in his service great poets such as Cem Sultan. He employed some poets in his high-council affairs. Among these, we know of Sehi, Necati, Şevkî, Sun'î, and Taliî (see the index of Âşık Çelebi). The famous poet Necati at first served the prince in his chancery and in time became his companion. Necati, who upon Mahmud's death went to Istanbul and looked for work, was assured a monthly salary of 1,000 *akçe*s.

The secretariats of the Royal Council and the statesmen's high councils provided many poets with an opportunity to present *kaside*s to them and thereby to obtain their proximity and companionship (for the case of Necati, see Âşık Çelebi 130b).

The biography of the poet Zatî, whom Âşık Çelebi called the "trailblazer among poets", is particularly illuminating (see Âşık Çelebi 277a-284a). Zatî, who lacked a proper post, was a poet who made poetry his complete livelihood. While handcrafting boots in Balıkesir, he "got an urge for poetry", came to Istanbul, and became one of the age's most sought-after poets.

It appears that Zatî received a *caize* of 2,000 *akçe*s for a *kaside* he first presented to the sultan on the date July 28, 1510 (Erünsal 332, no. 129). Without any "office, attachment, occupation, or job" like those of the other poets, he made his living solely by composing poems and collecting *caize*s; he developed his abilities by hanging around the poets of the age. He was poor; since poetry was his only livelihood, "whenever the dignitaries might require a *kaside* or *nazire*", he would draw upon his store of "old *kaside*s and ghazals". To make ends meet, he would concoct *kaside*s even for the low-ranking teachers and judges. The price of a *kaside* had dropped as low as one gold piece (60 *akçe*s). They say he composed as many as four hundred *kaside*s and seventeen hundred ghazals. In short, Zatî was a new type of poet, a poet who turned art into a commodity for open sale; he is the oldest representative we know of the modern poet/writer type who writes and sells volumes of poetry and tries to make a living thereby.

Why and Upon Whom *İnam* and Alms Would be Bestowed

On holidays, bonuses would be distributed. An additional gift would be made to those presenting an elegy on the occasion of a prince's death, or presenting a piece to hail a season like winter or spring, or those presenting a *kaside* or date-embedded couplet to commemorate a victory of the sultan. On the occasion of the death of an important personage's relative, the sultan would send the survivor a condolence of money and *hilat*s. A donation might also be made upon the recommendation of an influential scholar or *inşa* stylist. We know of people who made their living by routinely delivering *kaside*s. For this type of donation, the term *inam* is generally used. We know that the patron was known as a *velinimet* (benefactor), which derives from the Arabic root *na'ma*. In general, for donations by the ulema, the term *tasadduk* (alms-giving) was preferred. The *kaside*, elegy, date-embedded couplet, original book, or gift book would be delivered either personally by the writer or else in care of some intermediary, and the gift would be reciprocated with a gift.

In order to get *inam*, besides those works submitted directly to the sultan, works could alternatively be presented via the intercession of a sponsor. Upon the recommendation of the treasurer İsmail Ağa, Mihri Hatun, the daughter of Mevlâna Hasan of Amasya, was given 3,000 *akçe*s in *inam* for the work (*kaside*? divan?) she submitted (Erünsal 310-23). Thus, *inam* and alms-giving functioned as an institution that served the purposes of both social relations and the sponsorship of arts and letters.

As for the question of how written works circulated in society, one gathers that the works of poets and scholars would at first "circulate among polite society, banquets, and gatherings" (*Şakayık-ı Numaniye*, trans. Mecdî, 12), or the writer would send a copy of the work to the sultan, to dignitaries, or to his friends via some acquaintance. One must not forget that most mosque and madrasa complexes had charitable-foundation libraries open to the public. Thus, the institution of charitable foundations constituted a significant, separate avenue for the patronage of culture.[94]

The librarians (literally, "guardians of books") that sultans and the other endowers assigned to foundation libraries carried out their duties of storing these books, which were the property of the charitable foundation, meticulously, with a zeal befitting their religious obligation. From time to time, sultans would have these valuable treasure troves inspected and place them under conservation with their stamps of approval. Thus, the manuscript libraries of Istanbul foundations today constitute the world's richest collection encompassing products of arts and letters of Islamic civilization.

Besides patronage by dignitaries, meetings of poets amongst themselves formed an environment of exchange. Whenever they had the opportunity, poets of the age would assemble at a get-together and recite the poems they had composed. Prince Mahmud sent Necati to Edirne for his father on business, and Necati presented the sultan with a *kaside* and received a *hilat* and *caize*. Upon Necati's return, "the poets of the time—Revanî, Ferruhî, Mesihî, Şem'î, and Âhî—assembled in a gathering" in Istanbul and held a meeting among themselves. With the pen name he chose, a poet would be assured of the security of his brand of art.

A poet's use of another poet's pen name was forbidden, and the sultan enforced punishment for this crime (Âşık Çelebi 277b).

Poets in one of the court departments, especially those (for example, Ruhî) in the room of the *müteferrika*s (privileged ones) residing together with the hostage princes, ulema, and noblemen's children, would receive *inam* at certain times. Those serving as scribe to the Royal Council were ever endowed with skill in arts like *inşa*, poetry, and calligraphy. Among the likes of these, in our register's holiday-bonus lists of the year 914 A.H., we find new poet names such as Natıkî, Revanî, Şefiî, Edibî, and Basirî. Two new names, Mesihî and Sinanî, enter the rolls of the year 915 A.H. We find another new name, 'Iyanî, in the list of 916 A.H. Zatî and Kelamî were first added to the list that year as well.

Apparently, a hierarchy was consciously maintained in the ordering of the names on the lists. Azizî, who crowned the list nearly every year between 909 and 917 A.H., should be the top with respect to standing. He received a *came* (honorary robe) of *benek* silk. The two poets (Mailî and Ruhî) who came after Azizî were given *came*s of embroidered Bursa silk, the next three (Kâtibî, Sailî, and Şehdî) *mirahuri came*s of fine red woolen fabric, and the last five (Hamdî, Sa'yî, Şehdî, Sabayî, and Keşfî) *büri*s (*büri*s must be *hilat*s made from inferior-quality wool). One can accept the varieties of fabric from which the *came*s were made as evidence for the hierarchy. In a note, "benek" is described as Bursa's gold-threaded velvet, so it should probably be a very precious silk. In the 917 A.H. list, it is recorded that a *hilat* of this fabric was bestowed upon 'Azîzî (Erünsal 338, no. 163). The expression "mirahuri" likely refers to a style of stitching or attire. In Shawwal of 917 A.H., one layer "of gold-threaded Bursa *benek* velvet in the *mirahuri* style" was donated to Firdevsî, the author of the *Süleymanname* (Erünsal 339, no. 167). *Mirahuri came*s made of pied Bursa velvet or red fabric must have been of lesser worth. To Ruhî and Mesihî, in second place, *mirahuri came*s of variegated fabric were given, and to Kâtibî, in fourth place, one of red fabric (Erünsal 335, no. 145).

Nevertheless, it is worth noting that, in Shawwal of 915 A.H., Azizî took sixth place after Ruhî, Sabayî, Keşfî, Refikî, and Basirî. One wonders whether Azizî, who had previously always been at the top of the list and received *hilat* of precious golden velvet, was in that period a poet of *melikü's-şuara* (king of poets) standing. Those receiving the Bursa *benek* must have been people rewarded in a special manner. The author Derviş Mahmud (no. 93) and the *Süleymanname* composer Firdevsî (nos. 48, 80, 90) both, like Azizî, were rewarded with *came*s of Bursa *benek*. As for Sa'yî, who always received *büri*s, he must have occupied the lowest rung on the ladder: the donation made to Sa'yî in Ramadan of 915 A.H. was a paltry 500 *akçe*s. Sa'yî was perpetually given *büri*s. In 916 A.H., Sa'yî was expunged from the list. Bayezid II, who liked his poetry, first had him located and showered him with great generosity (Latifi 191) and subsequently raised him to the tutorship of the lads in residence at the royal palace.

From a book containing samples of Seljuk *inşa*, it is inferred that the *melikü's-şuara* was appointed to this station by way of a sultanic award decree.[95] This privilege was conferred upon *melikü's-şuara* Muhyiddin Ebu'l-Fezail on account of some private duties and services; we know that, in the Seljuk state, poets such as Nizameddin Ahmed and Bahaddin Kaniî were appointed *melikü's-şuara*. The post of *melikü's-şuara* established under the Seljuks continued under the Ottomans. The important duties expected of this rank were clearly expressed in the award decree conferred upon the Seljuk poet Muhyiddin: to serve as companion to the well-educated sultan; to earn everybody's admiration for poetry and eloquence with the flair of the preeminent poet in front of the scholars, writers, poets, and statesmen assembled at the sultan's gathering; and especially, on holidays and at other ritual functions, in front of the ready audience, recite poems, speak eloquently, and finally pray for the sultan's state (prayer was a most important duty at the end of every *kaside*; for Muslims, prayer is the most powerful avenue for securing God's blessing).[96]

Surprisingly, Latifi did not include the poet Azizî in his *tezkire*. Yet Âşık Çelebi lauds him as "outstanding among his peers" and says "his poetry is most inventive" (175a; in the margin). Azizî also wrote a *şehrengiz* about the well-known gorgeous women of Istanbul. In his *tezkire*, Âşık Çelebi likens Ruhî (d. 930/1524), who took second place in the years 909-914 A.H., to "a sun that has cast its rays upon the earth" (240); he reports that everyone would throng about Ruhî and that the latter was in an unrivaled position among his peers. Ruhî was a close associate of sultans, especially of Selim the Grim. At one point he attained a high office like kitchen superintendent to the court. Among the top-ranked poets, Mailî (actually Mealî: Latifî and Âşık Çelebi mention his name as Mealî) presented a *kaside* to the sultan in Muharram 914 and was rewarded with 3,000 *akçe*s and a *hilat* of embroidered Bursa velvet (Erünsal 320, no. 66). In the list of Shawwal 917 A.H., he is mentioned among the *müşaherehoran*, in other words, the group who draw a monthly salary at the court. In the year 914 A.H., Revanî was put in third place. He was in the *sipahi oğlanları* (court cavalry) company, that is, among the soldiers in the sultan's retinue, and he was rewarded with 3,000 *akçe*s and a silken *hilat* in return for the *kaside* he presented in Muharram 914 (Erünsal 320). From his register record (Erünsal 327, no. 102) we learn that he was successful in capturing the sultan's special favor as a poet and that he was added to the staff of *müşaherehoran* (court servants). Latifî (169) reports that Revanî was in the service of the sultans Bayezid II and Selim the Grim, was invited to the sultans' gatherings, and was deemed worthy of holiday bonuses and other *inam*s.

Holiday Bonuses

The group of poets who for the most part received silken or woolen *came*s (*hilat*s) at religious festivals must have been a group belonging to the sultan's court. For long years between 909/1503 and 917/1511, this group consisted of mostly the same names. Over time, some new names would be added to the group and some would be expunged from the list. On the other hand, those who belonged to the court and drew a monthly salary included; alongside the lords and vassals under the category of "*müşaherehoran* of the sultan's gate", who were in the direct service of the sultan at Enderun and Bîrun; *nedim*s, scribes, *nakkaş*es, carpet weavers, musicians, and poets. In the year 900/1495, during the reign of Bayezid II, there were five poets in this group.[97] The number of those receiving holiday bonuses rose to eleven in 909/1503 and to nineteen in 917/1511. We cannot know for sure that all of these were among the *müşaherehoran*, that is, drawing a monthly salary. For instance, it has been noted that the poet Talî, one of Prince Mahmud's *nöker*s, was in the executive service (Erünsal 306, no. 3).

Just as poets received regular gifts of attire/fabric on holidays, they also received *inam*s on newly arising occasions, for example for the elegies they would compose upon the death of one of the princes. *İnam*s consisting of money or garments were granted to Şehdî, Ruhî, Mailî, Revanî, Cevherî, and Sailî, who presented elegies on 15 Sha'ban 910 A.H. upon the passing of Prince Mehmed.

The list of those receiving bonuses on holidays is interesting for showing which poets were most in demand as of a particular date. The following is a list of these from the years 909-911 A.H. (according to Erünsal):

SHAWWAL 909 A.H.	DHU AL-HIJJAH 909 A.H.	SHAWWAL 12 910 A.H.	DHU AL-HIJJAH 19 910 A.H.	SHAWWAL 7 911 A.H.
Azizî	Azizî	Azizî	Azizî	Azizî
Mailî	Mailî	Mailî	Mailî	Mailî
Ruhî	Ruhî	Ruhî	Ruhî	Ruhî
Kâtibî	Kâtibî	Kâtibî	Kâtibî	Kâtibî
Sailî	Sailî	Sailî	Sailî	Sailî
Şehdî	Şehdî	Şehdî	Şehdî	Şehdî
Hamdî	Hamdî	—	Hamdî	—
Sa'yî	Sa'yî	Sa'yî	Sa'yî	Sa'yî
La'lî	La'lî	La'lî	La'lî	La'lî
Sabayî	Sabayî	Sabayî	Sabayî	Sabayî
Keşfî	Keşfî	Keşfî	Keşfî	Keşfî
—	Refikî	Refikî	Refikî	Refikî
—	—	Hânî	Hânî	Hânî

We see that within two years, two new poets, Refikî and Hânî, have been appended to the list of holiday-bonus recipients. The poet Hamdî does not appear in the recipient list of 910 A.H., but is restored to the list on the holiday of Dhu al-Hijjah 19, 910 A.H., two months after Shawwal 910 A.H., only to be expunged from the list again the following year.

The following are recipients of *came*s (*hilat*s) and/or woolen or silken garment fabric in Shawwal 917 A.H.:

Sabayî, Azizî, Mailî, Mesihî, Sailî, Nasibî, Keşfî, Zatî, Edibî, and Sinanî; upon these were conferred various garments (*came*) or woolen or silken garment fabric.

Those Appended on Shawwal 14:

Refikî, 'Iyanî, Natıkî, Sucudî, and Dilirî: to these was given only a small sum of money in the vicinity of 500 or 800 *akçe*s.

To Firdevsî, who was added on Shawwal 23, were donated both money (3,000 *akçe*s) and a silken garment. We know that, in Second Jumada 915 A.H., Firdevsî presented his work entitled *Süleymanname* to the sultan by way of the head treasurer and was rewarded with 3,000 *akçe*s and a silken garment (Erünsal 328). So it was as a result of this magnificent work that Firdevsî was included in the holiday bonus recipient list and financed anew.

Here is the list of those receiving *inam* during the years 909-917 A.H. for assorted reasons, such as producing *kaside*s or elegies:

POET PRESENTING THE SULTAN WITH A POEM	AKÇES	HİL'AT AWARDED
Taliî, *kaside*	2000	*benek came*
Mevlâna Sa'dî, teacher, *kaside*	3000	*murabba* of *çuka* fabric
Mevlâna Ruhî, his son died, *ta'ziye*	—	*benek*
Alâaddin, poet, *kaside*	1500	—
Sailî, brought a book	2000	—
Mevlâna İdris (Bidlisî), official stylist, his father died, *taziye*	—	Bursa *çatma*
Ömer Çelebi, scribe, poet, *kaside*	3000	*münakkaş*
Mehmed, *kaside*	3000	—
Mahmud, *kaside*	2000	*benek*
Mevlâna Sa'dî	3000	*murabba* of *çuka* fabric
Keşfî, *kaside*	500	—
Mailî, *kaside*	3000	—
Ahmed Çelebi, presented a book authored by himself	5000	*çatma*
Mevlâna Ruhî	3000	*benek*
Kâtibî, *kaside*	2000	—
Ruhî	2000	*münakkaş*
Mevlâna İdris, *inşa* stylist	10000	*çatma*
Mehmed Çelebi Cevherî, *kaside*	3000	*benek*
Şehdî, *mersiye*	1500	—
Ruhî, *mersiye*	2000	*münakkaş*
Mailî, *mersiye*	2000	—
Revanî, *mersiye*	2000	—
Cevherî, *mersiye*	2000	—
Sailî, *mersiye*	—	*mirahuri*, embroidered, of fine red woolen fabric
Refikî, *mersiye*	500	—
Kâtibî, *mersiye*	2000	—
Mihri Hatun	3000	—
İdris, official stylist	—	*mirahuri*, of plain red cloth
Mailî, *kaside*	3000	—
Kâtibî	2000	—
Ruhî	2000	*münakkaş*
Ahmed Çelebi, translation of the *Kıssa-i Yusuf*	5000	*murabba*
Mevlâna Sa'dî Çelebi, *kaside*	3000	—
Refikî, *kaside*	?	?
İdris, authorship of the *Târîh-i Âl-i Osmân*	50000	of *çatma*
Ömer Çelebi, *kaside*	3000	*murabba* of *çuka* fabric
Ruhî, *müşahere*	2000	*münakkaş*
Firdevsî, for the *Süleymanname*	3000	8 *benek*
Zamirî	3000	*murabba* of *çuka* fabric

Mailî, *kaside*	3000	—
Kâtibî, *kaside*	2000	—
Ömer, *kaside*	3000	*murabba* of *çuka* fabric
İdris	5000	—
Firdevsî	3000	*benek*
Sa'dî, *kaside*	3000	*murabba* of *çuka* fabric
Vasfi, *kaside*	2000	*murabba* of *çuka* fabric

914 A.H.

Mailî, *kaside*	3000	*münakkaş*
Revanî, *kaside*	2000	—
İdris, *inşa* stylist	4000	—
Kâtibî, *kaside*	2000	—
Ali Çelebi, son of Mehmed Beg, *kaside*	2000	*benek*
Haydar, brought the book authored by Sultan Korkud	5000	*murabba* of *çuka* fabric, and a *mirahuri came*
Ruhî	2000	*münakkaş*
Basirî, *kaside*	2000	—
Necati, *kaside*	2000	*benek*
Haydar Çelebi, former *defterdar* of Prince Şehinşah, *kaside*	5000	of *çatma*
İdris, *inşa* stylist	4000	—
Firdevsî, author of the *Süleymanname*	3000	*benek*
İdris, gave a book	10000	*murabba* along with a sable fur
Ömer, *kaside*	3000	*benek*
Kâtibî	2000	—
Sabayî	300	—
Keşfî	500	—
Sefayî	1500	—
Firdevsî	3000	*benek*
Refikî, *kaside*	1500	—
Ömer, brought a book	7000	*murabba* of *çuka* fabric
Derviş Mahmud, brought a book authored by himself	3000	*benek*
Prince Korkud Çelebi, sent a book authored by himself	2000	a *sikke* gold piece
Kâtibî	2000	—
Mailî, *kaside*	3000	*münakkaş*
Ruhî	2000	*münakkaş*
Kâtibî, *kaside*	2000	—
Basirî, *kaside*	2000	—
Mevlâna İdris, *taziye* for his son who died	—	*hilat* of *çatma*
Firdevsî, author of the *Süleymanname*	3000	*benek*
Mahbub Çelebi, *kaside*	3000	—
Sabayî	2000	—
Keşfî	800	—
Sa'yî	500	—
Kâtibî	4000	—

Sa'dî Çelebi, *kaside*	3000	—

916 A.H.

Kâtibî, *kaside*	2000	—
Refikî, *kaside*	1500	—
Ruhî	2000	*münakkaş*
Mailî	3000	*münakkaş*
Şefiî	1000	—
Sefayî	1500	—
İdris	7000	*murabba* of *çuka* fabric
İdris's mother	4000	of fine woolen fabric
İdris (again)	7000	—
Son of Mevlâna Yarhisarî, *kaside*	2000	—
Mevlâna Muzaffer, book authored by himself	10000	*murabba* of *çuka* fabric

917 A.H.

Kâtibî	2000	—
Sabayî, *kaside*	2000	—
Refikî, *kaside*	2000	—
Kâtibî, *kaside*	2000	—
Refikî, *mersiye*	2000	—
'Iyanî, *tarih*	1000	—
Şehdî, *mersiye* (upon the death of Şehinşah)	1000	—
Refikî	2000	—
Şehrî	1000	—
Kâtibî	2000	—
Şefiî	1000	—
Ruhî	2000	*münakkaş*
Süleyman Çelebi, book authored by himself	3000	—

NOTES

[1] Originally published in Turkish. İnalcık, Halil. *Şâir ve Patron: Patrimonyal Devlet ve Sanat Üzerinde Sosyolojik Bir İnceleme.* Ankara: Doğu Batı Yayınları, 2003.

[2] Graduate student in the Department of Turkish Literature, Bilkent University; *JTL* Assistant Editor.

[3] Editor's note: whereas this article's original Turkish version "did not employ a precise method of transcription", this English translation adheres to official *JTL* style guidelines in most respects. As per the original text, however, some Ottoman Turkish words and names containing hamzah, ayn, and long vowels have been explicitly spelled here using apostrophes ('), inverted apostrophes ('), and circumflexes (^), respectively, even where modern Turkish usage might omit them. In particular, Prof. İnalcık's transcription of the Ottoman verse passages has mostly been preserved.

[4] With the exception of this couplet, the freestanding passages of poetry were translated by Talât Sait Halman, *JTL* Editor-in-Chief.

[5] See İnalcık, "Comments on 'Sultanism' " 1-22.

[6] Regarding how Süleyman the Magnificent, who laid claim to superiority not just in the East but among European monarchs as well, engaged in political rivalry with Holy Roman Emperor Charles V, and patronage of European artists, see Necipoğlu, "Süleyman the Magnificent…".

[7] In particular, see Jardine and Hollingsworth.

[8] See both of Subtelny's articles listed in the Bibliography.

[9] On the nascence of Ottoman classical-period art: papers by A. Kuran, M. Rogers, N. Atasoy, and particularly Necipoğlu, "A Kanun for…".

[10] Editor's note: the birth, death, and reign dates of Ottoman sultans mentioned in this article have been taken from: Sakaoğlu, Necdet. *Bu Mülkün Sultanları: 36 Osmanlı Padişahı.* Istanbul: Oğlak, 2001.

[11] Editor's note: *JTL* romanizes names in a Persian context, such as "Jāmī", in accordance with the ALA-LC standard. Modern Turkish orthography, by contrast, transliterates the same name as "Câmî". As for the title "mullah", this has already passed into the English language. For further information on *JTL* style, see the "Style Guidelines" on pages 158-60 of the first issue of *JTL* (2004).

[12] *Münşeât* of Feridun Bey, I, Istanbul 1274, 305-06.

[13] Ibid. 306-07. On this subject, one should not overlook the articles by scholars Togan and Ritter treating Timurid-era Herat and Jāmī; further, Yarshater; Subtelny, "A Taste for…"; on patronage's importance for art in the Iranian and Central Asian courts in particular, Subtelny, "Socioeconomic Bases of…"; Golombek and Subtelny, eds., *Timurid Art and…*; on the Turkish poetry fragments of the great Islamic music theorist, poet, and calligrapher 'Abdül-Kâdir Merâgî, whose mother tongue was Azeri (Turkmen) Turkish, see Tekin, "Timur Devrine Ait…"; on the interest Tamerlane took in Turkish poetry, ibid. 866.

[14] See Manz.

[15] For a list of those exiled from Tabriz, see Uzunçarşılı, "Osmanlı Sarayı'nda Ehl-i…" 24-65.

[16] When Alâaddin Ali Kuşçu was summoned from Samarkand by Mehmed the Conqueror, he brought along with him as many as two hundred hand-picked Central Asian and Iranian men of learning (Taşköprîzade 183).

[17] Research of mine regarding inherited estates in Bursa ("XV. Asır Türkiye…") has shown that, even in this affluent commercial city, the richest class was the "military" class, whose wealth depended on land rents; the same circumstance has been proven for the Middle East, see Subtelny, "Socioeconomic Bases of…".

[18] In the *Şakayık-ı Numaniye*, after the scholars, a separate section was devoted to the biographies of heads of dervish orders.

[19] Aslanapa; Erdmann; on the use of court carpet motifs in folk weaving, see Acar; Raby; Denny; Köprülü, *Milli Edebiyat Cereyanının…*; as well as an important study by Çağman and Tanındı; for the continuity of Turkish folk literature, see Çavuşoğlu, "Fatih Sultan Mehmed…".

[20] During Mehmed the Conqueror's princeship in Manisa, his tutors were Molla Hüsrev, the famous scholar of jurisprudence, and İbrahim, the *nişancı*, and his mentor in military administrative affairs was General Zaganos.

[21] For a list of poet-sultans and sample poems, see Tayyarzade Atâ; also Mehmed Said (Şehrîzade); also Saadet Şanlı.

[22] "The books of recorded memory […] are devoted […] to being agreeable and seemly and to catching the farsighted gaze of the sultan's good graces", *Şakayık-ı Numaniye* translation, 12-13.

[23] İnalcık, "The Rûznâmçe Registers…".

[24] İnalcık, "Osmanlı Bürokrasisinde Aklâm…".

[25] For the thesis that Dehhanî came to Anatolia during the reign of Alâaddin I (1220-1237), see İlaydın.

[26] See Rogers.

[27] See the two studies by Subtelny listed in the Bibliography. Toward a definition of the Timurid Renaissance see Aubin; under the Ottomans the *soyural* was a deed of transfer and derived from the land transfers that Ottoman patrons usually turned into sources of wealth.

[28] See the studies by Subtelny, especially "Socioeconomic Bases of…" 490-92.

[29] Çavuşoğlu, "Fatih Sultan Mehmed…"; Sohrweide.

[30] Tursun Beg, *Tarih-i Ebülfeth.*

[31] See Çavuşoğlu, "Kanuni Devrinin sonuna…" 75-90.

[32] For an example of such a study, see Alpay.

33 See İnalcık, "Mehmed II".

34 Tarlan, *Şeyhî Divanını Tetkik*; according to Çavuşoğlu ("Fatih Sultan Mehmed…", 43), Şeyhî was the trailblazer of the "Iranianesque" style.

35 Concerning the idea that poets during the reign of Mehmed the Conqueror composed a new stage marked by self-confidence opposite the Persians, see Çavuşoğlu, ibid. 31-32. This awareness of equality, or even of superiority, first forcefully emerged in Central Asia; see Bodrogligeti 57; İlaydın; Akün. According to Âşık Çelebi; Şeyhî, Ahmed Paşa, and Necati caused posterity to forget their predecessors in the *mesnevi*, *kaside*, and ghazal genres, respectively.

36 An authoritative study of the *kaside* has recently been published: *Qasida Poetry in…*, edited by Sperl and Shackle; within this work, for the *kaside* and patronage, see Stetkevych; M. Glünz; here I am grateful to our esteemed literary historians Prof. Günay Kut and Dr. Mehmet Kalpaklı for bringing these publications to my attention.

37 The topic of patronage in Ottoman poetry was examined in a separate section of Walter G. Andrews's unpublished doctoral dissertation. Andrews firstly determined Latifi's worldview (*Weltanschauung*) and then attempted to analyze Latifi's criticisms within this framework. According to Prof. Andrews (dissertation, 3, 55, 103), Latifi desires a balance between material and spiritual values and complains of the importance placed upon the material in his day. Prof. Andrews attempted a new method for the analysis and evaluation of Ottoman poetry by establishing the poet's behavior and standards. Ultimately, he cautioned old and new researchers alike against the notion that Ottoman poetry was nothing but imitations of Iranian models.

38 Ibn Bībī, *El-Evāmirrü'l-'Alāiyye…* 459-61; İlaydın, 766, states that he came during the reign of Alâaddin I (1220-1237).

39 From Ibn Bībī via Yazıcızade 78-81, 137.

40 *Şakayık-ı Numaniye* 198-99, concerning the circles of poets see İpekten; Pala; Şentürk; Canım; Atasoy, *Hasbahçe: Osmanlı Kültürü'nde…*.

41 Most recently, after Metin And's and Özdemir Nutku's important treatments of this subject, Atasoy's *1582 Surname-i Hümayun…*. Mustafa Âlî's *Mevā'idü'n-Nefāis fī…* is a work on par with B. Castiglione's famous *Il Cortegiano*, which set out the labels and behaviors of high society in Renaissance Italy. In this work, Âlî reports the rules associated with banquets (347-49), poets (356), meetings (394), and sultanic donations (391-94); see also Âlî, *Cami'ul-Buhur der…*.

42 Barkan, "954-955 (1547-1548) Malî Yılına ait…" 307.

43 Seyyid Lokman, *Hünernâme* 43.

44 Kınalızade Hasan Çelebi, I, 422.

45 The monthly salaries paid to clergy were known variously as *vazife*, *cihet*, and *idrar*.

46 This overall approach was clearly expressed by independent historians such as Selânikî and Ali in *nasihatname*s and *layiha*s written especially to correct improprieties in state administration from the end of the sixteenth through the seventeenth century. The most famous work of the *nasihatname* genre is the *Koçi Bey Risalesi*.

47 An extant court record shows that he tried to purchase an attendant from one of Bursa's *hamam*s after being exiled to Bursa.

48 Regarding Korkud see Uzunçarşılı, "II inci Bayezid'in Oğullarından…".

49 The salacious work entitled *Dafiü'l-Gumum ve Rafiü'l-Humum*, which he composed in honor of Prince Korkud, became famous.

50 *Farsça Divan* 7: "Şuḥbat-i Salāṭīn sarmāyah-'i ḥasad ast va nash'ah-'i sharāb mūjib-i 'aẕāb-i abad ast va muṣāḥabat-i nudamā māni-'i khalvat-i khayāl ast."

51 *Mesîhî Dîvânı*; his correspondence (*Mesihî Münşeati*) is interesting; an article written by Necib Asım is also relevant.

52 Nonetheless, what flowery couplet of any divan poet is as poetic as the following refined, natural plaint of Karacaoğlan's: *Yeşil başlı ördek olsam / Sular içmem gölünüzden* (Were I a mallard duck / I'd not drink from your pond).

[53] See Bonebakker; Kuşcu; 'Abdalqāhir al-Jurjānī; for the textual analysis of Ottoman poetry with respect to the particular artistic conventions of poetry, see Tarlan, *Fuzûlî Divani Şerhi*; Çalışkan; Üzgör. In the introductions to his divans, Fuzulî boasts of having thoroughly scrutinized the "formulae" of poetic artistry. Concerning the importance of poetry as a science, compare Ali Şîr Nevâyî's *Mecâlisü'n-Nefâ'is* (1-2) with the introductions to Fuzuli's Turkish and Persian divans.

[54] *Türkçe Divan* 6-7; *Farsça Divan* 1-16.

[55] "Man az iqlīm-i 'Arab Ḥayratī az mulk-i 'Ajam".

[56] In contrast to the art of the court poets who received *caize* from the sultan and attended banquets, generally see Tekin, "Turkish Literature", regarding the Sufi literature that Sufi poets represented.

[57] *Heşt Bihişt: Sehī Beg Tezkiresi...*, critical edition prepared by Dr. Günay Kut along with analysis. Sehi appears to have followed the format of Ali Şîr Nevâyî. Nevâyî divided his *tezkiretü'ş-şuara* entitled *Mecâlisü'n-Nefâ'is* into eight *meclis*es. After providing background on a poet's life and character, Nevâyî would evaluate his work and quote sample passages. The Ottoman *tezkire* authors generally followed this precedent. A perusal of the *Mecâlis* establishes how important patronage was in the Middle East. See the eighth *meclis* treating Sultan Hüseyin Bahadır Han.

[58] Âşık Çelebi, *Meşâ'ir üş-şu'arâ...*, 106b-107b.

[59] A comparison of manuscripts and the most comprehensive study of Latifi's *tezkire*, Andrews, "The Tezkere-i Şu'arâ of Latifi as a Source for the Critical Evaluation of Ottoman Poetry"; here I am indebted to the author for sending me this valuable work and permitting me to use it. Professor Andrews compares 49 manuscripts and establishes that in 982/1574 Latifi made several additions and modifications to the original he had written in 953/1546, so that the manuscripts fall into two distinct categories. The modifications were limited not merely to style but included new information as well (for instance in the entry on Şükrî). Probably after A. Cevdet, *Tezkire-i Şu'arâ*, Istanbul 1314 A.H., a new, scholarly edition is called for. I have used the Cevdet edition. Generally regarding *tezkiretü'ş-şuara*s, the works of T. Banguoğlu (1930), Ş. Oktürk (1945), N. Çetin (1947-48), and Stewart-Robinson (1959) devote considerable space to Latifi; Sevgi; see also Aynur; a group at Erzurum Atatürk University who plan to publish critical editions of the Turkish *tezkiretü'ş-şuara*s has published Nevâyî's *Mecâlisü'n-Nefâ'is* as its first project (Erzurum, 1995).

[60] For instance, Necati (325-30), Nalişî (334), Gazalî (254-56), Mihri (319-22), Melihî (314-18), and Nişancı Celâlzade (335-37).

[61] Concerning whom see Köprülü, "Âşık Çelebi"; *Meşâ'ir üş-şu'arâ...*, edited by G. M. Meredith-Owens, Preface, IX-XXV.

[62] *Düstûrnâme-i Enverî*, 91: "Mîr Süleyman dün ü gün sohbet eder / Ahmedî'yle dembedem 'işret eder".

[63] For the other sources that indicate this, see İnalcık, *Fâtih Devri Üzerinde...* 59.

[64] These *inam* registers are discussed later.

[65] Barkan, "954-955 (1547-1548) Malî Yılına ait..." 262-65; look ahead to the section treating this source.

[66] Latifi 205. In the introduction and conclusion of his work, Latifi complains that in his day true poetry and poets go unappreciated. Taking this as a foundation, Professor Andrews agrees with Latifi's view concerning the breakdown of patronage in this period (Dissertation, Chapter IV). Latifi (205), who wrote his work in 1546 under Rüstem Paşa's viziership, emphasizes that state patronage and salaries paid to poets had been terminated; however, I find the notion that patronage had entered a new era somewhat exaggerated. It is known that donations were made in later periods under the names of *inam* and *teşrifiye*.

[67] In his *tezkire*, Sehi ranked the poets according to hierarchical "strata" spelled out in state protocol. First came the biographies of sultans and princes, next those of viziers and commanders, then those of ancient poets who had lived before Sehi's time, then those of poets whom Sehi had known personally, and finally those of young poets. Members of the religio-jurisprudential branch predominated in all eight strata. Contrast this categorization with those by Jāmī and Nevâyî.

[68] See Kalpaklı.

[69] For the Ottomans, in his *kaside* to İbrahim Musullu, the Shah's representative used the expression "pretentious apostate army" (Karahan 138; Fuzulî, *Külliyat* 44); Kınalızade Alâaddin Ali, in charge of the *Ahlak-ı Alaî*, considered Fuzulî a *rafizî*. During the Safavid period, many groups of Kalenderîs,

Melametîs, Bektaşîs, Mevlevîs, Kadirîs, Kızılbaşes, and Babaîs migrated from Anatolia to settle in and around Karbala.

[70] *Şikâyetnâme*, the text edited by A. Karahan; *Fuzûlî'nin Mektupları* 56-57; concerning his prose styling see Ahmet, "Fuzûlî'nin Nesri". A bibliography on Fuzuli: Cunbur, *Fuzûlî hakkında bir Bibliyografya Denemesi*. For more on his life, his *kaside*s and *mukattaât* ought to be carefully reexamined (see *Farsça Divan* 611-42).

[71] In this period, one ducat of gold was worth 60 *akçe*s. This means that Fuzuli's monthly annuity amounted to 4.5 gold pieces. At that time, 9 *akçe*s was the approximate daily wage of a master builder.

[72] Cf. İnalcık, "Osmanlı Bürokrasisinde Aklâm…".

[73] For a *mukatta* of Fuzuli's addressed to the director of the *Atebât-ı Aliye*, see *Farsça Divan* 611.

[74] On bribery in Ottoman administration, see İnalcık, "Tax Collection, Embezzlement…".

[75] In Iran, the condolence and the elegy have given rise to a broad literary style. Fuzulî was probably reciting *kaside*s of condolence to Shiite visitors. As for the Ottoman Turks, he mentions that they did not understand Persian and that therefore he composed the *Hadikatü's-Süeda*; for condolence literature, see Ayoub; And. In 763/1361 in Kastamonu, Yûsufî composed a *mesnevi* of 3000 couplets entitled *Maktel-i Hüseyin* in memory of Candaroğlu Bayezid Bey based on Abû-Mihne; Erzi. On the ceremony for the imam of the age in Hilla and on the visitors arriving from Anatolia, Ibn Battuta, II, 324-25.

[76] A detailed depiction of these sites: Seyyid Lokman, *Hünernâme*; see also the Bibliography section below.

[77] The *kaside*s that Fuzulî composed for dignitaries in the course of Süleyman's long residence in Baghdad, as well as the *kaside*s he composed for the Ottoman governors who arrived later, are an important topic that will be taken up separately. 'Abdülkâdir (Kadri) Efendi the *kazasker* especially sponsored Mevlâna Fuzulî.

[78] See Uzunçarşılı, "Onaltıncı Asır Ortalarında…"; Gökbilgin, "Celâlzade Mustafa Çelebi".

[79] According to Âşık Çelebi (Preface, XIV), the earlier famous *inşa* stylists had been Lamiî Çelebi and Cafer Çelebi.

[80] For details on these visits by Süleyman, see Seyyid Lokman's *Hünernâme*; *Ferdî Tarihi*; Nasuhü's-Silahî (Matrakçı).

[81] According to Sıdıkî; see Karahan 69.

[82] See Şerafettin Turan 47.

[83] The letter in all likelihood should date back to the time when Bayezid was sent to Konya; cf. Şerafettin Turan 45-46; in 1558, Bayezid was appointed to the *sancak* of Amasya. According to Dakuki (57-58, 59-60), Fuzulî died not in 1556 but rather in 1561.

[84] *Fuzuli Üzerine Makaleler* 167-80.

[85] *Meşâ'ir üş-şu'arâ* 198b-199a.

[86] *Tezkiretü'ş-Şu'arâ* 758-62; Kınalızade 631; the *tezkire* of Kınalızade, which contains the poet's biography and itself constitutes an example of *inşa*, was edited by İbrahim Kutluk, upon whose death first İbrahim Olgun and subsequently the late İsmet Parmaksızoğlu undertook the task of publication.

[87] For a concise and pithy analysis of the development of the general *inşa* language in the Middle East, see Roemer, *Staatsschreiben der Timuridenzeit*.

[88] Ahmet, "Fuzûlî'nin Nesri".

[89] No systematic study has yet been carried out on the subject of the formation of the official Ottoman court language. The *Menâhicü'l-İnşâ'*, the first important source in this respect, was edited by Ş. Tekin: *Menâhicü'l-İnşâ, The Earliest Ottoman Chancery Manual by Yahya bin Mehmed el-Kâtib from the 15th Century*. For Mustafa Özkan's essays, see the Bibliography. The Conqueror showed esteem beyond measure to Cezerî Kasım Paşa, the first great *inşa* stylist, who bore the pen name Safi and rose through the ranks as far as vice vizier in the reign of Bayezid II. According to Sehi (318-19), Safi hailed from Iran and "it was first he who introduced to the district of Rûm the *inşa* style, judgments, and official correspondence". Safi became a very generous patron of poets.

[90] See Sehi, *Heşt Bihişt* 319-20, in which Safi is incorrectly referred to as Vefayî, about whom see ibid. 321.

[91] There was begrudging rivalry between the Ottoman scribes and the *inşa* stylists from the East.

[92] See *Fuzûlî'nin Mektupları*, ed. Karahan, 258-59; Karahan points out that this might have been appended by a copyist.

[93] Erünsal, "II. Bayezid Devrine Ait…" and "Kanunî Sultan Süleyman Devrine Ait…".
[94] Cf. Faroqhi; Erünsal, ed., *Kütüphanecilikle İlgili Osmanlıca….*
[95] Osman Turan 57, no. 21.
[96] In the introduction to his Persian divan (6), Fuzulî speaks of the eliteness of the poets in attendance at the sultans' banquets, and says: "bamurā'āt-i salāṭīn-i ḥamīdah akhlāq va ikhtilāṭ-i akābir-i ṣāḥibmaẕāq u sayr-i bāghhā-yi bihisht āṣār va nishāṭ-i sharābhā-yi khvushguvār".
[97] Barkan, "Osmanlı İmparatorluğunda Bütçelere…" 309.

BIBLIOGRAPHY

'Abdalqāhir al-Jurjānī. *Asrār al-Balāgha: The Mysteries of Eloquence.* Ed. Hellmut Ritter. Istanbul: İstanbul Üniversitesi Edebiyat Fakültesi Yayınları, 1954.

Acar, Belkıs Balpınar. *Kilim, Cicim, Zili, Sumak, Türk Düz Dokuma Yaygıları.* Istanbul: Eren Yayıncılık, 1982.

Ahmet, Nevvar. "Fuzuli'nin Nesri". Thesis. Istanbul: Istanbul University Turkology Institute, 1938. No. 104.

Akün, Ömer Faruk. "Divan Edebiyatı". *Türk Diyanet Vakfı İslâm Ansiklopedisi.* Vol. 9. Istanbul: Türk Diyanet Vakfı, 1994. 389-428.

Ali Şîr Nevâyî. *Mecâlisü'n-Nefâ'is.* Ed. Hüseyin Ayan et al. Erzurum: Atatürk Üniversitesi Türkiyat Araştırmaları Enstitüsü, 1995.

Alpay, Gönül. "Yusuf Emiri'nin Beng ü Çakır adlı Münazarası". *Türk Dili Araştırma Yıllığı-Belleten* (1972): 103-25.

Anafarta, Nigâr. *Hünernâme Minyatürleri ve Sanatçıları.* Istanbul: Yapı ve Kredi Bankası, 1969.

And, Metin. *Minyatürlerle Osmanlı-İslâm Mitologyası.* Istanbul: Akbank, 1998.

Andrews, Walter G. "The Tezkere-i Şu'ara of Latifi as a Source for the Critical Evaluation of Ottoman Poetry". Doctoral dissertation. The University of Michigan, 1970.

Asım, Necib. "Mesîhî Dîvânı: Dîvânlarımızdan Tarihçe Nasıl İstifade Edilir?". *Türk Tarih Encümeni* 1 (February 1911): 265-69.

Aslanapa, Oktay. *Türk Halı Sanatının Bin Yılı.* Istanbul: Eren Yayıncılık, 1987.

Âşık Çelebi. *Meşâ'ir üş-şu'arâ or Tezkere of Âşık Çelebi.* Ed. Glyn M. Meredith-Owens. London: Luzac, 1971.

Atasoy, Nurhan. *Hasbahçe: Osmanlı Kültürü'nde Bahçe ve Çiçek.* Istanbul: Koç Kültür ve Sanat Tanıtım, 2002.

——. *1582 Surname-i Hümayun: Düğün Kitabı.* Istanbul: Koçbank, 1997.

Aubin, Jean. "Le mécénat timouride à Chiraz". *Studia Islamica* 8 (1957): 71-86.

Aynur, Hatice, ed. *Üniversitelerde Eski Türk Edebiyatı Çalışmaları: Tezler, Yayınlar, Haberler.* Nos. 1-2. Istanbul: Boğaziçi Üniversitesi, 1991.

Ayoub, Mahmud. *Redemptive Suffering in Islam: A Study of the Devotional Aspects of 'Ashura' in Twelver Shi'ism.* The Hague: Mouton, 1978.

Barkan, Ömer Lütfi, ed. "954-955 (1547-1548) Malî Yılına ait bir Osmanlı Bütçesi". *İstanbul Üniversitesi İktisat Fakültesi Mecmuası* XIX-1/4 (1957-1958).

——. "Osmanlı İmparatorluğunda Bütçelere dair notlar". *İstanbul Üniversitesi İktisat Fakültesi Mecmuası* XVII (1956).

Bodrogligeti, András J. E. "Orta Asya Türklerinin Kültür Mirası ve Klasik Orta Asya Türk Edebiyatı". *Toplumsal Tarih* 54 (June 1998): 53-64.

Bonebakker, Seeger A. "Materials for the History of Arabic Rhetoric from the Hilyat al-Muhadara of Hatimi". Supplement 4. *Agli Annali* vol. 35, fascicle 3. Napoli, 1975.

Canım, Rıdvan. *Türk Edebiyatında Sakinâmeler ve İşretnâme.* Ankara: Akçağ Yayınları, 1998.

Cem Sultan. *Cem Sultan'ın Türkçe Divan'ı.* Haz. İ. Halil Ersoylu. Ankara: Türk Dil Kurumu Yayınları, 1989.

Cunbur, Müjgân, ed. *Fuzûlî hakkında bir Bibliyografya Denemesi.* Istanbul: Maarif Vekâleti Yayınları, 1956.

Çağman, Filiz and Zeren Tanındı. "Osmanlı-Safevi İlişkileri Çerçevesinde Topkapı Sarayı Müzesi Resimli El Yazmalarına Bakış". *Aslanapa Armağanı*. Ed. Selçuk Mülayim, Zeki Sönmez, and Ara Altun. Istanbul: Bağlam Yayınları, 1996. 37-76.

Çalışkan, Adem. *Fuzûlî'nin Su Kasidesi ve Şerhi*. Ankara: Diyanet İşleri Başkanlığı, 1992.

Çavuşoğlu, Mehmed. "Fatih Sultan Mehmed devrine kadar Osmanlı-Türk Edebi Mahsullerinde Muhtevanın Tekâmülü". *Kubbealtı Akademi Mecmuası* 11.2 (April 1982): 31-43.

——. "Kanuni Devrinin sonuna kadar Anadolu'da Nevâyî Tesiri Üzerine Notlar". *Atsız Armağanı*. Ed. Erol Güngör et al. Istanbul: Ötüken Yayınevi, 1976.

Dakuki, Ibrahim. "Fuzulî al-Bagdadi et la vie culturelle en Iraq au XVIe siècle". *Revue d'Histoire Maghrébine*.

Denny, Walter B. "The Origin and Development of Ottoman Court Carpets". *Oriental Carpet & Textile Studies* 2 (1986): 243-259.

Düstûrnâme-i Enverî. Ed. M. Halil. Istanbul: 1929.

Erdmann, Hanna. *Orientteppiche: 16-19. Jahrhundert (Bildkataloge des Kestner-Museums Hannover 9)*. Hanover: Museen Islam, 1966.

Erünsal, İsmail E. "Türk Edebiyatı Tarihinin Arşiv Kaynakları I: II. Bayezid Devrine Ait Bir İn'âmât Defteri". *Tarih Enstitüsü Dergisi* 10-11 (1979-1980): 303-42.

——. "Türk Edebiyatı Tarihinin Arşiv Kaynakları II: Kanunî Sultan Süleyman Devrine Ait Bir İn'âmât Defteri". *Osmanlı Araştırmaları* 4 (1984): 1-17.

——, ed. *Kütüphanecilikle İlgili Osmanlıca Metinler ve Belgeler*. Istanbul: İstanbul Üniversitesi Edebiyat Fakültesi Yayınları, 1982.

Erzi, Adnan Sadık. "Bibliyografya: Beşir Çelebi, Tevarih-i Âl-i Osman". *Belleten* 13.49 (January 1949): 181-85.

Faroqhi, Suraiya. *Kultur und Alltag im Osmanischen Reich: vom Mittelalter bis zum Anfang des 20. Jahrhunderts*. Munich: C. H. Beck, 1995.

Ferdî Tarihi. Manuscript. Istanbul: Ayasofya Library 3317.

Firdawsī. *Şehname*. Trans. Necati Lugal. Istanbul: 1994.

Fuzulî. *Farsça Divan* [Persian divan]. Ed. Hasibe Mazıoğlu. Ankara Üniversitesi Dil ve Tarih-Coğrafya Fakültesi Yayınları 135. Ankara: Türk Tarih Kurumu Basımevi, 1962.

——. *Fuzûlî'nin Mektupları*. Ed. Abdülkadir Karahan. Istanbul: İstanbul Üniversitesi Edebiyat Fakültesi 1948.

——. *Külliyat*. Istanbul: 1315 A.H.

——. *Leylâ ve Mecnun: Metin, Düzyazıya Çeviri, Notlar ve Açıklamalar*. Ed. and trans. Muhammet Nur Doğan. İstanbul: Yapı Kredi Yayınları.

——. *Türkçe Divan* [Turkish divan]. Ed. Kenan Akyüz et al. Ankara: Türk Tarih Kurumu Basımevi, 1958.

Gazalî. *Dafiü'l-Gumum ve Rafiü'l-Humum*. Manuscript. Istanbul: Istanbul University Library. T. V. 9659.

Gelibolulu Mustafa Âlî. *Cami'u'l-Buhur der Mecalis-i Sur (Edisyon Kritik ve Tahlil)*. Ed. Ali Öztekin. Ankara: Türk Tarih Kurumu Yayınları, 1996.

——. *Gelibolulu Mustafa 'Âli ve Mevâ'idü'n-Nefâis fî-Kavâ'ıdi'l-Mecâlis*. Ed. Mehmet Şeker. Ankara: Atatürk Kültür, Dil ve Tarih Yüksek Kurumu Türk Tarih Kurumu Yayınları, 1997.

Glünz, Michael. "Poetic Tradition and Social Change: The Persian Qasida in Post-Mongol Iran". *Qasida Poetry in Islamic Asia and Africa I: Classical Traditions and Modern Meanings*. Ed. Stefan Sperl and Christopher Shackle. Leiden: E. J. Brill, 1996. 183-203.

Golombek, Lisa and Maria Eva Subtelny, eds. *Timurid Art and Culture: Iran and Central Asia in the Fifteenth Century*. Leiden: E. J. Brill, 1992.

Gökbilgin, Tayyib M. "Celâl-zade Mustafa Çelebi". *İslâm Ansiklopedisi: İslâm Âlemi Tarih, Coğrafya, Etnografya ve Biyografya Lugati*. Vol. 3. Eskişehir: Milli Eğitim Bakanlığı Yayınları, 2001. 61-63.

——. *XV. ve XVI. Asırlarda Edirne ve Paşa Livası: Vakıflar, Mülkler, Mukattaalar: Vakfiyeler*. Istanbul: İstanbul Üniversitesi Edebiyat Fakültesi Yayınları, 1952.

Hayretî. *Dîvan: Tenkidli Basım.* Ed. Mehmed Çavuşoğlu and M. Ali Tanyeri. Istanbul: İstanbul Üniversitesi Edebiyat Fakültesi Yayınları, 1981.

Hollingsworth, Mary. *Patronage in Renaissance Italy: From 1400 to the Early Sixteenth Century.* Baltimore: Johns Hopkins University Press, 1994.

Ibn Battuta. *The Travels of Ibn Battuta: A.D. 1325-1354.* Ed. H. A. R. Gibb. Vol. 2. Cambridge: Cambridge University Press, 1971.

Ibn Bībī. *El-Evāmirrü'l-'Alāiyye fi'l-Umūri'l-'Alā'iyye.* Ed. Adnan Sadık Erzi. Facsimile edition. Ankara: Türk Tarih Kurumu Basımevi, 1956.

İlaydın, Hikmet. "Anadolu'da Klasik Türk Şiirinin Başlangıcı". *Türk Dili* 277 (October 1974): 765-74.

İnalcık, Halil. "XV. Asır Türkiye İktisadi ve İçtimai Tarihi Kaynakları". *İstanbul Üniversitesi İktisat Fakültesi Mecmuası* XV (1953-1954): 51-57.

———. "Comments on 'Sultanism': Max Weber's Typification of the Ottoman Polity". *Princeton Papers in Near Eastern Studies* 1 (1992): 1-22, 49-72.

———. *Fâtih Devri Üzerinde Tetkikler ve Vesikalar.* Ankara: Türk Tarih Kurumu, 1954.

———. "Mehmed II". *İslâm Ansiklopedisi: İslâm Âlemi Tarih, Coğrafya, Etnografya ve Biyografya Lugati.* Vol. 7. Eskişehir: Milli Eğitim Bakanlığı Yayınları, 2001. 506-35.

———. "Osmanlı Bürokrasisinde Aklâm ve Muâmelât". *Osmanlı Araştırmaları* I (1980): 1-14.

———. *Şâir ve Patron: Patrimonyal Devlet ve Sanat Üzerine Sosyolojik Bir İnceleme.* Ankara: Doğu Batı Yayınları, 2003.

———. "Tax Collection, Embezzlement and Bribery in Ottoman Finances". *The Turkish Studies Association Bulletin* 15.2 (September 1991): 327-46.

———. "The Rûznâmçe Registers of the Kadıaskers of Rumeli as preserved in the İstanbul Müftülük Archives". *Essays in Ottoman History.* Istanbul: Eren Yayıncılık, 1998. 125-52.

İpekten, Haluk. "Türk Edebiyatında Edebi Muhitler, XV-XVI. Asırlar". Associate professorship dissertation. Istanbul: Istanbul University Faculty of Literature, 1969.

Jardine, Lisa. *Worldly Goods: A New History of the Renaissance.* London: Macmillan, 1996.

Jettmar, Karl. *Art of the Steppes.* Trans. Ann E. Keep. New York: Greystone Press, 1967.

Kalpaklı, Mehmet. "Nazire Geleneği Çerçevesinde Fuzûlî'nin *Enisü'l-Kalb*'i". *Bir* 3 (1995): 227-34.

Karahan, Abdülkadir. *Fuzulî, Muhiti Hayatı ve Şahsiyeti.* Istanbul: 1949.

Kınalızade Alâaddin Ali. *Ahlak-ı Alaî.* Bulak, 1248 A.H.

Kınalızade Hasan Çelebi. *Tezkiretü'ş-Şu'arâ.* Ed. İbrahim Kutluk. Ankara: Türk Tarih Kurumu Yayınları, 1981.

Koçi Bey Risalesi. Ed. Ali Kemali Aksüt. Istanbul: 1925.

Köprülü, M. Fuad. "Âşık Çelebi". *İslâm Ansiklopedisi: İslâm Âlemi Tarih, Coğrafya, Etnografya ve Biyografya Lugati.* Vol. 1. Eskişehir: Milli Eğitim Bakanlığı Yayınları, 2001. 695-701.

———, ed. *Milli Edebiyat Cereyanının İlk Mübeşşirleri ve Divanı Türkii Basit: XVIinci Asır Şairlerinden "Edirneli Nazmi"nin Eseri.* Istanbul: İstanbul Darülfünunu Türkiyat Enstitüsü, 1928.

Kuşcu, Ali. "Al-Risâla fi'l-İsti'ara". *İslâm Araştırmaları Dergisi* 3: 215-34.

Manz, Beatrice Forbes. *The Rise and Rule of Tamerlane.* Cambridge: Cambridge University Press, 1989.

Mazıoğlu, Hasibe. *Fuzuli Üzerine Makaleler.* Ankara: Atatürk Kültür Dil ve Tarih Yüksek Kurumu, 1997.

Mehmed Sa'id (Şehrîzade). *Mahzenu's-Safâ ve Kunz-i Dürer.* Manuscript. Papers of Muallim Cevdet, no. D. 74. Istanbul: Atatürk Library.

Mesîhî Dîvânı. Ed. Mine Mengi. Ankara: Atatürk Kültür Dil ve Tarih Yüksek Kurumu, 1995.

Mesîhî Münşeatı. Es'ad Efendi 3351. Istanbul: Süleymaniye Library.

Nasuhü's-Silahî (Matrakçı). *Beyân-ı menâzil-i sefer-i Irâkeyn-i Sultân Süleymân Hân.* Ed. Hüseyin Yurdaydın. Ankara: Türk Tarih Kurumu Yayınları, 1976.

Necipoğlu, Gülru. "A Kanun for the State, A Canon for the Arts: Conceptualizing the Classical Synthesis of Ottoman Arts and Architecture". *Soliman le Magnifique et son temps.* Ed. Gilles Veinstein. Paris: La Documentation Française, 1992. 195-216.

———. "Süleyman the Magnificent and the Representation of Power in the Ottoman Hapsburg-Papal Rivalry". *The Art Bulletin* 71 (September 1989): 401-27.

Özkan, Mustafa. "Osmanlıca Nasıl bir Dil idi?". *Türkçe Kültürü* (1994): 75-80.

——. "Osmanlıcanın Değişim Süreci Nasıl Bir Seyir İzlemiştir". *Türkçe Kültürü* (1994): 81-86.

Pala, İskender. *Şürler, Şairler ve Meclisler*. Istanbul: Ötüken Yayınevi, 1997.

Raby, Julian. "Court and Export, Part 2: The Ushak Carpets". *Oriental Carpet & Textile Studies* 2 (1986): 177-87.

Roemer, Hans Robert. *Staatsschreiben der Timuridenzeit*. Wiesbaden: FranzSteiner Verlag, 1952.

Rogers, Michael J. "Centralization and Timurid Creativity". *Oriento Moderno* N. S. XV (LXXVI): 533-50.

Ruhî. *Bağdatlı Rûhî Dîvânı: Karşılaştırmalı Metin*. Ed. Coşkun Ak. Vol. 1. Bursa: 2001.

Sehi. *Heşt Bihişt: The Tezkire by Sehî Beg*. Ed. Günay Kut. Sources of Oriental Languages and Literatures 5. Turkic Sources V. Ed. Şinasi Tekin and Gönül Alpay Tekin. Cambridge: Harvard University Printing Office, 1978.

Seyyid Lokman. *Hünernâme*. Hazine 1524. Istanbul: Topkapı Palace Library. Ed. Zekeriya Eroğlu: "Şehnâmeci Lokman'ın Hünernâmesi", master's thesis, Boğaziçi University, Department of Turkish Language and Literature, 1998.

Sevgi, Ahmet. "Latîfî (Hayatı ve Eserleri) İnceleme-Metin". Doctoral dissertation. Ankara: Gazi University, 1987.

Sohrweide, Hanna. "Dichter und Gelehrte aus dem Osten im osmanischen Reich (1453–1600): Ein Beitrag zur türkisch-persischen Kulturgeschichte". *Der Islam* 46.3 (1970): 263-302.

Sperl, Stefan and Christopher Shackle, eds. *Qasida Poetry in Islamic Asia and Africa I: Classical Traditions and Modern Meanings*. Leiden: E. J. Brill, 1996.

Stetkevych, Suzanne Pinckney. "Abbasid Panegyric and the Poetics of Political Allegiance: Two Poems of al-Muttanabī on Kāfūr". *Qasida Poetry in Islamic Asia and Africa I: Classical Traditions and Modern Meanings*. Ed. Stefan Sperl and Christopher Shackle. Leiden: E. J. Brill, 1996. 35-63.

Subtelny, Maria Eva. "A Taste for the Timurid Period: The Persian Poetry of the Late Timurid Period". *Zeitschrift der Deutschen Morgenländischen Gesellschaft* 136 (1986): 56-79.

——. "Socioeconomic Bases of Cultural Patronage Under the Later Timurids". *International Journal of Middle East Studies* 20 (November 1988): 479-505.

Şanlı, Saadet. "Şehnameci Taliki Zade'ye göre Osmanlı Padişahlarının Şairlikleri -Taliki-Zade Şehnamesi (V. Hassa)'nın Edisyon Kritiği". Doctoral dissertation. Istanbul University Faculty of Literature, 1989.

Şentürk, Ahmet Atilla. *XVI. Asra Kadar Anadolu Sahası Mesnevîlerinde Edebî Tasvirler*. Istanbul: Kitabevi, 2002.

Tarlan, Ali Nihad. *Fuzûlî Divanı Şerhi*. Ankara: Kültür ve Turizm Bakanlığı Yayınları, 1985.

——. *Şeyhî Divanını Tetkik*. Istanbul: İstanbul Üniversitesi Edebiyat Fakültesi, 1964.

Taşköprîzade, Ahmed. *Şakayık-ı Nu'mâniyye*. Trans. Mecdî. Istanbul, 1269 A.H.

Tayyarzade Atâ. *Atâ Tarihi*. Vol. I. Istanbul, 1291/1874.

Tekin, Gönül Alpay. "Timur Devrine Ait İki Türkçe Şiir: Two Turkish Poems of the Timur Period". *Harvard Ukrainian Studies* 3-4 (1979-1980): 850-67.

——. "Turkish Literature". *Islamic Spirituality: Manifestations*. Ed. Seyyed Hossein Nasr. New York: Crossroad Publishing Company, 1991. 350-61.

Togan, Zeki Velidi. "Herat". *İslâm Ansiklopedisi: İslâm Âlemi Tarih, Coğrafya, Etnografya ve Biyografya Lugati*. Vol. 5. Eskişehir: Milli Eğitim Bakanlığı Yayınları, 2001. 429-42.

Togan, Zeki Velidi and Hellmut Ritter. "Câmî". *İslâm Ansiklopedisi: İslâm Âlemi Tarih, Coğrafya, Etnografya ve Biyografya Lugati*. Vol. 3. Eskişehir: Milli Eğitim Bakanlığı Yayınları, 2001. 15-20.

Turan, Osman. *Türkiye Selçukluları Hakkında Resmî Vesikalar: Metin, Tercüme ve Araştırmalar*. Ankara: Türk Tarih Kurumu Basımevi, 1958.

Turan, Şerafettin. *Kanunî'nin Oğlu Şehzâde Bayezit Vak'ası*. Ankara: Ankara Üniversitesi Dil ve Tarih-Coğrafya Fakültesi Yayınları, 1961.

Tursun Beg. *Tarih-i Ebülfeth* [The History of Mehmed the Conqueror]. Ed. and trans. Halil İnalcık and Rhoads Murphey. Minneapolis: Bibliotheca Islamica, 1978. Text published in facsimile.

Uzunçarşılı, İsmail Hakkı. "II inci Bayezid'in Oğullarından Sultan Korkut". *Belleten* 30.120 (October 1966): 539-601.

——. "Onaltıncı Asır Ortalarında Yaşamış Olan İki Büyük Şahsiyet: Tosyalı Celâl Zâde Mustafa ve Salih Çelebiler". *Belleten* 22.87 (July 1958): 391-441.

——. "Osmanlı Sarayı'nda Ehl-i Hıref (Sanatkârlar) Defterleri". *Belgeler* 11.15 (1981-1986): 23-76.

Üzgör, Tahir. *Edebiyat Bilgileri*. Istanbul: Veli Yayınları, 1983.

Yahya bin Mehmed el-Kâtib. *Menâhicü'l-İnşâ: The Earliest Ottoman Chancery Manual by Yahya bin Mehmed el-Kâtib from the 15th Century*. Ed. Şinasi Tekin. Roxbury, Massachusetts: Community Art Workshop, 1971. Text in facsimile with introduction by Şinasi Tekin.

Yarshater, Ehsan. "Persian Poetry in the Timurid and Safavid Periods". *The Cambridge History of Iran Volume 6: The Timurid and Safavid Periods*. Ed. Peter Jackson and Laurence Lockhart. Cambridge: Cambridge University Press, 1986. 965-94.

Yazıcızade, Ali. *Tevarih-i Âl-i Selçuk*. Topkapı Palace Library copy, Revan 1390.

The *Seyahatname* of Evliya Çelebi as a Literary Monument

Robert Dankoff

The study of the *Seyahatname* as a literary monument has hardly begun. This essay focuses on issues relating to genre, form, and style. With regard to both contents and structure, designating the work as travel literature is too simplistic; the most exact generic description would be: Ottoman geographical encyclopedia structured as travel account and personal memoir. The first-person account of Evliya's itinerary and adventures forms the armature within which he builds up his main structure consisting of description. Evliya's descriptive style is expansive and digressive, with frequent use of alliteration, jingles, wordplay, and similes, all of which add charm to a text that is otherwise admittedly quite tedious. Evliya's literary flair comes out in the narrative sections, which reveal him as a master prose stylist. His occasional sallies into verse, on the other hand, are perfunctory.

Evliya Çelebi (1611-1685?) is one of those authors more quoted than read. The vast size of his work and its encyclopedic nature invite skimming and probing rather than concentrated and extensive perusal. Also, the lack of a reliable edition until now has discouraged serious analysis.[1] Thus, there has been little effort to try and characterize the work as a whole. In this essay, I leave aside the broader contextual questions relating to Ottoman cultural history[2] and focus on strictly literary issues relating to genre, form, and style.

THE QUESTION OF GENRE

The *Seyahatname* recounts journeys over a forty-year period (roughly 1640-1680). To that extent it falls in the category of travel literature. But there are two kinds of difficulties with this designation, one based on internal, the other on external considerations.

1. The main point deriving from internal considerations relates to contents. The *Seyahatname* is by no means simply a straightforward travel narrative. Rather, the roughly chronological travel account merely provides the armature within which the author does many other things. These other things—mainly description, but also narratives of various sorts, such as historical and hagiographical, as well as elegies and other kinds of insertions in verse—make up the bulk of the work, and so cannot be considered simply as digressions to the travel account.

Another point relates to structure. The division of the work into ten "books", while perhaps required because of its voluminous nature, is by no means a mechanical one based simply on a chronological division. Rather, there are organizing principles both within each book and among the books that are different from the chronological principle of the travel narrative which provides the armature of the work.

The framing books, Books I and X, are devoted to Istanbul and Cairo respectively, the major metropolises of the Ottoman Empire, where Evliya spent the parts of his life before and after his forty-year period of travel. These two books are the only ones provided with a chapter organization, and appear to be modelled on each other in various respects. For example, the description of the shops and guilds in Cairo (Book X, ch. 49) is a reduced and more straightforward version of the corresponding sections concerning Istanbul (Book I, ch. 270). Further, the survey of quarters and villages up and down the Golden Horn and the Bosphorus (Book I, chs. 235-66) has its analogue in Evliya's trips up and down the Nile (Book X, chs. 65-74).

While Books II-IX do not have the same tight structure as the frame books, there is clear evidence that the author intended to provide a kind of shape to each book. Although his itineraries over forty years repeat and crisscross, his accounts of them tend to be coherent and interrelated. It is not wrong to characterize Book II by the rubric "Anatolia and the Celâlî Rebels", Books III and V by "The Career of Melek Ahmed Pasha", Book IV by "Safavid Borderlands", Book VI by "Hungary and the German Campaign", Book VII by "Habsburg Borderlands", Book VIII by "Greece and the Conquest of Crete", and Book IX by "Pilgrimage". It is also no accident that several of the books end with saga-like accounts like those of the lives and deaths of the Celâlî rebel and bandit Kara Haydaroğlu in Book II and of the brave and tragic commander Seydi Ahmed Pasha in Book V, or the account of the author's own adventurous escape from Istanbul when threatened by the dangerous grand vizier İpşir Pasha in Book III.

Thus, with regard to both contents and structure, designating the work as travel literature would be too simplistic. Yet the author called it *Seyahatname* or "Book of Travels" and presented it in the first place as a literary record of his achievement as *seyyah-ı âlem* or world traveler.

2. This brings us to the external considerations, relating to Islamic and Ottoman conventions. *Seyahat* (Ar. *siyâha*) traditionally refers to the journeys undertaken by a Sufi adept seeking mystical guidance and illumination, such as travel in search of a shaikh or at the behest of one's shaikh[3], also the visiting (*ziyaret*) of the tombs and shrines of *evliya* (holy men, saints, or friends of God). While this motivation is certainly present in the *Seyahatname*, and also relates to the author's name (Evliya) and to his self-characterization as dervish, it is by no means the primary driving force. Nor is the description of such journeys a well-founded literary genre; on the contrary, Evliya's designation of his work as *Seyahatname* is unprecedented (according to his own account, the title was suggested by his father; II 241b23).[4]

The other traditional type of travel in Islam is *rihla*. The term designates both a journey motivated by the hajj (pilgrimage to Mecca) as well as a genre of literature devoted to recording such a journey. This motivation is also present in the *Seyahatname*, especially in Book IX, but again it is subordinate.

Rather, Evliya's primary motivation was to provide a complete description of the Ottoman Empire and its neighboring regions. His model was less the *rihla* tradition of the Arab travelers (such as Ibn Jubayr and Ibn Battuta) and more the *masalik wa mamalik* and *khitat* traditions of the Arab geographers (such as al-Muqaddasi and al-Maqrizi). The *rihla* mode is personal or autobiographical: Evliya's junkets and adventures, while often following recognizable narrative patterns, tend to be quirky and anecdotal, sometimes sliding into satire or fantasy. The geographical mode, imperial in scope, embraces history, customs, folklore, and much else, all tending to fit into pre-established formulas and grids.

In the Ottoman context, with the partial exception of Mehmed Âşık of Trabzon (d. ca. 1600), Evliya would have found little precedence for what he undertook. Thus, the most exact generic description of the *Seyahatname* is: Ottoman geographical encyclopedia structured as travel account and personal memoir. It is a genre without precedent and without imitation.

THE POETICS OF DESCRIPTION

If you open the *Seyahatname* at random, your eye is likely to light on a section heading (set off in the original mss. by indentation, large letters, or red ink) beginning with the word *evsaf* (description)—or, less commonly, *sitayiş* (praise)—and including the name of a town. These town descriptions are the most characteristic literary unit of the work. They generally follow the same pattern, beginning with the history and administrative organization of the town, its names in various languages and their etymologies, and its geographic position. They then continue with a description of the town's topography, with particular attention to fortifications, and including descriptions of houses, mosques, madrasas, schools, inns, baths, and fountains. These sections are followed by comments on town quarters and religious affiliations; climate; the appearance, dress, manners, and customs of the populace; proper names and speech habits; the ulema, poets, physicians, and other notables; markets, shops, products, and comestibles; and parks, gardens, and picnic spots. Town descriptions are usually concluded with comments on graves and shrines, along with biographies or hagiographies of the dead.

Some tendencies of Evliya's descriptive style, as also pointed out in Hanneke Lamers's article "On Evliya's Style" and Nuran Tezcan's article "Bir Üslup Ustası Olarak Evliya Çelebi" (Evliya Çelebi as a Master of Style) are the following:

1. The scope of the work being encyclopedic, the treatment of a topic, and also the transitions from one topic to another, are expansive, digressive, and leisurely. These tendencies extend to the narrative portions of the work. Evliya is in no hurry. Even word choice and phraseology are unconstrained by considerations of directness and concision. Thus, speaking of someone's brother or daughter, Evliya seldom uses *karındaş* or *kız* but rather *bürâder-i cân-berâber* or *duhter-i pâkize-ahter*. A school is rarely simply *mekteb*, but rather *mekteb-i sıbyân-ı tıflân-ı ebced-hân*. If he mounts his horse he might say *ata binüp* but he might also say *esb-i sabâ-reftârlarımıza süvâr olup* (IX 201a20).

2. Rhyme and Persianate phrasing are common throughout (as in the above examples) but particularly in headings and/or at the end of sections. E.g., IX 87a8: *ve iki yüz dükkândır, ammâ bezzâzistânı iki aded hândır, ve bir hammâmı önünde bir çemenzâr musallâ-yı gülistândır, cânib-i erba'ası kavak dırahtları ile ârâste olmuş ibâdet-hâne-i ehl-i irfândır, ve etrâfı kârgîr binâ-yı amâristândır.*

3. There is frequent use of alliteration, jingles, wordplay, etc. E.g., VI 161a16: *berrâk ve ak-pak bir âb-ı muravvakdır*; VII 95a31: *dağları cümle bâğlar ve bâğlarında zâğlar bâğların üzümlerin yedikce bâğlar sâhibleri zâğlardan feryâd edüp ağlarlar*; IX 148b2: *gayet girdâb sapa yoldur, sıpasın gâ'ib eden gelmez ve gelen gülmez ve sıpasın bulmaz, böyle bir bî-emân yollardır.* This tendency also extends to the narrative portions of his work. E.g., IV 263a11: *Erzurum beğleri ve behadırânın Rum yeğleri*; V 13b26: *beyaz kar üzre kara kuş gibi şikâr üzleyüp gelirler*; V 144a25: *anlar bizlere biz anlara bizler sokup kırarken.*

4. There is frequent use of similes and other images that add vividness to an otherwise standard account. Thus, the seeds of a certain fine pomegranate are "as large as partridge eggs" (IX 87a18: *âbdâr ve dânedâr hoşgüvâr ve la'lgûn Nif kirazı derler bir gülnârı var kim her dânesi keklik beyzası kadar vardır*); and, in a legend, the fourth caliph Ali slices a certain stone with his sword "like a cucumber" (IV 378a5: *hîn-i fetihde hazret-i Ali* [...] *düşmana karşu ol taşı Zülfikar ile iki pâre etmişdir, bi-emri-hudâ gûyâ mânend-i hıyâr dilmişdir*).

5. In his town descriptions Evliya typically uses *cümle* to introduce the number of mosques, madrasas, baths, etc., but sometimes he gets tired of *cümle* and substitutes other terms, and once he gets started doing this, he often runs out of standard terminology and has to create terms of his own, quasi-Turkish or quasi-Arabic. E.g., VIII 248a34-249a3: *cümlesi, kamusı, hepsi, umûmisi, olancası, barısı, olandası, hemusı, hamusı, emetası, âmmetası, hemisi, hemetası, yekûnisi, cem'âsı, olanısı, götürüsi, herbarısı.*

6. An analogous technique is to assume the narrative style of a different persona, thus alerting or awakening the reader. E.g., V 180a12-180b17 (shrine of Memi Bey Sultan in Eğribucak): assuming a dervish style, he ends each period with an endearment, as though addressing the reader: *imânım, cânım, gülüm, ömrüm, cânımın cânı, pîrim, cânânım*, etc.

While Evliya constantly employs such devices in order to add charm, it must be admitted that even with these techniques at play, most of the descriptive sections of the *Seyahatname* (and therefore most of the work) make for very tedious reading. There is little to distinguish the description of one mosque from that of another. Even (as often) when Evliya waxes ecstatic over the beauty of a building's structure or decoration, his language tends to cliché. A fine minaret is always "well-proportioned" (*mevzûn*). A crevice or precipice is always likened to an abyss of hell (*gayyâ, derk-i esfel*). If he mentions a garden we can expect a reference to the Koranic "İrem of the pillars" (usually reduced to *irem-i zât*), and if he mentions fragrances we can be sure that they "perfume the brain" (*demâğ-i benî-âdem mu'attar eder*). In soup-kitchens (*imaret*) and hospices (*tekke*) we invariably find that hospitality is extended to all visitors (*âyende vü revendegânlara ni'meti mebzûl*), and musical performances, where they occur, always resemble those at the Timurid court of Herat around 1500 (*Hüseyin Baykara fasılları*).

EVLİYA AS VERSIFIER

As pointed out in Osman Horata's article "*Evliya Çelebi Seyahatnâmesi*'ndeki Manzum Kısımlar" (Verse Portions of Evliya Çelebi's *Seyahatname*), Evliya frequently cites verses by others. These are usually Turkish, although Arabic and Persian are not infrequent, and he also cites poems in Greek, Kurdish, Syriac, and some African languages (including one that he calls "Hebrew" and that is perhaps invented). Aside from chronograms—whether noted down from the monuments observed or else relating to battles, births and deaths, etc.—he cites verses relating to places or events that have caught his fancy, and occasional favorite verses illustrating the working of fate or expressing his point of view.[5] None of these displays any marked literary sensibility. Usually he quotes from memory and therefore inaccurately (example of Yahya below). Occasionally he names his source, but as far as poets are concerned, he is clearly more interested in anecdotes about their lives than he is in their verse.[6]

Turning now to his own compositions, aside from occasional short chronograms and throwaways, we find the following more ambitious examples:

1. I 214b29-33: On spiritual intoxication as opposed to drinking wine; *mesnevi*, 7 *beyt*s; meter: · − − − + · − − − + · − −.

2. IV 347b: Eulogy (*şehrengiz*) of Baghdad; *kaside*, 59 *beyt*s; meter:

· − − − + · − − − + · − − − + · − − −.[7]

3. V 146b6-14: Chronogram on the conquest of Ribnİçse; *mesnevi*, 12 *beyt*s; meter:

· − − − + · − − − + · − − − + · − − −.

4. VII 182b30-183a2: Elegy (*mersiye*) for a dead slave boy; *mesnevi*, 14 *beyt*s; meter:

− · − − + − · − − + − · −.

5. IX 79a25-79b15: Eulogy (*sitayiş*) of Bal-bınarı in Aydın; *kaside*, 16 *beyt*s; meter:

· − − − + · − − − + · − − − + · − − −.

In general, Evliya's verse is uninspired. He mainly resorts to it in order to display his ability to eulogize a place (*sitayiş, şehrengiz*) in verse, in the manner of Cemâlî and other poets, just as he can in prose.

THE ROLE OF NARRATION

While Evliya was an indifferent versifier, he was a master of prose, as has been pointed out in Pertev Naili Boratav's article "Evliya Çelebi'nin Hikâyeciliği" (Evliya Çelebi's Narrative Art) and Mine Mengi's article "*Evliya Çelebi Seyahatnamesi'*nin Birinci Cildinde Tahkiye" (Narration in the First Volume of Evliya Çelebi's *Seyahatname*). His literary skills were based firstly on a gift for narrative, honed over the years in his capacity as entertainer and companion of sultans, viziers, and pashas; and secondly on a superb education in Ottoman and Islamic culture, including Koran and commentaries, biographies and hagiographies of the prophets and saints, chronicles, epics, travelogues, belles-lettres, etc.[8] Since he aimed as much to entertain as to inform, he had no compunction about inflating numbers and spicing his otherwise sober travel account with exaggerations, humorous anecdotes, tall tales, and other fictions or embroidered truths. Some of these are highly polished narratives, indicative of literary sensitivity and ambition, and appealing to a sophisticated Ottoman audience. The one instance where his narrative flair spills over into verse ("Hebrew"—i.e., an unidentified African language—poems in Books IX and X attributed to the "prophet" Kaffah) seems to be an elaborate juggling of outlandish linguistic and prophetic lore, calculated to appeal to a recherché Ottoman taste for whimsicality.[9]

As mentioned above, the first-person account of Evliya's itinerary and adventures forms the armature or scaffolding within which he builds up his main structure which consists of description. This narrative core occupies roughly five percent of the whole. Most of the other narratives that we find in the *Seyahatname*—whether historical, legendary, or hagiographic—are subordinate to the descriptive sections. The main exceptions are the two saga-like accounts mentioned above, the heroic biographies at the end of Books II and V.

In the case of some of the narratives, the autograph manuscripts (i.e., those prepared by Evliya himself, which we have for Books I-VIII) show evidence of very careful editing and revision. For example, Evliya recounts the last days of Sultan İbrahim in two different places (A: I 78a13-78b24; B: II 369b29-370a19, 370b6-373a3). Comparing the two accounts, it is plain that B is based on A, with many elaborations. Sometimes there is only a change in wording. Most of the changes are outright additions, making B nearly twice the length of A (not counting the lengthy interpolation of Evliya's visit to Cinci Hoca's palace). These changes lend color and detail to the narrative, and additional personal reference. Thus, to the list of items which Cinci and the other courtiers caused the sultan to waste money on, B adds a troupe of gypsy musicians. B also includes a list of bad consequences to the sultan's prodigality. When it comes to Cinci being put to death, B mentions how much of his wealth was confiscated by the state, and also the fact that Evliya continued to use the horse which he had received from Cinci as a gift (mentioned in the interpolation). Finally, B spins out the sultan's macabre conversation with his own executioner, adding the remark that he too would join in the funeral prayer. But version A shows reworking as well: additions made at the final fair copy stage are noted in the margin. Thus, Evliya specifies the date of the events leading up to the sultan's execution, adds the information that the conspirators tried to obtain a decree in their favor from the mad sultan but were unsuccessful, and also includes a rather long note concerning the sultan's funeral. All this demonstrates that Evliya had second thoughts about this narrative two different times, recorded separately and without any overlap. This instructive example, which is analyzed at greater length in the article "Şu Rasadı Yıkalım mı? Evliya Çelebi ve Filoloji" (Shall We Demolish That Observatory? Evliya Çelebi and

Philology) by Robert Dankoff, offers a way of demonstrating Evliya's method of composition by comparing his two versions of the same account.

One can also compare Evliya's recounting of certain events with the standard Ottoman histories. Thus, Evliya's account of Melek Ahmed Pasha's fall from the grand vizierate can be compared with that of the major historian of the period, Naima. When this is done, as on pages 12-15 of *The Intimate Life of an Ottoman Statesman: Melek Ahmed Paşa (1588-1662)* by Robert Dankoff, we can see how Evliya inflates the human drama, colors the narrative with the use of dialect, resorts to the epic mode for battle descriptions, and lightens the whole with his personal touch.

Evliya's account of his adventures in Bitlis, from the beginning of Book V, can serve as an example of Evliya's literary art on a somewhat larger scale (text and English translation in Dankoff, *Evliya Çelebi in Bitlis*). Far from being a mere string of personal anecdotes, this account is a well-structured narrative with careful setting of scenes, clear transitions, and cumulative mounting of tension, interrupted by comic relief and issuing in a climax and denouement. It can be outlined as follows:

1. The stage is set in Book IV with Melek Pasha's defeat of Abdal Khan. Abdal Khan flees, and the Pasha appoints as puppet khan Abdal's lovable and compliant young son, Ziyaeddin. At the homage ceremony we are introduced to the latter's elder brother, Nureddehir, whom Evliya, in a kind of novel-like foreshadowing, characterizes as "bloodthirsty" (IV 273b36). At the beginning of Book V Melek Pasha learns he has been removed from office as governor of Van. He immediately sends Evliya to Bitlis to help his other agents collect some arrears. Shortly after Evliya arrives, news reaches Bitlis that Melek Pasha has been removed from office, and the following day Abdal Khan himself returns. The situation becomes critical for Evliya.

2. Prelude (V 9a36-9b1): In Evliya's dream, his father reassures him that he will escape.

3. Breakfast scene (9b7-10a22): The khan's wife sends him a warning to leave, he is tested by the khan's sons Bedir and Nureddehir, murder of the "treacherous" steward Haydar Kethuda.

4. Transition (10a22-35): He betrays his apprehensions, exercises his horses daily in the snow to prepare for his escape.

5. First conversation with Abdal Khan (10b1-31): He flatters the khan, who gives him gifts and promises more.

6. Transition (10b32-35): "When I came out, I displayed these gifts to all the courtiers and pretended to be deliriously happy at this good fortune. But the truth was that all joy had vanished from my heart ever since Haydar Agha was cut up at my side. I

could only think about mounting my horse, girding my sword, and running away. My joy had turned to sorrow, my wine to poison, as in the verse: Not everyone knows what pain I suffer / Only I know, and God knows [*Derdin nice düşvâr idigin her kişi bilmez / Bir ben bilirim çekdicegim bir de bir Allâh*].[10] I remained in Bitlis two more months in this state, unable to go anywhere, since we were completely snowbound".

7. Second conversation with Abdal Khan (10b36-11a16): The khan curses Melek Pasha, Evliya tries to mollify him.

8. Transition (11a16-22): The situation daily grows more dangerous, the khan having everyone killed whom he suspects of collusion with Melek Pasha.

9. Skiing scene (11a23-12a4): Murder of the "treacherous" Molla Mehemmed.

10. Transition (12a5-27): Elegiac remarks on Molla Mehemmed, another month of agitation and planning escape while entertaining the khan.

11. Bath scene (12a27-12b20): Nureddehir becomes riotous and makes threatening overtures to his brother, the "new khan" Ziyaeddin.

12. Transition (12b20-13a1): Passing the time playing cards and eating candies and fruit, Evliya excuses himself to urinate, checks his horses and gives instructions to his retinue.

13. Scene in Ziyaeddin's sleeping quarters (13a1-15): That night Ziyaeddin has trouble sleeping and asks Evliya to keep him company. In the course of conversation, Ziyaeddin says that he would flee to Melek Ahmed Pasha in Van if only it were not the dead of winter. Finally he falls asleep.

14. Transition (13a15-18): Evliya lies down with his clothes on, as usual, but cannot sleep himself.

15. Climax (13a18-13b2): At two hours past midnight he sees Nureddehir enter the chamber, with a dagger in his hand. Evliya, pretending to be asleep, watches as Nureddehir approaches first himself, then two other sleepers, pausing to address each one in monologue fashion, until he comes before his brother Ziyaeddin. Suddenly he flares up and stabs his brother to death.

16. Evliya's escape (13b2-14a35).

Aside from its value as a sheer adventure story, the most memorable aspects of this narrative are the fine characterizations of the key players. Abdal Khan, depicted earlier as genial host and Renaissance man, is now revealed as a cantankerous and suspicious tyrant, revengeful and bitter over the loss of his wealth and the great bloodshed among his followers. Evliya manages to stay on his good side through jokes and flattery, while revealing to the reader his own fears and apprehensions. Then there is the blustery Haydar Kethuda, the ancient functionary whom Melek Pasha had appointed as the child khan's steward, who spits at Bedir and Nureddehir when they rebuff him and suffers the consequence. Especially poignant is the contrast between Nureddehir, the violent elder brother who has taken his father's side, and Ziyaeddin, the meek and compliant younger brother who confides in Evliya. Nureddehir's nervous tension and violent thoughts, and Evliya's own Falstaffian character, are wonderfully sketched in the climactic scene (13a18-13b2):

> It was two hours past midnight.
>
> [...] I was lying in bed, and my eyes were on the door. Suddenly, who should appear there but Nureddehir Beg, with a waistband round his middle and his sleeves rolled up. Softly he crept in, stretched and yawned, cracked his knuckles and snapped his lower vertebrae, then fingered his dagger and straightened his belt. As I lay there watching, he first came over to me, saying, "Evliya the dervish. What are you doing in this land?" My heart was in my throat. Taking refuge in God, I gave a snort as if in my sleep, and began to snore like a pig, just as the others were. I was really trumpeting in a comical fashion. Seeing me thus, Nureddehir said, "This dervish's beauty-sleep is also like the sleep of swine", and he passed me by.
>
> Moving on to the story-reciter Molla Dilaver at the foot of the closet, he said: "You pimp from Isfahan, get to work, or go to your house down in the city and sleep there!" He passed him also and went over to the coffee-server Rüstem, lying next to the khan, and looked him over too. Then his eye fell on his own "dear" brother the khan, who was lying on the couch and slumbering peacefully, "bedded on roses and covered with hyacinths". He glanced about furtively, then returned to gaze at the khan. I was peering out from under my coverlet like a dog from under the skirting-board of a privy, wondering if they had some private matter to discuss. Suddenly he drew the dagger from his belt, flung off the khan's gold-embroidered quilt, and gave him a kick, shouting, "Get up, you catamite!"
>
> Groggy with sleep, the khan opened his eyes and saw that it was his own "dear" brother. As he cried out, Nureddehir plunged the sharp dagger in his breast, then again at the midriff, twisting it into his belly. Grasping in terror and futility for his own dagger, the khan fell to the floor, where his brother stabbed him once again.[11]

While there are many other sustained narratives in the *Seyahatname*—e.g., sagas of the Celâlî rebels at the end of Book II, and a Grimmelshausen-like account of adventures during the battle on the Raab at the beginning of Book VII—none of these approaches the Bitlis narrative for novel-like richness and coherence. One notes the fine pacing of exposition and narration, dialogue, and transitional elements; the density of setting, character, and plot; and the interaction of various social types on the same plane, each retaining his own voice or dialect (heteroglossia).

Another direction in which Evliya carries his narrative flair is satire. An example is "The Girl Who Gave Birth to an Elephant", which comes at the end of the very full description of Sivas (III 79a6; text and German translation in Korkut Buğday, *Evliyâ*

Çelebis Anatolienreise 204-09; English translation in Robert Dankoff, *An Ottoman Mentality*... 173-74). Evliya grounds the narrative in a historical moment, characteristically plays up his mediating and peace-making roles, uses dialect and other kinds of verisimilitude to portray the hapless and hilarious plight of the Anatolian villagers, disavows fantasy by appealing to popular theology, and directs his satirical barbs against the greed and corruption of the Ottoman officials on the scene. Other examples of satirical fiction are his account of Genghis Khan's conversion to Islam, directed against the fanaticism of the religious authorities (VII 131a; English translation in Dankoff, *An Ottoman Mentality*... 73-75), and his description of the Kadızadeli Çelebis who come out to view the battle against Celâlî Gürci Nebi in Üsküdar in 1648 (III 31a25).

CONCLUSION

The study of the *Seyahatname* as a literary monument has hardly begun. I have suggested here a few of the possible directions in which such a study may go. Others may wish to analyze this protean text as an anatomy, or a picaresque; or may wish to apply more novel approaches of literary criticism. Now that a reliable edition is in the process of completion, one may at least hope that the *Seyahatname* will in the future be read, even enjoyed, as much as it is quoted.

NOTES

[1] The text published by Yapı Kredi Yayınları can be considered a critical edition beginning with Book V; there is a plan to re-edit Books I-IV.

[2] For evaluations of these questions, see the following works: "Evliya Çelebi" by M. Cavid Baysun, "Evliya Çelebi" by Mücteba İlgürel, "Evliya Çelebi and the *Seyahatname*" by Robert Dankoff, and *An Ottoman Mentality: The World of Evliya Çelebi* by Robert Dankoff.

[3] Editor's note: Both the spelling of some originally Arabic words which have entered common English usage and all transliterations from Ottoman Turkish are according to the preferences of the author rather than official *JTL* style.

[4] References to Books I-VIII are to the following autograph mss.:

Bağdat 304	Books I and II
Bağdat 305	Books III and IV
Bağdat 307	Book V
Revan 1457	Book VI
Bağdat 308	Books VII and VIII

References to Book IX are to Bağdat 306. References to Book X are to İÜTY 5973. References include book number, folio number, and sometimes line number. All mss. are preserved in the Topkapı Palace Library, with the exception of Book X, which is to be found in the manuscript collection of Istanbul University.

[5] E.g., *Görelim âyîne-i devrân ne sûret gösterir* (I 38a3, II 261b9, 363b25, III 182b14, V 73b25, VI 54a7, 183b18, VII 165b24, X 183b18—only here as the second *mısra* of a *beyt* beginning: *İdgâha varalım ol günde dollab seyrine*). The longest poetic text quoted by Evliya is Cemâlî's eulogy (*sitayiş*) of Ereğli (III 17a-18a).

[6] Mustafa İsen, in his article "Edebiyat Tarihimizin Kaynaklarından Evliya Çelebi Seyahatnamesi" (The *Seyahatname* of Evliya Çelebi as a Source of Our Literary History) shows that in Book I Evliya depends on

Mustafa Ali. In Manisa, where he names ten living poets, he seems to depend on his own judgment (IX 38a29-38b18). This is pointed out on pages 120-23 of Nuran Tezcan's work *Manisa nach Evliyâ Çelebi*.

[7] Contrary to Jessica Lutz's assertion in her article "Evliya Çelebi's Qasîda on Baghdad" that the *kaside* is devoted to Ma'ruf Karkhi (63), only line 18 (verse 25) is devoted to him. Rather, the poem is a *şehrengiz* devoted to Baghdad, recounting its praises. Line 22 (verse 32) should be rendered: "They chant its (i.e., Baghdad's; not his, i.e., Ma'ruf Karkhi's) praises". In the following lines Evliya is speaking (as he often does in his praises of various cities) of the lovely boys of the town and their lovers.

[8] While some attention has been paid to Evliya's sources of information, there have been few studies concerned with literary influence. The epic style adopted in battle narratives seems to echo popular Turkish genres like *Battalname* rather than chronicles, and some expressions favored in the hagiographical accounts perhaps derive specifically from *Menâkıb-ı İbrâhîm-i Gülşenî*, but these suggestions need to be confirmed.

[9] More information on this literary phenomenon can be found in chapter 5 of *An Ottoman Mentality: The World of Evliya Çelebi* by Robert Dankoff.

[10] By Şeyhülislâm Yahya (not named). On page 244 of *Divan-ı Yahya*, we find the following lines: *Aşkın nice düşvâr idügin her kişi bilmez / Bir ben bilürim çekdüğimi bir de bir Allâh.*

[11] *Nısfü'l-leyli iki sâ'at geçmişdi. [...] Yatdığım yerde iki gözlerim kapuda idi. Anı gördüm, Nûre'd-dehir Beg orta kuşak ile bâzuların sığamış kapudan içeri yap yap girüp bir kerre gerindi ve sündi, ve parmakların çatırdatdı ve belin kütürdetdi, ve elin hançerine koyup kemerin onarup gördüm, ibtidâ bana doğrı gelirken eydir: "Ey fakîr Evliyâ, sen bu diyârda nişlersen" dedikde cânım dişime alup "İlâhî sana sığınıram" deyü derûnumdan bir teveccüh edüp uykuda hûzlar gibi muş muş uyur şekilli olup hınzîr-vâr öbirleri gibi horuldamağa başladım, ammâ şaka-gûne nefîr-i hâb çekerdim. Bu hâl üzre Nûre'd-dehir hakîri görüp eydir: "Garîbün hâb-ı nâzı dahi hâb-ı hınzîr gibidir" deyüp hele beni geçüp yüklük dibinde kıssa-hon Monlâ Dilâvere varup "Ey gidi İsfahânî, işine yâ aşağı şehirde hânene gidüp yatsana" deyü anı da geçdi ve hânun yanında yatan kahveci Rüsteme varup ana da bakup hânun serîri yanına varup gördi kim serîr üzre hân hâb-ı nâzda nâz-ı na'îm ile gül döşenüp sünbül örtünen bürâder-i cân-berâberidir, bir kerre cânib-i erba'asında bizlere bakup yine hâna bakdı. Hakîr yine ihrâm altından nazar edüp "Âyâ bir tenhâ müşâvere edecek kelimâtleri mi var ki?" deyü kadem-gâhda etek tahtası altından av zağarı bakar gibi hakîr nigerân edüp dururken hemân Nûre'd-dehir belinden hançerin çıkarup hânun üzerinden zer-ender-zer yorganın serpüp hâna bir depme urup "Kalh bire hey hîz götlek" deyince hân dahi nevm-âlûd serâsîme kalkup nigerân etdikde gördi kim bürâder-i cân-berâberidir, hay derken hânun memesi üstine bir hançer-i ser-tîz ve tîz bir dahi bağrına urup hançeri karnında burdı, hân cân havlıyle başı altından hançerin çıkaram derken serîrden aşağı düşüp hâna bir hançer dahi urunca* (a transcription and English translation of this passage can also be found in Dankoff, *Evliya Çelebi in Bitlis* 376-79).

WORKS CITED

Baysun, M. Cavid. "Evliya Çelebî". *İslâm Ansiklopedisi.* Vol. 4. Istanbul: Millî Eğitim Basımevi, 1948. 400-12.

Boratav, Pertev Naili. "Evliya Çelebi'nin Hikâyeciliği". *Folklor ve Edebiyat.* Vol. 1. Istanbul: Adam Yayıncılık, 1982. 297-303.

Bruinessen, Martin van and Hendrik Boeschoten, eds. *Evliya Çelebi Diyarbekir'de.* Trans. Tansel Güney. Istanbul: İletişim Yayınları, 2003.

——. *Evliya Çelebi in Diyarbekir.* Leiden: E. J. Brill, 1988.

Buğday, Korkut, ed. *Evliyâ Çelebis Anatolienreise.* Leiden: E. J. Brill, 1996.

Dankoff, Robert. *An Ottoman Mentality: The World of Evliya Çelebi.* Leiden: Brill, 2004.

——. "Evliya Çelebi and the *Seyahatname*". *The Turks.* Eds. Hasan Celâl Güzel et al. Vol. 3: Ottomans. Ankara: Yeni Türkiye Publications, 2002. 605-26.

——. "Evliya Çelebi ve Seyahatnâmesi Işığında Osmanlı Toplum Hayatı". *Türkler.* Eds. Hasan Celâl Güzel et al. Trans. Nasuh Uslu. Vol. 10. Ankara: Yeni Türkiye Yayınları, 2002. 268-91.

——. "Şu Rasadı Yıkalım mı? Evliya Çelebi ve Filoloji". Tezcan and Atlansoy 99-118.

——. *The Intimate Life of an Ottoman Statesman: Melek Ahmed Paşa (1588-1662).* Albany, New York: State University of New York Press, 1991.

Dankoff, Robert, ed. *Evliya Çelebi in Bitlis.* Leiden: E. J. Brill, 1990.

Gökyay, Orhan Şaik et al., eds. *Evliya Çelebi Seyahatnâmesi.* Vols. 1-9. İstanbul: Yapı Kredi Yayınları, 1996-2005.

Horata, Osman. *"Evliya Çelebi Seyahatnâmesi'*ndeki Manzum Kısımlar". Tezcan and Atlansoy 155-67.

İlgürel, Mücteba. "Evliya Çelebi". *İslam Ansiklopedisi.* Eds. Tayyar Altıkulaç et al. Vol. 11. Istanbul: Türkiye Diyanet Vakfı, 1995. 529-33.

İsen, Mustafa. "Edebiyat Tarihimizin Kaynaklarından Evliya Çelebi Seyahatnamesi". *Türklük Araştırmaları Dergisi* 4 (1988): 229-33.

Lamers, Hanneke. "On Evliya's Style". *Evliya Çelebi in Diyarbekir.* Eds. Martin van Bruinessen and Hendrik Boeschoten. Leiden: E. J. Brill, 1988. 64-70.

——. "Evliya Çelebi'nin Üslubu". *Evliya Çelebi Diyarbekir'de.* Eds. Martin van Bruinessen and Hendrik Boeschoten. Trans. Tansel Güney. Istanbul: İletişim Yayınları, 2003. 117-25.

Lutz, Jessica. "Evliya Çelebi's Qasîda on Baghdad". *De Turcicis Aliisque Rebus Commentarii Henry Hofman dedicati.* Ed. Marc Vandamme. Utrecht Turcological Series, vol. 3. Utrecht: Instituut voor Oosterse Talen en Culturen, 1992. 59-77.

Mengi, Mine. *"Evliya Çelebi Seyahatnamesi'*nin Birinci Cildinde Tahkiye". Tezcan and Atlansoy 197-208.

Şeyhülislâm Yahya. *Divan-ı Yahya.* İstanbul: Matbaa-i Âmire, 1334 A. H.

Tezcan, Nuran. "Bir Üslup Ustası Olarak Evliya Çelebi". Tezcan and Atlansoy 231-43.

Tezcan, Nuran, ed. *Manisa nach Evliyâ Çelebi.* Leiden: Brill, 1999.

Tezcan, Nuran and Kadir Atlansoy, eds. *Evliya Çelebi ve Seyahatname.* Gazimağusa: Doğu Akdeniz Üniversitesi Yayınları, 2002.

Images of the Woman in Turkish Drama as Illustrated by the Plays of Adalet Ağaoğlu[1]

Sevda Şener

This article, which was originally read as a conference paper, presents an introductory and general overview of a complex and oft-neglected field: the treatment of women in Turkish drama. The first part of the article follows a broadly historical approach, in which common images of the woman in Turkish drama as well as the developments and changes in these are traced across the decades of the twentieth century, starting from the 1920s. While the archetypical nature of many of these images is emphasized, their origins and development are also placed in a specific social and historical context. Thus, the emergence of images as varied as "the sinful woman of the modern nouveau riche middle class" and "the venerable, wise old peasant mother" is connected to important events reshaping Turkish society, such as wars and constitutional change, and to newly adopted trends in theater, such as European political drama. In the second part of the article, some of the most important images listed above are traced in the works of Adalet Ağaoğlu, an acclaimed Turkish woman playwright who wrote the majority of her plays during the 1960s before shifting her creative focus toward novels and short stories. The picture that emerges from the article's general observations, combined with its case study of Ağaoğlu, indicates that portrayals of the woman in Turkish drama, especially thanks to the growing contribution of women playwrights since the 1960s, have developed from socially conditioned stereotypes toward individual, complex, and controversial identities.

Analyzing images of the woman in Turkish drama affords us clues about the conception of the woman and the estimation of her role in society across different periods of social development. To that end, this article first sketches the development of female character types over the twentieth century, tying them to classical archetypes where possible, and then demonstrates the extent to which Adalet Ağaoğlu, a pioneer among

Turkish women playwrights, has embroidered these types to produce complex images for the stage. Ağaoğlu makes an apt case study because, as a woman herself, she offers a uniquely female perspective on the images of the woman at a time in Turkish history when women playwrights were just coming into their own.

Before delving into the history, however, it is important to be aware of some terminology. In theater, a character "type" is a surrogate, either realistic or traditionally accepted, for some real-life counterpart, generalized to subsume minor variants. Whether realistic or traditional, a type is inflexible, resistant to the changes that accompany social development. An "image", on the other hand, is an interpretation of a traditional type. Although the images of certain groups of characters vary with social conditions and values, they retain some archetypal attributes in common. Naturally, playwrights tend to stress some traits over others in order to render characters' types more interesting and for comical or tragical effect. Such distortions reflect types' socially accepted images, exaggerated according to the taste and requirements of the spectator of the times. Since excessive detail might obscure the bird's-eye view, this article will tend to err on the side of simplicity and generalization.

1920-1950

The plays written for and produced at the Istanbul Municipal Theater in the 1920s and 1930s highlight the political and economic problems experienced during the first World War and the occupation of Istanbul by foreign forces. Topical themes of the plays of this period include political conflict, rapid changes in the traditional ways of life, snobbery, and the domination of materialistic tendencies over humanistic values. Beginning in the 1930s and continuing into the following decade, plays also voice the nation's confidence in Atatürk (the founder of modern Turkey and the leader behind a new program of reforms) and popular expectations for the future.

Three types of women predominate in the plays of these decades: the innocent victim girl captive to social oppression and abuse; the sinful woman of the modern nouveau riche middle class; and the educated, progressive young woman of the new republic.

The victim girl type is passive and emotional. Neither childhood nor marriage has brought her a chance of happiness. Restrictive economic conditions and traditional rules imposed upon women are to blame for her plight. Her nearest archetype is Io.

The sinful and guilty woman type abuses her husband and even her children. Addicted to luxury, gambling, and drinking, she does not keep house and cannot bring up her children properly. She is the root of her family's ills. Her archetype is Gaia.

In stark contrast to this sinful type stands the idealist young woman type, who represents the staunch young generation of modern Turkey. Educated, conscientious, and intelligent, she follows the program of reforms. Her archetype is Athena. She features in the didactic plays written and produced at the Folk Lodges founded in many Anatolian towns in the 1930s to celebrate the tenth anniversary of the Turkish Republic.

Two observations are in order regarding these types. Firstly, the victim girl type does not always remain helpless. In some plays, such female characters are presented as being able to overcome their difficulties, usually with the help of a good-natured male character. The other observation is that both the conservative and the progressive writers of this period dwell on the guilty woman type in their plays. The conservative writers hold the new wave of modernization responsible for her moral corruption. They also portray the woman as lacking in sexual self-control. Because she gives in to lust, the woman is traditionally considered more liable to sin. Some progressive playwrights, on the other hand, focus on the economic causes of moral decay and accuse a certain segment of the wealthy upper class, who grew rich through the black market in the days of armistice while Istanbul was occupied by foreign forces. In this fashion, the image of the sinful woman is used to point out the threat of Western imperialism and the moral consequences of slavishly imitating Western customs.

THE 1950s

From the 1950s on, the tension between traditional and modern ways of life grows in importance for playwrights, providing them with dramatic situations easy to handle in both tragical and comical terms. Two principal types emerge. On the one hand, as traditional moral values yield to the aspirations of a nouveau riche middle class, a greedy and unreliable woman type develops. On the other hand, faced with financial hardships in the wake of World War II, a strong, ideal housewife type emerges to hold her family together. The loyalty and perseverance exhibited by this latter type suggest the Penelope archetype.

It is in this period that modern Turkish playwrights begin to demonstrate a mastery of their craft. In character terms, what distinguishes this period from preceding decades is a fundamental mistrust of the weaker sex due to the former type above. In many plays the middle-class housewife is ridiculed for her tastelessness, vulgarity, and irresponsibility. These selfish, intriguing, insatiable housewives are the cause of their entire families' troubles.

The more active the images of this type, the more greed stands out. For instance, a popular target of social criticism is the social climbing wife, dissatisfied with her husband's income, who wants to live in a well-to-do part of town. In more moderate versions of the same type, it is sneaking selfishness, gossipiness, and laziness that come out. In more passive images, irresponsibility is emphasized. The vulgar and showy wife of the nouveau riche, the scheming and manipulative wife of the bureaucrat, and the educated woman who cannot develop a strong personality are the main variations of this undependable woman type. Another variation is the uneducated eligible girl type, of middling family, whose sole aim is to marry a man who can provide her with a luxurious lifestyle.

Balancing these images is the cherished type of the ideal housewife, a self-sacrificing, patient wife and mother. Content with what she has, she holds the family together. She deserves her husband's gratitude and receives the spectator's sympathy.

A popular playwright's comment on one of his positive women characters is telling: "She is the housewife and mother type of the past. She is a high school graduate. She lives in the past rather than in the present. Simple and sensitive, she is devoted to her children. Although she looks weak, she can be energetic and dominant when necessary. She is delicately beautiful, worn out from years of sorrow." This description illustrates the popular expectations of the ideal woman in this period: educated, but not above high school level; capable of intervening should something go wrong, but not supposed to intervene too often; beautiful, but only so as to reflect traditionally passive and feminine qualities. The dramatic impact of the play is usually reinforced by the poor health or death of so sensitive a person.

1960-1980

After the declaration of a more liberal constitution in 1960, Turkish theater develops rapidly as writers deal with social and political problems more freely. Plays by Turkish writers are welcomed by state- and municipally subsidized theaters. Several new theater companies are established, and the number of spectators increases. Women playwrights spark a new interest in women's problems.

European political drama markedly influences the treatment of political questions. In the theatrical medium, few new approaches to social matters besides Bertolt Brecht's epic theater are accepted as valid. Dwelling on the social insecurity and poverty of the working classes, politically committed playwrights attract attention to the troubles of prison inmates, miners, and factory workers. Nor do they neglect the rural poor, with obvious allusions to the economic order behind their misery. A certain distrust is discernible toward intellectuals, who are taken to task for indifference and selfishness.

As well as new themes, this period sees new character types introduced to Turkish drama. Equally important, though, is the way character portraits begin to take the places of stereotypes. While playwrights depend much on realistic observation, deeper causes of individual and social problems are detected, and writers avoid easy interpretations. Domestic drama remains the favorite kind, but socially-oriented domestic conflicts are no longer interpreted from the viewpoint of the traditional conception of social harmony. Family relationships that face collapse under the pressure of financial difficulties, and psychological crises experienced at such crucial times, are dealt with in increasingly subtle ways. Comedies tend toward satire.

The woman character types of this period generally share a frustrating barrier of some sort but differ in their abilities to cope with it. On the victim end of the spectrum stand a variety of villager images. The tradition that obliges a girl to marry the man chosen by her parents; oppression by the mother-in-law; the custom of marrying the widow of the dead husband to his younger brother in order to keep her at home and force her to work on the farm; contempt for the childless woman; the traditional right of a husband, although strictly forbidden by law, to have a second wife; the kidnapping of the daughter of the family against which one feels enmity because of a bloodfeud between the families; and the death sentence imposed upon the woman who has been raped against her will, have all formed dramatic material for plays spotlighting the problems of women in underdeveloped, rural parts of the country. The daily lives of women living in shantytowns who have to work hard to earn their living yet still have to obey the orders of their fathers and husbands, or those of young poor girls who fall prey to the lust of men, are brought to the stage as images of the exploited woman.

Another weak type of woman, whose positive traits merit a happier life but whose world of rigid rules against her kind prevent her from attaining that life, is visible in the hard-working, patient, self-sacrificing wife of the urban worker. All of the weak types may become frustrated to the extent of nervous breakdown from oppressive middle-class conservatism, exploitation by elders, or spousal maltreatment.

On the stronger end of the spectrum stand two types: the venerable, wise old peasant mother and the urban professional woman. The former type, who will not be intimidated by the threats of the rich landowner, is a popular figure in the plays that deal with life in poor villages. She represents Anatolian people's strength of character and their potential for resisting social injustice.

From the 1970s on, the latter type of woman, who holds down a job, thus contributing to the economy of her family, has been brought to the stage frequently. As men are traditionally not supposed to take part in housework, the main problem this professional woman faces is being held responsible for housekeeping no matter how tired she is. Here also recurs the self-sacrificing woman image, willing to care for her elderly parents even after she is married and has her own family.

The strongest extension of the professional woman type is that of the self-supporting, intelligent woman who can stand against the old customs and rules that used to deprive her of her essential rights. Women playwrights are endowing this type, one of the more common characters of recent plays, with traits that render the image realistic and credible.

BACKGROUND ON ADALET AĞAOĞLU

One of Turkey's foremost modern playwrights, Adalet Ağaoğlu dwells on women's issues without neglecting the social and economic factors that affect men as well. She serves as an excellent case study for this article because, through the characters of her plays, she manages to present a woman's perspective on woman types.

Ağaoğlu begins to write for the theater in the 1960s, before turning to novel and short-story writing toward the end of the 1970s. Although plays by women playwrights had been staged before, Ağaoğlu becomes the first woman to write consistently for the theater and have her plays successfully staged by the State Theater in Ankara and the Municipal Theater in Istanbul as well as private theater companies. What is more, these plays receive overwhelmingly favorable reviews from drama critics.

Ağaoğlu discovers her interest in the theater when she is appointed as a dramatist for radio plays soon after graduating from Ankara University. She adapts conventional plays for broadcast and writes a few radio plays of her own. Her first conventional play, *Bir Piyes Yazalım* (Let's Write A Play), is written in collaboration with a friend by the name of Sevim Uzgören and in 1953 produced at the Ankara State Theater. Next, she visits the United States for two years, where she writes *Babaları Adına* (In the Name of Their Father), which is never produced. Upon returning to Turkey, she co-founds a private theater called Meydan Sahnesi (Arena Stage), where she works as both a manager and a dramaturg from 1961 to 1963. Meanwhile, she writes three of her main plays: *Evcilik Oyunu* (Marital Game), *Çatıdaki Çatlak* (The Crack in the Roof), which are respectively produced in the years 1964 and 1965, and *Tombala* (Bingo), which is produced in 1969, six years after it is written. These plays are followed by three one-act plays, *Bir Kahramanın Ölümü* (Death of a Hero), *Çıkış* (Way Out/Escape), and *Kozalar* (Cocoons), and three long plays, *Sınırlarda* (At the Border), *Sessiz Adam* (A Silent Man), and *Kendini Yazan Şarkı* (The Song that Writes Itself), between 1967 and 1971. Above all, Ağaoğlu's last play, *Çok Uzak—Fazla Yakın* (Very Far—Too Near), demonstrates her mastery of her craft.

IMAGES OF THE WOMAN IN AĞAOĞLU'S PLAYS

The images in Ağaoğlu's plays are representative of the contemporary conception of the woman and her roles, especially from a female point of view. In *Evcilik Oyunu*, for example, there are two types of women. One is the traditional mother type, who insists on bringing up her daughter according to the established conception of sexual morality, which forbids any premarital relationship with the opposite sex. In other words, she is the rigid and oppressive mother type identified with the conservative, middle-class woman. This mother's strict attitude can seem omnipresent: a young girl is under the watch not only of her parents but also of her neighbors. Even the keeper of the city park forbids boys and girls to sit together on the riverbank.

The second woman image in *Evcilik Oyunu* is the grown-up daughter raised under these conditions. At the beginning of the play, she and her husband are presented as a loving couple who nonetheless seek a divorce, because they get on each other's nerves when they are together, for which reason the wife refuses to live under the same roof with her husband. This scene takes us back to the couple's childhood, when they used to get scolded for not obeying the rules against casual interaction between boys and girls. Here is the image of a girl who, afflicted by the notion that she must always guard her chastity and watch out for likely assault by men, cannot suppress her deep-rooted fear of the opposite sex, thereby dooming her married life both for herself and for her husband.

Ağaoğlu's one-act play *Çıkış* also addresses the aftermath of overprotective parenting, but this time in the form of absurdist theater. In this play, a girl is constantly kept at home by her father to safeguard her against the dangers of the outside world. In her seclusion, she has developed a strong fear of bugs and snakes, which seem to crowd the windowless room she occupies. She persistently busies herself with killing them and cleaning the house. At the same time, she insists on going outdoors no matter how dark it may be. In the end, the girl emerges from the house only to discover that it is not so dark outside after all. Then, however, she cannot help worrying that her father is all alone inside.

The problem of the inevitable loneliness of old people is dealt with in *Tombala*, in which an elderly couple pass their days quarreling, eating, playing bingo, and above all, waiting in vain for their grown-up children to come and visit them. As the old woman attempts to occupy herself with cooking, housekeeping, and worrying about her children, her husband simply reads an old newspaper over and over again.

A traditionally patient and submissive housewife image is the delicately treated protagonist of *Çatıdaki Çatlak*. Middle-aged and unmarried, she lives with her brother, a man of moderate income. Her character exemplifies the traditionally raised woman who not only feels responsible for all the housework but still feels so indebted to the man, who earns money to support the family, that she neglects her own health problems. She balances this submissiveness, however, by taking the initiative to help a poor working woman who has to simultaneously earn a living and take care of her baby all by herself.

In Ağaoğlu's intriguing one-act play *Kozalar*, selfish middle-class women take the stage in an unusual situation. Unaware of the social turmoil outside their homes, three women sip tea and gossip until they discover that their children are missing. The play ends as unseen spiders spin webs around them until they are wrapped up like cocoons.

The next play, *Kendini Yazan Şarkı*, is the drama of the lost generation of the 1970s. We encounter a peasant mother figure who never complains despite having her hands full with three generations to care for: her baby grandson, her gruesome young daughter, and her sullen, crippled father-in-law. In this image of a patient and loving peasant mother, the hidden strength of character of womankind is emphasized in contrast to the intelligent-but-dependent girl of rich, middle-class family.

Finally, Ağaoğlu's *Çok Uzak—Fazla Yakın* is a masterpiece. Through a very delicately handled structure, feelings of love, jealousy, and hatred are all detectable in a complex relationship between a twin brother and sister. With indirect allusions to the contrasting values of the artistic and material worlds, the woman is portrayed as shouldering the burden of the latter. On the one hand, it is she who toils for professional promotion while her brother is content with the modest lifestyle of a poet. On the other hand, it is also she who undertakes to care for her parents in their old age and during their illnesses, while her brother remains aloof in his artistic seclusion.

CONCLUSION

This overview has explored the particular example of Adalet Ağaoğlu in order to show how modern women playwrights have contributed to Turkish theater in general: especially since 1960, they have presented a uniquely feminine perspective on social life as a whole, while raising popular awareness of women's issues through an ever more rich and complex portrayal of classical character types. Ağaoğlu in particular has gone beyond familiar feminist themes like victimization and empowerment to holistically explore, for example, the long-term effects on adult society of traditionally conditioning and indoctrinating girls.

NOTES

[1] Originally delivered in mid-December 1998 at Ohio State University on the occasion of the awarding of an honorary doctorate to Adalet Ağaoğlu. The author wishes to express her thanks to Arif Nat Riley for his editing of the article.

A Multicultural Biography of an Era
in *The Other Side of the Mountain*
Yasemin Alptekin

The Other Side of the Mountain is a reconstruction of the history of the Turkish Republic through three generations, from the beginning of the twentieth century to the present day, not in the way a history book would present it, chronologically, but through the human condition and all its contrasting universals: love-hate, hope-despair, poignancy-expectation, ambition-dissatisfaction, success-failure, dynamism-fatigue, happiness and tears. The setting of the novel covers a vast geography including Europe and the Balkans; thus, the human condition of the characters in the novel, as reflected by the geography in which characters' experiences take place, is more global than provincial.

> Anybody can make history; only a great man can write it.
> *Oscar Wilde*

There are not very many Turkish novels available for non-Turkish readers of English; usually, the ones that have been translated have appeared in English quite a few years after the originals made their names on the Turkish book market. Yet *Dağın Öteki Yüzü* (The Other Side of the Mountain) by Erendiz Atasü became available in both Turkish and English without much delay: both the fourth edition of the Turkish version from Bilgi Yayınevi and the English version from Milet Publishing Company were published successively in the years 1999 and 2000. The novel, as stated on the cover, "tracing the lives of three generations of a Turkish family from the end of the Ottoman Empire to the 1990s", won the Orhan Kemal[1] Novel Award in 1996. The story of the novel is as interesting for English readers as it is for Turkish readers, for the first part of the book takes place in the United Kingdom. Above and beyond that, the English version is more than a translation—it is an edition rewritten in English by the novelist herself along with the assistance of Elizabeth Maslen, the translator.

The author's letter to the reader at the beginning of the Turkish version, which is placed at the end of the book in the English edition, provides the reader with an important piece of inside information as to what the author's motivations were as she penned the novel. After her mother's death, the author finds a pile of letters exchanged between her parents throughout the 1930s and 1940s. She says:

> The letters unlocked a door for my own insights, intensified by the pain of loss. Crossing this threshold, I seemed to enter into my innermost self, into a domain of my own being of which I had not been aware. My parents' generation stood there, the anguish of their lost motherland, the anguish of migrations. In that domain were the orphans of the First World War, children of a nation condemned to death by the world powers, and also the generation of rebirth, young citizens of a young and eager Republic, the endurance and effort that carried them from their schools for orphans and set them among the creators of the 'resurrection', their faith in the ideals of their youth, their disappointments, their hurt silences … all these were there. (277)

The voice of the narrator reflects the excitement, the idealism, and the innocence of the three-generation-long struggle to create the Turkish identity. "*The Other Side of the Mountain* is a history of modern Turkey", says Elizabeth Maslen in her article in *Cumhuriyet* (August 24, 2000). "It was like a journey into the heart of Turkish culture", she adds. It was an opportunity for her to realize and evaluate what Mustafa Kemal Atatürk meant for modern-day Turkey in general, and for women in particular.

The weaving of actual events into a stylistic expression of literary narration does not relegate the reader to remote corners of history, but rather brings reality closer to the heart. Indeed, the novel is a reconstruction of history not in the way a history book would present it, chronologically, but through the human condition and all its contrasting universals: love-hate, hope-despair, poignancy-expectation, ambition-dissatisfaction, success-failure, dynamism-fatigue, happiness and tears.

The setting of the novel covers a vast geography including Europe and the Balkans; thus, the human condition of the characters in the novel, as reflected by the geography in which characters' experiences take place, is more global than provincial. Another dimension of the human condition in the novel which transcends the national is the sophisticated allusions to world literature, not to mention the literary references to the Turkish letters of the "idealist era". Finally, the human condition presented in *The Other Side of the Mountain* includes an array of international actors as well as the local players of the times.

> I should have been in Paris in the twenties, painting pictures in a garret. Hemingway would have fought with his wife in the café below. Picasso, dressed in a picturesque sailor's outfit, would have sworn vividly as he passed along the street smelling of cheese, wine, and crêpes, where I lived. I should have been as delicate and free as my fellow countrywoman, the painter, Hale Asaf … I should have hidden my bleeding heart, like her … (13)

The way Atasü brings Hemingway, Picasso, and Hale Asaf[2] onto the same stage to perform in the above paragraph represents the common ground those artists shared at some point in their lives transcending culture, nationality, and gender. This common ground can be summarized in the "liberty, equality, and fraternity" of Paris. In other words, the virtual meeting of the artists in Paris is also the meeting place of the "idealism" where the Turkish Republic found its origins with the Young Turk movement at the beginning of the twentieth century. In this sense, the foundation of the Turkish Republic bears resemblance to the struggles of many nations to achieve sovereignty with freedom, equality, peace, and the progress of its people in the world through an anti-imperialist war. What succeeded the foundation of the Republic was not some second-rate revolution limited solely to the national and regional welfare of an elite group of power-hungry rulers. It was more of a national, grassroots fight against the world powers, not only on the war front but on all levels of life. Such idealism, however, as represented in the novel by the two young Turkish women studying at Oxford, is not something easy to comprehend for those who have not had a similar experience in their own country during their lifetime. Miss Meadow is one of those characters in the book who tries to extrapolate the devotion of women to Mustafa Kemal by religious similes:

> [S]uch devotion did not lie within Miss Meadow's field of experience, and in order to comprehend it fully, she had to compare it with emotions she had known or had witnessed. She could only compare the love Vicdan and Nefise cherished for Mustafa Kemal to the emotion felt for Jesus, that burned in the hearts of Catholic nuns, the virgins wearing Christ's ring. (67)

Miss Meadow cannot conceive of any love more powerful than one can cherish for Christ as Savior redeeming his disciples of their sins. However, "a revolutionary way of loving" is what she names the love the girls have for Mustafa Kemal. The European obsession with Hitler in the mid-1930s is another transitory instance of "fad politics", unlike the devotion the "girls felt for the hero who had cured their country's ravaged flesh" (67).

> Frankly, Nefise and Vicdan were not interested in politics or in political leaders. They had faith in their own country and their own leader, and were light-hearted. Could this little man called Hitler, so small and ugly, offer the conquered German nation what Mustafa Kemal Pasha, the war veteran, their 'Gazi', had achieved for the Turks? Well,

the Germans should be thankful then. All these roaring voices, the continual shouting, must be characteristic of the German nation. Well, you could not expect every society to be as impassive as the British. (42-43)

As stated in *Telling the Truth About History*[3]:

> Where the word 'kingdom' indicated a territory belonging to a single ruler and 'country' suggested a land where people had lived long together as subjects, 'nation' evoked the very modern concept of men and women self-consciously banded together into a political union. With nationalism as an engine of political and social reform, people looked to national history to illuminate the course of human progress that had brought the modern nation into being. (92)

Atasü's account of historic events is brought together with the lives of her characters in the novel in such a way that despair and hope, expectation and disillusion keep revolving in a universal cycle. From the Turkish War of Liberation arises a young nation with hopes of further westernization; however, the two young Turkish women Vicdan and Nefise are not very happy with everything they experience in Europe, in Berlin. "Berlin was turning from an enjoyable adventure into a chilling nightmare. […] Berlin was a clown with an angst-ridden heart, walking a tightrope, which was destined to break" (43). When the two girls witness a Jew beaten up in the middle of the street by Nazi soldiers and cannot do anything to help the victim, they once again feel the hidden poignancy. "The children of peoples who have suffered for a long time have bitter memories they would rather not confess even to themselves" (44-45). The pain one feels of war and violence is never limited to within the borders—it goes beyond the borders and hits those human beings with similar experiences even more harshly.

Along the same line of thinking, the presentation and the representation of Republican idealism are thoroughly realistic in the novel. The disheartened souls and the wounded hearts are not prepared to face the reality. Love and disillusionment of people with one another is also the disillusionment with expectations as the Republic ideal transforms itself from a hard-won battle into an elusive reality. Peace is not long lasting; not only in the world but in the lives of people as well. Vicdan's daughter's divorce parallels Vicdan's despair of the times.

Vicdan's daughter, the narrator, analyzes her mother's feelings as follows:

> My mother was one of those who retreat into themselves when hurt. That was how she reacted when the '*grand amour*' of her life, the Republic, started to slip down the incline. According to my parents' shared opinion, the Republic had deviated from its destined path; they were truly unhappy, I knew, they felt wounded. Their common hurts bound them more closely together. […] Who knows, probably mother approved of my breaking my shell, severing my ties, and flinging them away! (211)

In his *History*, Emerson says, "There is properly no history, only biography", and his words prove to be true in the saga of three generations in the novel, which in turn presents a historical account of an era, or a cross-cultural biography of an epoch. The biographies of the characters interplay in such a fashion that cultural lending and borrowing project a present-day global human condition, approaching it from the 1930s. It is the global dimension of the events and the cross-cultural presence of the characters that bring the history to life—that is, into reality, transcending the boundaries of a work of fiction.

The chapter entitled "At the Summit" is the true summit of the novel. In that section Atasü describes the two events that actually took place, as she stated in the letter to the reader: one is ascending Uludağ (Mount Olympus in Turkey), and the other is Vicdan's meeting with Mustafa Kemal at Dolmabahçe (Palace)[4] prior to his falling fatally ill. The "summit" and the "visit" are the "real" top experiences in Vicdan's life, with an impact that no other experience could even come close to. Starting with the ascent, the reader sees the depth of Vicdan's soul, which is invisible and impenetrable even to her own brothers, who admire her as a phenomenal woman and loving sister. The scaling of the summit also represents a contrast between the "ideal" image of Vicdan and the ordinary dreams of her brothers. Vicdan's universality is a projection of how far ahead the Turkish woman has ascended, whereas the conventional position of her brothers is a sad reality of where the men still stand in Turkish society. Vicdan, the idealist woman of the young Turkish Republic, reaches the summit and finds herself looking up to an idol: Mustafa Kemal.

> Burhan and Reha are aware of their bodies, agile and strong. The images of women they have touched or dreamed of touching appear and vanish. Reha sees the slender, supple body of Yildiz, that beauty of beauties; scents the smell of the women he visits in Beyoglu brothels, in Istanbul. Burhan thinks for a moment of the young girl, daughter of his mother's neighbor, who is in love with him. A quiet, placid girl, very suitable for the wife of an army officer whose demanding life would be full of hardships. Then he thinks of Vecdet. Is he in love with her? Vecdet is not one of those women created to complete a man; she is already a wholeness in herself. Vecdet is not for Burhan.
>
> Vicdan thinks of the Gazi … (86)

At the summit, Vicdan remembers her visit with Atatürk. She remembers his vividly saying, "No nation is better or worse than the rest. World politics is a bloody fight for spoils […]. We have to consider what is beneficial for Turkey above our petty personal aims" (89). She goes through a fascinating realization of a new identity that captures her soul and body. "After the meeting with the Gazi, a whole new, liberating vista has opened before her: the world of men and the range of responses it arouses within her. [...] She has abandoned the old world of women and moved on. [...] Vicdan has no intention of going back to that old world of women! [...] Vicdan is drunk with happiness" (93).

The ascent to Mount Olympus creates different sensations for each of the three individuals who join the hike. As for the brothers Reha and Burhan, although the day is memorable, the experience is more of an incomprehensible one in size and affects them like a child's joy with an uncommon sight, rather than an experience of an adult combined with something deeper and bigger in the memory:

> Reha and Burhan will always remember this day, remember the infant joy they tasted on the summit of Uludağ, their adult minds not really comprehending the mysterious ecstasy. They will always remember that hot summer day when their sister, stroking the dark head of one, the fair head of the other, told them the legends of Uludağ and of Mother Cybele who had made her home on its summit, of Troy on the Sea of Marmara, and of Hector, the brave martyred son of Priam of Anatolia. They listened to her soft voice, relating all those ancient legends, of Troy stabbed in the back, and of Kemal Pasha taking revenge for Troy. (96)

Vicdan's identity transformation at the summit is not incidental. The ascent marks the multicultural fabric of Anatolian history and its people both symbolically and historically, wrapped in a narrative of fantasy by the author depicting all the universal images that the mountain carries with it:

> Mother Cybele, squatting on her heavy haunches and suckling, for thousands of years, the child – both husband and son – pressed to her ample bosom!... Oh, Mother Goddess, Daughter of Anatolia, called Artemis on the Aegean islands, Demeter where the sea opens into the Mediterranean, Isis at the Nile delta, Lat in the Arabian desert! Mother Earth, symbol of endless life and of endless death ... Mountains, plains, plateaus and hundreds of husbands are yours! You set up home on the summit of Uludağ, our Anatolian Mount Olympus, and fed the rich Mysa plain. (83)

The universal legends and what they symbolize for Anatolia take the reader to one of the most striking images of the novel and what it represents for the protagonist: "the other side of the mountain". "The southern face of the mountain was sheer, but the northern face, looking over the Bursa plain, rose in a series of slopes" (85). According to Taoist philosophy, a single principle, the Tao, or Great Ultimate, runs the universe. This principle is divided into two principles that oppose one another in their actions, yin and yang. Some examples of the opposites that yin and yang represent are front-back, day-night, and male-female. The opposites exist in pairs, and one of them cannot be present in the absence of the other. Originally, yin and yang represented the two sides of a mountain: yin (female) was the shadowy northern side, yang (male) the sunny southern side. All the opposites one perceives in the universe can be reduced to one of these opposite forces. In general, these forces are distinguished by their role in producing creation and producing degeneration: yang is the force of creation and yin the force of completion and degeneration. In this respect, the creation of the Republic and the degeneration of it as experienced by its young people perfectly fit the pattern described.

All opposites that one experiences—health and sickness, wealth and poverty, power and submission—can be explained in terms of the temporary dominance of one principle over the other. Since no one principle dominates eternally, it follows that all conditions are subject to change into their opposites. The yin and yang are further differentiated into five material agents, or *wu hsing*, which both produce one another and overcome one another. Accordingly, all change in the universe can be explained by the workings of yin and yang and the progress of the five material agents as they either produce one another or overcome one another. In an effort to explain the universal, the five agents *explain everything*, including the progress of change in the universe. And the progress that interests most human beings is history, since human history paradoxically appears to be both in human control and out of human control.[5]

The universal and the opposites that exist in the universe as presented in a multicultural context in the novel seem much in line with the fundamental division of yin and yang in Eastern philosophy. As seen from the summit, the other side of the mountain is nothing but "continuation" and "transformation", as well as the "opposite" and the "change". The cycle is complete at the top when Vicdan ascends the summit of Uludağ, and when she meets her idol and her ideal, Mustafa Kemal. The yin in her transforms into yang as she abandons the old world of women and moves on (93).

The interculturality of times and people is also a representation of change and continuity in the lives of the characters in the novel. As certain things change over time, certain other things remain the same. During the transformation of the Ottoman court culture into a national one, the high-cultural components are to be preserved as inheritance from the multi-cultural fabric of the Ottoman Empire, and the educated protectors of the Republic hold those multicultural elements precious as part of the "ideal cultural mosaic" of the newly born nation:

> İzzet was listening to the song Reha was murmuring. It was a lyric composed by Bimen Şen. İzzet started to ponder on what it was like to be an Ottoman. What was the impulse stimulating Bimen, the son of an Armenian priest, to compose one of the finest pieces of Turkish music? How much of the Ottoman had the Turkish republic inherited? What fragments of those Ottoman qualities that formed a kind of sympathetic synthesis could have survived the destructiveness of the Great War, and the cruelties the Turkish-speaking population both suffered and perpetrated? (110)

There are certain other "culture-specific" phenomena, which the protagonist(s) expect to disappear or change for the better in time, but unfortunately the undesirable prevails. In a letter that Nefise writes to Vicdan on November 20, 1934, she mentions her new position at Gazi Teacher Training College. Although she has applied for a post, her papers have not been processed in a timely manner; therefore, she has not been assigned a teaching position by the Ministry of Education. She complains of the situation as follows: "With these new documents, I travelled to Ankara and appealed to the Ministry of Education – in vain! I cannot find words to convey the chaotic state the Ministry is in!" (36).

Despite the love of country and the republican idealism to give back what she has received from her country, Nefise cannot help missing her good old days in England. "Vicdan, I miss you, miss England and Cambridge so profoundly, you cannot imagine … Dear Cambridge … I am so far away from her" (36). Here, what Nefise radiates is a new set of multiplicities in the novel alongside the setting and the culture, and they are, the "multiple identities" along with "multiple loyalties". Atasü reveals in her letter to the reader that "[a]mong the other characters in the book, Vicdan's friend Nefise, with whom she shares the England experience, is completely imaginary" (279). However, the way Nefise is presented in the novel is like the other half of Vicdan, the suppressed and hidden half. The narrator's account of events is more of settling score with her mother Vicdan. We have some blurred scenes of the life of the narrator and her life philosophy, but barely the actual life. Protective mother Vicdan is an interfering character, and the narrator criticizes Vicdan, not the daughter. "Oh mother, why do you hide yourself from me? Why? Isn't it unfair to me? I want to get to know you, the mother whom I have never known …" (23).

Nefise and Vicdan are depicted as two "very close" friends at the beginning of the book, even with some implications of same-gender attraction to one another. "Nefise's head rests on Vicdan's lap, Vicdan's hand on Nefise's brow. The love they feel for each other is clearly visible. Whom do they have except each other? A pair of young women, two fatherless girls in a foreign land" (35). The picture displayed here is all very innocent when presented in an Oriental cultural context, whereas it may allude to further homosexual associations in Western cultures. A similar "closeness" takes place when both girls share the same bed in Berlin (66).

Nefise's role as the "other half" of Vicdan is in tune with yin and yang as well, in the original sense of a mountain's two sides. The physical and spiritual existence of Vicdan show similar split and opposing characteristics as her daughter describes her:

She was gentle …	She was tough …
She was merry …	She was morose …
She was full of the joy of living …	She was sad … (23)

The distinct opposites in Vicdan's personality, and the differences between Nefise and Vicdan as two young women devoted to the same idealism, are in congruence with the way they are contrasted. Vicdan finds freedom in her asexual existence just as she found freedom at Cambridge: "Remember how we used to walk in the moonlight in Cambridge? We felt safe. We never worried that we were women …" (37). In fact, the following is almost like a revelation on Vicdan's part when it comes to assessing her gender and body:

> The former limits of our lives disappear when we throw away or let life snatch from our grasp the good and the bad that we possess, or when we endure enforced separations. The last property we own is our bodies. Throw that away … and freedom! (23)

Another area of multicultural presence is the power of literature and the power of words that are celebrated in Vicdan's insights as she passes judgments on her daughter's husband and other men. She says: "I know people. I know writers and poets as well. I have taught literature to students from all over Turkey. Literature's subject is humanity, don't forget" (210-211). And the daughter cannot help but accept the fact, "She really knew!" (211). What is interesting here is that Vicdan does not make any culture-specific reference to literature and words. She definitely means the universals of literature and what words have to offer to humanity on a global scale. In fact, her love of literature is illustrated by the examples chosen as the poetry she reads. "Vicdan turns to poetry. Her new hobby is to search for poems on Korea, in newspapers and journals, and to analyse them. Disappointing … she will not be able to find what she is looking for. She will only be able to keep grief and anger at bay by dissecting the poems with her relentless criticism" (141). Idealism is reflected in the poetry of Nazım Hikmet and William Wordsworth and in the epistolary form of the novel.

The euphoria of looking to Europe for a civilized world, and the pride of the Republic with an invincible leader envisioning "peace at home, peace in the world", die almost simultaneously as Atatürk loses his joy of living!

> He had been pessimistic for some time, ever since the Depression of 1929 to be exact, when he lost all hope that world peace could be achieved in the twentieth century. The Depression had been the final, decisive stroke, crushing the last chance of those nations which had emerged, battered, from the Great War, to realise that their new leaders were nothing but puny souls in thrall to the compulsive appetites of their own personal ambitions. (245)

The pessimism that comes with the Depression continues well into the following decades and after, both in Europe and in Turkey. World War II and the Korean War are two of those conflicts where the peace in the world proves to be unattainable. Just as the world cannot settle itself into a permanent peace, the characters in the novel find themselves in different types of struggles in their lives. The alcohol problem of Burhan leaves that officer of the young republic in ruins in his old age. "Towards the end, memory moves towards the point from which it started … Memory is like the setting sun, whose last rays are bright, but light a diminishing field" for Burhan (198).

Disillusionment starts with Fitnat, Vicdan's mother, and goes on with Vicdan and her daughter, the narrator. Vicdan's ability to see people through their souls and what happens in the world is paralleled by a visionary's clandestine post at the summit. The difference between Atatürk and his army officers lies in the fact that the President was at the summit; others were limited to the areas where they fought: "A fighting man is only aware of a small part of reality, of what he is living through at any precise moment. But the President, from his summit, has a bird's eye view" (248).

Where is hope in the cycle? Hope is an ever-recurring dream relayed on to the following generation, just as Mustafa Kemal's baton of responsibility could be said to have passed to the youth Vicdan represented. "I wait in vain, yet grief is out of place. Time never closes the circle; time flows in spirals. Now, let me repeat my former question. Has nothing changed? I am that change!" (274). The change is there with the narrator and the author, and within the biography of an epoch lasting for three generations.

> What a vast contradiction exists between myself and my suffering, bleeding, miserable and merciless country! But I am made up of that contradiction. I, who am the offspring of the wounded children of a people felled in the short, spiralling interval between the beginning and the end of the twentieth century, of those children who became the creators of their people's miraculous resurrection, I am the change. (274-75)

The multicultural context of the novel displays additional difficulty both in translation and in addressing the reader. In the Turkish version there are quite a few references that may be unfamiliar to the Turkish reader, and the same is true for non-Turkish readers of English. The significance of certain factual information and place names in the novel may easily go unnoticed by those readers barely knowledgeable in the history and geography of Turkey. A map of Turkey at the beginning of the book, and a glossary at the end, would make a major difference in underscoring some historical and geographical facts as well as the names in the novel. As an example to the argument, names and terms such as "War of Independence"[6] (38), "seven hills of Istanbul"[7] (50), Bosphorus[8] (50), Koca Hill[9], and "bey"[10] (141) would have been more meaningful had their significance been explained.

Sociolinguistic nuances in any work of translation always present a challenge to the translator, and Turkish is no exception in creating such a challenge. The language of the translated version flows very well, except for a few areas where culture-specific expressions and idioms are used in the letters.

It could have been more meaningful to give some explanation to the verbatim translations of: "[P]lease try not to catch cold"[11] (24); "No other man's hand has touched me, and none shall"[12] (24); "I pray to God that you and your family are in good health, and kiss your sea-green eyes lovingly"[13] (38); "There she is, Vicdan's mother, standing at the Istanbul harbour, on the verge of collapse, sniffing at lemon cologne and essence of mint"[14] (51).

There are additional problems with the inconsistent transliteration of some Turkish words, such as "black charshaf"[15] (51) and "shalvar"[16]. In those words, Turkish *c* and *s* with a cedilla[17] are spelled as "ch" and "sh", whereas with the word "kasar[18] cheese" the same spelling is not used. Furthermore, the name of a hill, "Conk Heights"[19], is halfway translated without any transliteration to help the reader.

Similarly, there is an inconsistency in the way some Turkish words are kept while others are translated. For example, "big brother" is used for *ağabey*[20]; but *potur*[21], *Laz*[22] in "Raik, the Laz" (236), *mevlit*[23], and *hüzzam*[24] keep their original spellings, again in the absence of any translation to help the reader.

The Other Side of the Mountain takes the reader on a fascinating journey through times and cultures and through the lives of its characters. The multicultural fabric of Turkish society and the intercultural involvement of its people create a multidimensional story of a global nature with factual events presented in a fictional guise. The international geography illustrates the close proximity among the people of the world and among the nations through connections of biographies of people, and thus the history they create. The issues presented in that multi-environment, however, reflect the universals of the human condition, with its problems of gender, sexuality, love, despair, ideals, failures, hopes, and expectations. Despite the interlingual problems, and translation inconsistencies and challenges in places, the novel woven into the biographies of the characters with their factual and fictional presence generates the biography of an era with cross-cultural perspectives. *The Other Side of the Mountain* displays the interconnectedness of the people and the events that take place in history at any point in time, as well as the isolation of the individual when it comes to dealing with his or her problems. There is one Planet Earth that we all share, and there is one life that we all live. A multicultural biography of an era is what we read through the lives of those people who play a part in history.

Notes

[1] Orhan Kemal (1914-1970) a prominent Turkish novelist; a prestigious annual award to honor his literary contributions.

[2] Hale Asaf was born in 1905 in Istanbul. At a very young age she developed her painting skills in Berlin at the Fine Arts Academy, specializing in still-life paintings and portraits. After returning from Berlin, she continued her studies at the Fine Arts Academy in Istanbul. Later, Hale Hanım furthered her studies in Paris. She married there and came back to Turkey. For a while she worked as a teacher in Bursa. Paris, which was the center of the art world, held great attraction for her, so she returned to Paris but had a difficult time there. She met an Italian political writer; however, a short time before their planned wedding, she died on the operating table at the age of 33, on May 31, 1938. Unlucky Hale had had five surgical procedures performed during her short life. She is buried in Thiais Cemetery, in Paris. *Antik & Dekor* 50 (January 1999).

[3] By Joyce Appleby, Lynn Hunt, and Margaret Jacob, 1995.

[4] An Ottoman Palace in Istanbul built on the coast of Bosphorus, on the European side, in the nineteenth century and where the last Sultan resided. Atatürk, the founder of the Turkish Republic, had a room of his own in the Palace after the Republic was founded; he lived and governed Turkey from his simple, modest bedroom and office at this palace for just three months. He was cared for in that Palace during his illness, and he died in his room there. The Dolmabahçe Palace was built between 1843 and 1856 when the Ottoman Empire was losing its power. This superb palace displays the richness and power of the Sultans.

[5] http://www.wsu.edu:8080/~dee/CHPHIL/WUHSING.HTM

[6] The Turkish War of Liberation fought between 1919 and 1922 against French, British, Italian, and Greek armies who occupied Istanbul and most of Anatolia.

[7] Istanbul is believed to have been built on seven hills; those seven hills are represented in the city logo of Istanbul.

[8] The strait that divides the European and Asian sides of Istanbul, connecting the Black Sea to the Marmara Sea.

[9] Great Hill (*Kocatepe*) is where Mustafa Kemal commanded the Great Offensive which brought victory for the Turkish armies.

[10] Word of respect used succeeding a male name of either older age or higher rank.

[11] An expression of care and concern.

[12] An attestation of virginity and a pledge to remain a virgin till she marries her fiancé.

[13] An old-fashioned cliché line and salutation used in letter-writing to express cordial affection.

[14] Turkish people believe in the utility of eau de cologne of lemon or mint as smelling salts.

[15] The *çarşaf* is "a large cloth worn as a combination head covering, veil, and shawl usu. by Muslim women esp. in Iran" (Langenscheidt 1998).

[16] Baggy pants worn by Turkish peasant women.

[17] *ç* (ch) as in the word *chair*, and *ş* (sh) as in the word *shine*.

[18] Turkish *kaşar* cheese is a yellow sheep cheese.

[19] *Conkbayır* (*c* in Turkish reads *j* as in the word *jam*).

[20] The word *ağabey* is actually used in addressing an older brother or sometimes an older male.

[21] Baggy pants worn by men in some regions in Turkey.

[22] An ethnic group of the Black Sea region.

[23] A religious chanting (recitation of the life of Prophet Muhammad composed in poetic form by Süleyman Çelebi in the fifteenth century) at Turkish memorial gatherings after a deceased one.

[24] A mode of classical Turkish music.

Making History, Fiction, and Theory Reconcile:
An "Aesthetic Reading" of *The Other Side of the Mountain*[1]

Dilek Doltaş

By coining the term "historiographic metafiction", Linda Hutcheon wishes both to confront modernism critically and to incorporate the postmodern views on history, fiction, and theory into her readings of narratives bordering on them. Hutcheon's theoretical arguments, however, overlook the postmodern premise that no conceptual differentiation between history, fiction, and theory is possible. Murray Krieger's phrase "reading aesthetically" addresses the issues brought forth by such texts without falling into the same conceptual traps. When read aesthetically, Erendiz Atasü's *The Other Side of the Mountain* allows the reader to see how this can be done.

Linda Hutcheon's term "historiographic metafiction", as a way of reconciling history, fiction, and theory in discussing narratives bordering on them, is quite problematic (5). Murray Krieger's critical phrase "reading aesthetically" (144), inspired by Wolfgang Iser's theories on interpretation, addresses the issues brought forth by such texts without stumbling into the same conceptual pitfalls as Hutcheon. Analyzing Erendiz Atasü's quasi-historical, quasi-fictive narrative *Dağın Öteki Yüzü* (The Other Side of the Mountain), I will try to show how in this book a certain period in Turkish history is read aesthetically, allowing so-called historical and fictitious facts and personages to be interpreted dynamically and subjectively, on the one hand, and impersonally and consistently, on the other. Furthermore, an aesthetic reading of the narrative enables the reader to problematize simultaneously the "facts" and establish epistemologies of the period, and to acknowledge the significance of adhering to them. In other words, as Krieger explains, while ascribing meaning to a text, "reading aesthetically" can allow attitudes that are historically contingent and arbitrary to coexist with essentialist, formalist ones (143-46).

In her book *Dağın Öteki Yüzü*, Atasü situates social, theoretical, ideological, and literary issues in history in a way that allows for literature's ability to generate paradoxes in them all. By generating a dialogical relationship among these issues, Atasü both participates in the making of history and problematizes the actuality of historical facts. Therefore, a study of *Dağın Öteki Yüzü* is useful in illustrating how the term "aesthetic reading" and not "historiographic metafiction" contributes to the discussion of those texts that deal self-consciously with history, literature, and theory.

At the beginning of *A Poetics of Postmodernism*, Hutcheon states that in this book she will be "privileging the novel genre, and one form in particular, a form that [she] want[s] to call 'historiographic metafiction'" (5). She then explains that, "In most of the critical work on postmodernism, it is narrative—be it literature, history, or theory—that has usually been the major focus of attention. Historiographic metafiction incorporates all three of these domains: that is, its theoretical self-awareness of history and fiction as human constructs [...] is made the grounds for its rethinking and reworking of the forms and contents of the past" (5). In the chapters that follow, Hutcheon continues to expand on the implications of the term, saying, "What the postmodern writing of both history and literature has taught us is that both history and fiction are discourses, that both constitute systems of signification by which we make sense of the past.... In other words, the meaning and shape are not *in the events*, but *in the systems* which make those past 'events' into present historical 'facts'" (89). Then she expands on her presuppositions about the distinction between present "facts" and past "events" as well as between constructed and non-constructed knowledge, embedding her coinage "historiographic metafiction" in those distinctions. She says:

> Historiographic metafiction refutes the natural or common-sense methods of distinguishing between historical fact and fiction. It refuses the view that only history has a truth claim, both by questioning the ground of that claim in historiography and by asserting that both history and fiction are discourses, human constructs, signifying systems, and both derive their major claim to truth from that identity. [....] The "real" referent of their language once existed; but it is only accessible to us today in textualized form: documents, eye-witness accounts, archives. The past is "archeologized" (Lemaire, 1981, xiv), but its reservoir of available materials is always acknowledged as a textualized one. (93)

As can be seen from the long passages quoted from her book, Hutcheon relies upon the terminology, therefore to some extent upon the epistemology, of modern poetics to highlight postmodern concerns. She employs static, descriptive, and classificatory terms such as "the novel genre", "history", "historical fact", "past event", "fiction", and "identity" to discuss postmodern issues like the cognitive status of historical knowledge and the ontological nature of historical documents. Furthermore, she makes two statements which challenge her own postmodern presuppositions. First, she says that "the natural and common-sense methods of distinguishing between *historical fact* and *fiction*" are to be rejected, and "both *history* and *fiction* are [to be considered as] discourses, human constructs"; then she claims that "the 'real' referent of [historical] language once existed; but it is *only* accessible to us *today* in textualized form."[2] If the "real" referent of the past becomes fictionalized as it is reconstructed in the present, then we are led to assume that because the referent of the immediate experience is direct, it is nonfiction, and therefore real. However, as Rey Chow in discussing Joan Scott's article "The Evidence of Experience" aptly argues, "by privileging experience we are leaving open the question as to what authorizes experience itself" (27). Scott, somewhat in line with Jean Baudrillard, problematizes the "evidential", essentialist nature of personal experience and draws attention to the contiguous nature of visual perception, knowledge, and identity (776). In "The Evidence of Experience", Scott explains that experience and writing are equally constructed, and that, "When experience is taken as the origin of knowledge [...] questions about the constructed nature of experience" are put aside (777). Quoting Donna Haraway, Scott says, "Vision is not passive reflection [...]. 'All eyes, including our own organic ones, are active perceptual systems, building in translations and specific ways of seeing—that is ways of life'" (777). So, by assuming that "seeing is knowing", we allow the technology of seeing or seeing-as-technology to dominate our thinking about identity and reality. In the same way, Hutcheon, by taking immediate experience as the "bedrock of evidence" in the attainment of knowledge, privileges experience and considers it to be real, not fabricated as the knowledge of history.

In short, through the term "historiographic metafiction", Hutcheon is displaying a very ambiguous position: one that, while seeking to critically confront modernism, remains deluded by its distinctions and definitions. As both Chow and Scott suggest, "the appeal to experience as incontestable evidence and as an originary point of explanation for historical difference" (Chow 27) in fact undercuts the necessary task of the writer, which for postmodern thinkers is the exploration of "how difference is established, how it operates, how and in what ways it constitutes subjects who see and act in the world" (Scott 777).

"How difference is established, how it operates, and in what ways it constitutes subjects" seem to be the preoccupation of Atasü in *Dağın Öteki Yüzü*, published in Turkish in 1995 and in English in 2000.[3] Atasü explores these questions in the context of historical contingencies, and, being aware of the interdependence and the transformational nature of fact-and-fiction and past-and-present, she reads her own history "aesthetically", trying to construct from it a unity of form and meaning which deconstructs itself the moment that unity becomes aesthetically recognizable.

In a note printed on the title page, right after the title, of the first Turkish edition of the book, Atasü says that this is a "narrative that strolls waywardly between a story and a novel". The book in fact strolls through many other forms of writing as well. *Dağın Öteki Yüzü* borders on the genres of autobiography, biography, history, literary theory, scholarly research, and ideological writing. As Atasü strives to put versions of the past to present uses in examining difference—be it personal, ideological, educational, or exploratory—questions of narrative, most obviously those of style, form, and point of view, surface as of great importance. Because Atasü is aware that each of these is itself constitutive of our ways of seeing and understanding so-called facts and events, she never lets one form, style, or point of view dominate. Instead, she continuously constructs and deconstructs them, making them sometimes overlap, sometimes transform, and sometimes undercut one another. Krieger's description of what he calls "reading aesthetically" is very helpful in understanding how Atasü deals with both the historic material she uses and the narrative constrictions she faces in writing *Dağın Öteki Yüzü*.

In his article from the issue of *New Literary History* commemorating Wolfgang Iser's work, Krieger says:

> From Aristotle to Coleridge to the New Criticism, there is a striving toward an organicism that would claim the perfect harmony of part and whole [....] [H]ow to have an assembly of wayward elements that surrender nothing while the illusionary whole is constructed out of them as well as being deconstructed by them? We find these only in the fictional literary artifact, or so this tradition maintains. It presents the illusion of "free play" of total breakthrough, […from] the teleologies latent in the human power to impose form, the power to create an order we cannot find, an order in which we can only half believe. And it is for this momentary glimpsing of a logo-utopia, a utopia of words, that only the aesthetic can serve as our guide and companion. (142-43)

Krieger next discusses the paradoxical nature of understanding the world and the text. Man both desires to find an order, a form, in that which is historically contingent and arbitrary, and at the same time, wants to resist this desire. For Krieger, Iser's characterization of the aesthetic as a way of reading seems to supply an acceptable formula. "The simultaneity of the mutually exclusive", a phrase Iser uses to point to a distinction between the aesthetic forms of reading and "non-aesthetic readings", is key to this formula. According to Krieger, "reading aesthetically" is indeed not only another way of talking about readers' "willing suspension of disbelief" when they think they are to interpret self-professed fiction, but it also explains how interpretations can simultaneously procure formalistic, totalizing *and* arbitrary, historically contingent meanings for one and the same text. While reading aesthetically, we see that one reading is continuously undercut by the other, creating a tension between opposing views. Briefly for Krieger, those texts that lend themselves to aesthetic readings are best able to convey subversive, arbitrary, and heteroglossic sensibilities. "[N]onaesthetic readings", unlike aesthetic readings, "expect to keep the opposition between exclusives distinct and consecutive" (144), giving rise to more monolithic and monoglossic ways of seeing and interpreting.

In *Dağın Öteki Yüzü*, Atasü herself reads historical material aesthetically, and she creates a narrative which is "heteroglossic" with respect to forms of writing, language, and style, and "dialogical" with respect to characterization and history. The illusion or delusion of the significance of an event, which presupposes a historical order, is given simultaneously with the arbitrariness, the contingency of the historical situation to which that significance refers. The past is viewed and recreated by different characters at different moments in history, as well as by the writer, who narrates sometimes what she remembers, sometimes what she imagines, sometimes what she reads, and sometimes what she is told. Each time the same event is loaded with a different significance.

In the section of the book entitled "Letter to the Reader", the writer explains that for her "incidents in themselves, either in fiction or in real life, are not terribly important. My memory for factual detail has always been rather weak. But the essence of things that happen, the reasons for them and the results, the impact they have on individual psyches, the impressions on inner selves, have always been the issues of paramount importance to my mind" (279). In *Dağın Öteki Yüzü*, the meaning and importance of an event changes both from person to person and in time for the same person, pointing to the dynamic and continuously renewed significance of all historical material. Therefore, in this book, historical facts and events are novel to those for whom they are significant at the moment of their significance. Conversely, the present gains significance when set in the context of the present significance of past events. In short, Atasü's writing, which dramatically suggests the "novelty of the past and the antiquity of the present" as a way of interpreting history, is in some ways reminiscent of T.S. Eliot's aesthetic theory in *Tradition and Individual Talent*. Eliot claims that "No poet, no artist of any art, has his complete meaning alone. His significance, his appreciation is the appreciation of his relation to the dead poets and artists. ...I mean this as a principle of aesthetic, not merely historical, criticism" (526). But while Eliot concentrates on the continuities in historical texts that make up a tradition, Atasü reads history aesthetically and displays "how difference is established, how it operates, how and in what ways it constitutes subjects [...]" (Scott 777).

Its table of contents divides *Dağın Öteki Yüzü* into six sections, almost all carrying a subheading with a main heading which are simultaneously related and not related to each other. The first section[4] has the headings "Introduction" and "Letter to the Reader", the second "The Last Decade of Innocence" and "Towards Freedom", the third "The Wave" and "Towards the Open Sea... Memories and Illusions", the fourth "The Kemalists" and "Islands of the Past... Photographs and Letters of Bygone Days...", the fifth "Journal for my Daughter" and "On Another Shore", while the last consists of a dictionary[5] and carries a single heading, "Dictionary". The heading "Introduction" suggests that what we are to read is a formal and possibly a scholarly text. When this heading is coupled with "The Kemalists", which is the heading of the largest section of the book, we seek to associate the book with a certain period in Turkish history and perhaps a certain ideology—namely, that of Atatürk. The subheading of this first section, "Letter to the Reader", however, undercuts this formal, scholarly presentation and is suggestive of an informal and intimate approach reminiscent of personal (auto)biographical or confessional writing. This informal, personal tone present in the subheading of the first section is repeated in "Journal for my Daughter", the main heading of the fifth section, which narrative-wise is the last section of the book. Similarity of tone in the first and last sections suggests of a kind of aesthetic unity and closure which is again challenged by the supplementation of the section "Dictionary".

In the "Letter to the Reader", we are told with the precision of a historian which characters and events that appear in the narrative are tailored after which real events and people, and which ones are entirely fictive. The writer goes so far as to give full reference for the historical and scholarly data she used, how she procured it, and what use she made of it. However, she then shifts her tone and goes on to thank her friends, acquaintances, and relatives by name for their various contributions to the writing of her book. This personal and intimate style is abandoned once again as she starts using the more formal language of an editor, a translator, a linguist, and explains what norms and principles of writing she has employed and why:

> It is my impression that because Turkish was in the shadow of the Ottoman which was spoken by the educated middle class—probably because of its wealth of words—it remained as a functional language in the first half of the century. (I must say I did not have difficulties forming sentences in the language of that day.) But [that language] does not fit one closely like one's skin, it feels only as tight as one's costume! I think

language—itself an intrinsic part of manners—plays as great a role as old-fashioned manners in the timid and fearful nature of older generations.

> In all the passages referring to the past I consciously made use of a mixed language. To use the language of the day [that is, early twentieth-century Ottoman] carried with it the danger of making the text inaccessible [to present-day readers]. As we approached the present, I was careful to use a simpler form of Turkish [purified of the influence of Arabic and Persian]. If read carefully, it can be seen that in those passages told by the "I-narrator", who lives today and speaks the Turkish of today, there is no veil of costume! (First Turkish edition[6] 20-21)

This translator/scholar goes on to cite the numerous intertextual references present in the book, commenting on why she chose to include them and why they are where they appear. We understand, for example, that she has been inspired by Friedrich Wilhelm Nietzsche's *Thus Spoke Zarathustra* but that she read that book in its Turkish translation (282). The name of the translator, and the date and place of publication, are cited next to the title of the book, in the style of formal scholarly writing (first Turkish edition 22). This formal tone shifts again as Atasü tells the reader not to be surprised by the apparent non-feminist slant in the book:

> My reader will know me as a feminist writer, and this book he or she is holding at the moment may come as a surprise. The feminist sensibility of this book is masked, and reveals itself only to the observant. I discovered something about myself while writing it, which I should like to share with my reader. Both my mother and father were among the orphans of the First World War and Armistice (i.e. our occupation) years. By force of circumstance, their families were transformed into matriarchal households, and this may be the starting-point for my feminist awareness. (282)

Even while a formal, scholarly style is being constructed, it is undercut by the intimate personal tone employed by the writer as she addresses her readers. On the other hand, when Atasü talks about her personal tastes, her ideological choices, and her emotional relationship with her parents, their generation, and their history in a very confessional tone, she again refers to scholarly data and historical material in ways that are highly formal and analytic. The "Letter to the Reader" ends with an expression of Atasü's gratitude to the three people whom she says she owes much and greatly admires:

> Let me once more call to mind with respect, admiration and love the three great people whose influence on my heart and mind resonate through this book: Mustafa Kemal Atatürk, whose being supplied the sap which has sustained my country's life; that major poet, Nazım Hikmet; and the major writer Virginia Woolf, whose work has drawn me ever closer to the writer hidden within me. (283)
> […]
> And Dear Reader, of course I thank you too. (First Turkish edition 24)

The second section's main heading is "Last Ten Years of Innocence". In terms of style and content, this section is neither formal nor personal. If anything, it can be loosely associated with biographical writing. The subheading of this section again deconstructs the main heading, as the conceptual significances of the two are ethically pitted against each other. "Towards Freedom", read against "The Last Decade of Innocence", seems to imply that liberation and innocence are mutually exclusive. Furthermore, in this section, we are not given, as the title promises, an account of the events and impressions associated with only the last ten years of the writer's life, but we read of the writer's comments on, and her split-self's corrections or additions to, the events, persons, dreams, frustrations, and hopes that pertain to the forty-odd years of her entire life. The significance of these events, however, is continuously transformed. The formal balls that her parents diligently attend year after year in celebration of the Republic, for example, look comical to her in the 1970s; she says today they seem tragic. For the Kemalists, who believed in the significance of the revolution and of the Republic which was its most visible result, those balls carried ideological importance; therefore, they were taken very seriously. The writer's split-self reads this difference in attitude between herself and her parents as ironic. She says it is touching how one generation seems to take everything in life seriously while the other, nothing. In the same section, we are also told that the writer, after many travels, gains knowledge of life and loses her innocence. She then understands the world, which too has lost its innocence. The parents, who were innocent enough to take life and ideologies very seriously, on the other hand come to be respected by the writer only after she says she has lost her innocence. Hence, not only does the significance of historical events and people change continuously, but the meaning of concepts also becomes fluid as they are used to describe those changing events and identities.

"The Wave", the heading of the third section, calls to mind Virginia Woolf's *The Waves*. The subheading of this section is "Towards the Open Sea… Memories and Illusions". It is possible to see a parallelism between "Towards the Open Sea…" and "Towards Freedom". Both metaphorically suggest a point of departure in one's life; both look forward to the future. The subheading "Towards the Open Sea…", however, is immediately followed by a reference not to the future but to the past: "Memories and Illusions". In this section, Atasü concentrates on the character of her mother as it came to be known to her in all its contradictions. The mother's character is described differently by each of the people who knew her and who organize a ceremony to commemorate her contributions to the educational life of the country. She is "pliable and severe, full of joy and sad…" at the same time. Furthermore, we understand that her contributions are being acknowledged while she is on her deathbed. The daughter who attends the ceremony in her mother's name lives mentally in several historical times, including the present and a double, in fact a triple, life: her own life and memories, those of her mother, and those of Woolf, the writer of *The Waves*. The lives of these three women are contiguous with one another, sometimes merging into one but then quickly separating, as at the end of the section, when the writer signs off a piece of writing with the words: "She put her mother's name on the manuscript, and underneath her own, together with a dedication: 'To all women who have committed suicide and to those who have returned from the brink'" (28).

"The Kemalists", the main heading of the fourth and major section of the book, refers not only to the followers of an ideology, but also to a period in Turkish history as it was lived, known, and interpreted by those who were alive at the time of Mustafa Kemal Atatürk, the leader of the Turkish War of Independence and the founder of the Republic and of modern Turkey. But in line with her dynamic understanding of history, which is as much related to the present as to the past, Atasü incorporates into this section the sensibilities and attitudes of those who, like the writer, were born after Atatürk. The subheading of this section is "Islands of the Past... Photographs and Letters of Bygone Days...". Ironically, one of the main figures in this section, Nefise, the mother's best friend, is a purely fictive figure; therefore, she could not have been present in any of the photographs presented to us as real.

This section problematizes all the assumptions based on the distinction between the real and the fictive. We can see how Hutcheon's presupposition that "The 'real' referent of the (language of the past) once existed; but it is only accessible to us today in textualized form" (93) obviously needs to be revised upon treating so historiographic a piece of writing as "The Kemalists". "The Kemalists" is further divided into nine subsections. "The Other Side of the Mountain", the title of the book, appears here as the heading of the last subsection. In this last subsection, Atatürk is presented in person, and his ideology, vision, and expectation concerning the future of the country are given supposedly in his words. But even here, the events and characters of the future are presented simultaneously with those of the past, each commenting on and transforming the significance of the other.

"Journal for my Daughter", the main heading of the last narrative section, as pointed out earlier, brings us back to the subheading of the first section, "Letter to the Reader". But this section does not directly address the daughter as the first section addresses the reader. Here, the writer is at her parents' graves. She has with her the memories, as well as the materials, of her past (her parents' letters); she thinks of her daughter, in a sense her own future awaiting her, and goes to meet with her outside the cemetery. Since the writer's registered history also constitutes some of the historical materials of the daughter's history, it is not inappropriate to call this section "Journal for my Daughter". The subheading of this section, "On Another Shore", refers us directly to the writing at the end of section three, where we see that the life stories of the writer, her mother, and Woolf somehow intersect. We read: "Now I am on another shore. Am I a water-drop in this universe, that ends up on the spot where it started to form? Do I have to fall and mingle with the earth?" (28). But as we are made to see in that section and throughout the book, "ending up on the spot where it started" is never possible. In "On Another Shore", the writer lies on the graves of her parents and waits for the century, which began at about the time of their births, to come to an end and for the cycle to be completed. But what she means by "cycle" is left particularly ambiguous; therefore, as in *Waiting for Godot*, her waiting is in vain. In the passage that follows this scene, she vaguely associates "cycle" with time and points to the futility of her action. She says, "I wait in vain, yet grief is out of place. Time never closes the circle; time flows in spirals. Now, let me repeat my former question. Has nothing changed? I am that change!" (274). Indeed, since time always moves on, never makes a loop, never comes full circle, and does not have a material existence of its own, the materials and people who exist in time constitute time and change. In other words, in *Dağın Öteki Yüzü*, it is not only impossible to attain a static or cyclical, orderly understanding of history, reality, and identity; it is also not desirable; it is not even desirable to arrive at artistic unity. A kind of artistic unity, totality, seems to be achieved at the end of section five, as the writer moves from the fictional biography of her mother to that of herself and finally looks forward to a biography of her daughter. But by making the section that follows, with the heading "Dictionary", an integral part of the narrative, the sense of artistic closure is denied. The sixth or last section, "Dictionary", when read aesthetically, turns into a commentary on our simultaneous desire for and resistance to closure and order, or a form implied by some order. Here art imitates the contingent, dynamic, and constructed nature of history, reality, and identity. In explaining her reasons for calling an "imaginative reconstruction" of the past a "historical metafiction", Hutcheon says:

> 'Imaginative reconstruction' or intellectual systematization [...] is the focus of the postmodern rethinking of the problems of how we can and do come to have knowledge of the past [...]. Postmodernism returns to confront the problematic nature of the past as an object of knowledge for us in the present [...]. It puts into question, at the same time as it exploits, the grounding of historical knowledge in the past real. This is why I have been calling this historiographic metafiction. (92)

It is my contention that, by reading history aesthetically, Atasü is able to address much more competently than Hutcheon the postmodern problematization of the past as an object of knowledge for us in the present. As Krieger explains, reading aesthetically "permits the text to create beyond what its surrounding discourse has made available" (156), be it history, literature, or theory.

NOTES

[1] This is a revised version of a paper entitled "The Novelty of the Past and the Antiquity of the Future in the 'Historiographic Metafiction' *The Other Side of the Mountain*" which was presented at the Eighteenth Annual Conference of the Poetics and Linguistics Association held at the University of Berne in April 1998.

[2] Stresses and the phrases within the brackets are mine.

[3] Editor's note: translations have been taken from the English edition except where otherwise noted.

[4] Editor's note: this is the order of the first Turkish edition; the English edition places this section at the end.

[5] Editor's note: this three-page glossary, less meaningful for readers of English, does not appear in the English edition.

[6] Editor's note: the translation of this passage, which is omitted from the English edition, is by Doltaş, and the bracketed phrases are clarifications introduced by Doltaş.

WORKS CITED

Atasü, Erendiz. *Dağın Öteki Yüzü*. 1st ed. Istanbul: Remzi Kitabevi, 1995.

———. ———. 4th ed. Ankara: Bilgi Yayınevi, 1999.

———. *The Other Side of the Mountain*. Trans. Erendiz Atasü and Elizabeth Maslen. 1st ed. London: Milet Publishing Limited, 2000.

Chow, Rey. *Ethics After Idealism: Theory-Culture-Ethnicity-Reading*. Bloomington: Indiana University Press, 1998.

Eliot, T.S. "Tradition and Individual Talent". *Criticism: The Major Texts*. Ed. Walter Jackson Bate. New York: Harcourt, Brace & World, Inc., 1952.

Hutcheon, Linda. *A Poetics of Postmodernism: History, Theory, Fiction*. London: Routledge, 1988.

Iser, Wolfgang. *Prospecting: From Reader Response to Literary Anthropology*. Baltimore: The Johns Hopkins University Press, 1989.

———. *The Fictive and the Imaginary: Charting Literary Anthropology*. Baltimore: The Johns Hopkins University Press, 1993.

Krieger, Murray. "The 'Imaginary' and Its Enemies". *New Literary History* 31.1 (Winter 2000). 129-62.

Scott, Joan. "The Evidence of Experience". *Critical Inquiry* 17 (Summer 1991), The University of Chicago Press.

I, Hoca Nasreddin, Never Shall I Die

Hande A. Birkalan-Gedik

Associate Professor of Folklore, Department of Anthropology, Yeditepe University

Başgöz, İlhan and Pertev Boratav. *I, Hoca Nasreddin, Never Shall I Die: A Thematic Analysis of Hoca Stories.* Turkish Studies Series 18. Bloomington: Indiana University, 1998. 165 pages.

The present book brings together an introductory folkloric essay by İlhan Başgöz and research samples that Pertev Naili Boratav entrusted to Başgöz at Indiana University shortly before his death. Başgöz's essay, on the thematic analysis of Hoca stories in historical perspective, paves the way for an introduction to the world of Hoca. Boratav's two essays, both of which were originally presented at the *Centre national de la recherche scientifique* in Paris, contribute to scholarship on the Hoca tradition and to the popularization of Hoca tales worldwide. The book concludes with a sampling from Boratav's collection of over five hundred Hoca tales compiled from various manuscripts. Boratav himself already published these stories in Turkish in 1996; nonetheless, there is no contextual information on the individual texts in the present volume.

Two incidents in the field of folkloric Hoca research place this collaboration of Başgöz and Boratav in perspective. As part of his opening address at the Fifth International Conference of Turkish Folk Culture, Başgöz recounted an obscene Nasreddin Hoca joke. The rendition outraged Saim Sakaoğlu, another Turkish folklorist at the conference, who protested, "This is an insult to our Turkish identity!". The ensuing row among conference attendees spilled over onto the international scene. The

American folklorist Joann Conrad referred to this incident in an article in the *Journal of American Folklore*. The second incident concerns the research of Boratav, who, until his death in March 1998, was working on Hoca's celebrated audacity. Boratav's aim was to compile every tale in the Hoca tradition as well as to catalog the analogs in foreign oral traditions. Upon the publication in Turkey of this extensive research on Nasreddin Hoca, Boratav's book was recalled because it contained "unspeakable" jokes.

Both of these instances present us with an attitude that reflects a strong conservatism and a subverted sense of nationalism inherent in Turkish folklore studies. Known mainly for the didactic tales that feature him in oral tradition and children's storybooks alike, how may Nasreddin Hoca, our "national hero", appear as an obscene character? The quest for nationalism, and consequent eschewal of thorough analysis, seem to be the pivotal elements in these discussions. "Objectivity" and the "scientific approach", the two key concepts which Boratav sought to preserve for the field of folklore studies in Turkey, prove crucial in the task of analyzing folklore materials. For Boratav, folklore needs to be "objective", not because it is a science like physics or mathematics, but because it needs to rid itself of obliviousness that prevents analytical accuracy. Hence the significance of the present book: it unveils some of the "obscene" aspects of the Hoca character.

Some of these "unspeakable" tales are under examination in Başgöz's essay, "A Thematic Analysis of Hoca Stories in Historical Perspective". Calling for a sound analysis of both the historical and the popular characters of Nasreddin Hoca; and carefully examining both the textual and the *con*textual elements of the creation, development, and transmission of Hoca stories; *I, Hoca Nasreddin, Never Shall I Die* is a book that promulgates many tenets. For instance, the essay purports to provide a meaningful cultural, societal, and historical analysis. In this respect, Başgöz discusses the historical aspects of Nasreddin Hoca; the relationship between Hoca and religion, his family, his donkey, and his authority within the justice system; and his involvement with societal problems, such as poverty, famine, and so forth. Another example is a brief survey, of the Hoca tales in relation to other folklore forms such as proverbs and riddles, which aims to show an *intertextual* link between various genres. These two sections of the essay, however, are presented only in brief; much in the intertextual nature of the Hoca stories still awaits attention.

Another important part of this essay is where Başgöz examines the stylistic changes in the Hoca stories over time. This part is very important for two reasons: First, it describes the progress of the written forms, and the stylistic differences between narrated and written texts. Başgöz maintains that early stories represent a short body of text, in question-and-answer form, while the later stories are much longer. Second, another important aspect of the discussion of style deals with the relationship between literature and society. The interesting change in style is also prompted by societal changes in the lifestyles of the era. Whereas sexuality themes in the tribal period are more permissive, a taboo is imposed on the narration of sexuality in the later period, a time of sedentary society. Başgöz's essay, which makes up about half of the book, concludes with an appendix, listing eleven manuscripts consulted by the author and a bibliography on Hoca.

Hoca's involvement in society, besides his being a religious figure, further illustrates the above-mentioned relationship between literature and society. At the least, he is a human being with his own desires, actions, and responsibilities, all of which are apparent in the creation of Hoca tales. Through him, the populace can participate in the social life of the Sultanate, albeit vicariously. This attitude is also apparent in the creation of other Turkish folk heroes, such as Keloğlan of the folktale, Köroğlu of the romance, and Karacaoğlan of folk poetry. In the context of authority, Hoca is an antihero. Like Keloğlan, who might protest societal injustice, Hoca criticizes religious blasphemy.

Additionally, perhaps one of the most useful points of the book is the reference to the Hoca tales in terms of "tradition". This approach considers stories not only as texts; it also aims to explain them within the framework of "continuity". This understanding was previously employed by Başgöz, in his analysis of Karacaoğlan; and by Boratav, in his analysis of Köroğlu. Whether or not we can prove the existence of historical evidence of any folk character, it is important to note that these tales have long been alive in the minds of people, who create a continuous tradition of their own by narrating them, transmitting them, and writing them down. Considered from the perspective of a folklorist, this emphasis on continuity marks a unique contribution to the field by distinguishing itself from the perspective of a solely textual analysis.

Başgöz makes scattered reference to the medieval era, and especially he culls examples from the works of the Russian formalist Bakhtin and his work on Rabelais. Bakhtin notes that the medieval carnival functioned like a social valve, a multi-vocal platform upon which the masses could release their anxieties and desires. Defecation, farting, and vomiting became the basic sources of laughter, a concept which was looked down upon by the upper class. The way that Hoca acts certainly, though not always, creates a *carnivalesque* for laughter. At worst, Hoca's stories involving bodily functions can be called "jokes"!

The second part of the book opens with Boratav's essay, "The Spread of the Nasreddin Hoca Tradition", and begins with a survey of scholars who have thus far worked on the Hoca stories, especially those foreign ones who came from the Orientalist school. Boratav again does a thorough job by presenting a detailed list of the academics who have worked on the subject, which is a very useful source of information for those researchers who want to pursue the Hoca tradition further. The extent of Boratav's interest in documenting the tales is illustrated by his inclusion of early references to Hoca in the works of foreign authors, as well as by a compilation of Hoca tales in manuscripts and published works by Muslims and non-Muslims in Turkey and abroad.

In this section, Boratav also lists the themes of the Hoca stories, referring to manuscripts in both Turkish and European libraries. Here one can also find detailed notes on editions, literary adaptations, and the influence of oral tradition. Boratav concludes that written works have been far more important than oral tradition in contributing to the Hoca repertoire. Istanbul, especially, was the center for circulating the tales. In addition, libraries in Cairo, Baku, and Tabriz became very influential in the spread of the tales. As for oral tradition, Boratav advances the following view: the fifteenth century maintained a certain Nasreddin, and this character was a mixture of a saint and sage, but he also had some eccentricities. Moreover, historically speaking, Ottoman expansion augmented the spread of the Hoca tradition, especially through a large circulation of the written Hoca stories. Known under different names around the world, such as Juha al-Rumi or Molla Nasreddin, the figure of Nasreddin Hoca has been appropriated or claimed as a national hero in a variety of cultures. Boratav also notes that an in-depth analysis of this matter is necessary in order to draw certain conclusions about the spread of the jokes.

The second and relatively brief essay by Boratav, "The Turkish, the Muslim, and the Universal in Nasreddin Hoca Stories", suggests several "emergences" of the tales, instead of possible "origins". Analyzing the language, expressions, idioms, and clichés of the stories in particular, Boratav navigates through the categories of the Turkish, the Muslim, and the universal, drawing particular attention to national and regional characteristics. Much of this sort of analysis by Boratav has been published as articles or delivered as papers at international conferences and colloquia. For further details, readers with access to Turkish can certainly benefit from Boratav's book, *Nasreddin Hoca*.

I, Hoca Nasreddin, Never Shall I Die uniquely contributes to the scholarship on Nasreddin Hoca, despite its relatively short length. Not only does it offer an introductory analysis of the Hoca character, but it also comes in handy for the methods and sources it suggests for further research.

The Unreadable Shores of Love

Erdağ Göknar

Visiting Assistant Professor, Turkish Language and Culture, Duke University

Holbrook, Victoria Rowe. *The Unreadable Shores of Love: Turkish Modernity and Mystic Romance.* 1st ed. Austin: University of Texas Press, 1994. 187 pages (excl. bibliography).

How do we interpret an Ottoman literature fixed in the vise of Turkish nationalist discourse and an orientalist philological tradition? In *The Unreadable Shores of Love: Turkish Modernity and Mystic Romance* (Aşkın Okunmaz Kıyıları; below referred to as *Unreadable*), Victoria Rowe Holbrook explores this question in light of Mevlevî[1] sheikh-cum-poet Şeyh Galib's 1783 *mesnevî*[2] masterpiece, *Hüsn ü Aşk* (Beauty and Love). Setting out to write "a first poetics of Ottoman Turkish romance", Holbrook devotes the introduction and the first ("Inventing Difficulty: Modern Reception of Ottoman Poetry") and last ("Subjectivity and Interpretation") chapters[3] to introducing the reader to the political landscape where Ottoman literature and Turkish republican literary discourse negotiate complex and sustained relationships. As Holbrook maintains, the relationships between the two are predicated on the political disappearance of the Ottoman Empire, the rise of Turkish nationalism, and on nineteenth- and twentieth-century Ottoman-Turkish "occidentalization". She specifically highlights the literary-critical effects of the official discourse of the Republic, which defines the Turk against the Ottoman, the modern[4] against the religio-traditional, and the culturally eclectic (Ottoman-Persian, -Arabic, -Turkish, -Armenian, -Greek, -Jewish, etc.) against the culturally pure (Turkist). In short, what contributes to "unreadability" for Holbrook is a political and discursive taboo against the Ottoman that not only informs, but defines, modern Turkish literary scholarship. With regard to the Young Ottoman, Young Turk, and finally, republican reception of Ottoman poetry, Holbrook states:

> Ottoman language and literature were critiqued as metonym for Ottoman government more dangerous to challenge. […] The concept Ottoman, with its elaborate cultural and institutional accoutrements, was gradually discarded in favor of the occidentally correct concept "Turkish." "Difficulty" became a euphemism for qualities of the politically incorrect, to be tutored by the essentially simple, pure, and true. (22)

In her second chapter ("Intertextuality and the Fortress of Form"), Holbrook theoretically engages *Hüsn ü Aşk* while attacking traditional philological evaluation in a multilayered analysis of Rumi's "influence" on Galib. Here, she also begins modeling a postmodern method of Ottoman literary evaluation that serves as the engine of her book.[5] That is, she employs literary theory to "triangulate" out of the binary impasse between the republican and the Ottoman, in which the Ottoman becomes sublated for the good of modern Turkish progress. By interpreting Galib's *mesnevi* in this manner, she avoids the dialectical pressure between the two cultural entities, as well as diverts the synthetic (tending toward synthesis) force of sublation, which works negatively against the Ottoman. In her third chapter ("Poethood, Art, and Science"), Holbrook begins a critical discussion of *Hüsn ü Aşk* that also emphasizes Şeyh Galib's own theory of poetics, an aspect of his *mesnevi* which has been overlooked in the pertinent scholarship. Generally, in the third, fourth ("Philosophy of Language against Imitation"), and fifth ("Originality and Realism") chapters of her book, Holbrook brings together "post-philological" literary theory and Galib's *Hüsn ü Aşk*—while emphasizing its theoretical "Digression" (*Mebahis-i Diğer*)—with the intent of removing that *mesnevi* from the discursive vise of Western Orientalist and Turkish Nationalist scholarship.[6] The attack on discursive "unreadability" in *Unreadable* is organized around three major themes: the link between the political and the scholarly vis-à-vis the Republic's reception of the Ottoman, Holbrook's literary theory-based exploration of *Hüsn ü Aşk* and its "Digression", and Republican intellectuals' critical understanding of *Hüsn ü Aşk*[7].

Throughout her book, Holbrook intimates and underscores the need for scholarship and "generating new categories of information": on subjects such as the linguistic and literary history of Ottoman, Arabic, and Persian; on the history of the Ottoman "allegorical" tradition; on the allegory of the dervish path as a genre of Ottoman writing; on the framing "commentary" sections of *mesnevi* verse narratives; on the influences of Ibn Arabi's philosophical system in Ottoman intellectual history; on the intellectual history of the Mevlevî and Melâmî[8] sects; and on Ottoman literary style with respect to *tekke* (dervish lodge) and *medrese* (madrasa) culture. The following sequence of provocative sentences from Holbrook's text gives an idea of the matrix of her thought:

> Although Turkey was never colonized in the geographical way, it has, like other nations which preceded it in emerging from the empire (notably Greece), been powerfully described by outsiders whose discursive practices signified attitudes of the colonial master. Colonization in this case is of an ideal territory: of the country of a people's thoughts, their dream-land. In the process the hermeneutic view of Ottoman poetry was overwhelmed by the emblematic. (16)

> *Beauty and Love* has held a special place in modern Turkish critical consciousness; in the late nineteenth century evaluation of Galib's work became an evaluation of the Ottoman poetical past. Galib has been praised as a superlatively original genius and disparaged as a reactionary, according to critics' readings of his work. (52)

> Modern criticism of Ottoman romances has concentrated on determining the textual sources of works, paying less attention to their intrinsic qualities, and by this preoccupation and its omissions critics have created the impression that Ottoman poetry was more imitative of precedent, therefore (by nineteenth-century Romantic standards) less original than *Western* poetry. (76)

> The Ottoman institution of *Masnavi* readings following the Friday communal prayer has all but escaped modern notice. It would have occasioned discussion at once more personal and philosophical than recitation of the Koran or the weekly sermon could have. (109)

> Galib's judgment of the social value of poetry depended on relations between the individual and the divine, and [Namık] Kemal's, on relations between the people and the nation. (122)

> This is the late Ottoman eighteenth-century difference of Galib's Mevlevi-*Melami* bent: spiritual realization is to be enjoyed in *this* world. (146)

> Galib considered poetry and poetical imagination a kind of link between "worlds" of form and meaning. Gabriel's role in Muhammed's *miraj* parallels that of Poetry in Love's quest—and the role of poetry in Galib's quest. All take a "journey back" from form and language through imagination to awe in their source. (149)

As challenging as *Unreadable* is, however, the matrix of thought contained in its mere 187 pages is overwhelming and includes subjects such as philology, nationalism, cultural imperialism, orientalism, intertextuality, allegory, symbol, textual voices, imitation, poetic imagination, representation, subjectivity, and the paradigms of love and of the *miraj* (the ascension of Prophet Muhammad). It is no easy task for the writer or the reader to manage such topics in such a short book.[9] As an additional complicating factor,

Holbrook begins each sub-heading and each chapter heading with a couplet from *Hüsn ü Aşk*, intending to set up a kind of intertext of her own, whereby the subject of her analysis "speaks" to the analysis. Rather than elucidate the book, these couplets become distracting and their relationship to the analysis inscrutable.[10]

Holbrook's attempt to re-situate scholarship away from an Orientalist/Nationalist episteme is an important one in the history of Ottoman-Turkish studies. She invites us to "read" what is rhetorically presented as "unreadable". *Unreadable* and its Turkish version (*Aşkın Okunmaz Kıyıları*, Istanbul, İletişim Yayınları, 1998) are invaluable for what they provide, not only to scholars and aficionados of Ottoman and Turkish literature, but to all scholars of the Middle East.

NOTES

[1] An Islamic sect started in the name of Mevlana Celaleddin Rumî in the late thirteenth century; the disciples/dervishes of the Mevleviye sect are commonly known in the Western world as the "whirling dervishes".

[2] Rhyming couplets all sharing the same meter.

[3] Holbrook, who argues that scholars dealing with *mesnevi*s tend to ignore commentary sections at their beginnings and endings, frames her own discussion of Galib's *mesnevi* with similar commentaries.

[4] Here, I use "modern" as a localized discursive formation: in the Ottoman-Turkish cultural sense of an ontological and epistemological project involving "progress" and "occidentalization".

[5] For example, Holbrook transforms philological concerns about "origin" into theoretical and poetic concerns about "originality".

[6] Other reviews (see Sarah G. Moment Atiş and Selim S. Kuru) have focused on the unsuccessful meeting of theory and literature in the Ottoman case, basing the critique on a theory-literature binary which Holbrook attempts to avoid. Atiş writes: "It [*Unreadable*] addresses two audiences who speak separate and often mutually unintelligible tongues—language of post-modern literary theory and that of traditional Orientalist expertise. The book will be faulted from both directions" (162). Kuru writes: "There are various inherent problems with the encounter between critical theory and Ottoman literary studies, and it is as if this encounter develops in favor of the theoretical. [....] Rather than further elucidate Ottoman literature, it invariably turns into [the act of] reflecting well-known theoretical knowledge through a little-known literature" (7-8).

[7] One of the more interesting subtexts of *Unreadable* is the genealogy of Abdülbaki Gölpınarlı's critical thought with respect to Şeyh Galib. Holbrook writes of Gölpınarlı: "his oeuvre bequeaths a private map to republican literary politics" (126), and "[h]is final introduction to Galib in 1976 brought together the body of detail he had amassed over thirty-six years regarding the life, works, and the spiritual, intellectual, and political loyalties of an at last inscrutable poet. It was this inscrutable Galib the writer [Holbrook] met in 1983" (129).

[7] A Sunni sect known for its renouncement of worldly concerns and all forms of ostentation.

[8] This reviewer found an earlier article by Holbrook in the *Journal of the American Oriental Society* that contains a clearer explication of some of the ideas in her book.

[10] Holbrook's language is idiosyncratic: she often drops articles and writes asyntactic sentences some of which verge on the ungrammatical. Other reviews have complained about this phenomenon, even going as far as blaming copy editors. Though one's first reaction might be to read these as mistakes, Holbrook might have had something else in mind entirely. For example, her playing with English syntax might have been an attempt at showing a Turkish linguistic influence on her own text. One clue pointing to this possibility is the "asyntactic" nature of Turkish which is an agglutinative language and allows for flexibility in syntax. Furthermore, the definite article, *per se*, does not exist in Turkish, which may be the reason it was dropped in some of Holbrook's English sentences.

Works Cited

Atiş, Sarah G. Moment. "Reviews". *International Journal of Middle East Studies* 28.1 (1996): 159-62.

Holbrook, Victoria. *The Unreadable Shores of Love: Turkish Modernity and Mystic Romance.* Austin: University of Texas Press, 1994.

——. "Originality and Ottoman Poetics: In the Wilderness of the New". *Journal of the American Oriental Society* 112.3 (1992): 440-454.

Kuru, Selim S. "Aşkın Okunmaz Kıyıları". *Virgül* 15 (Ocak 1999): 7-10.

The Travels of Evliya Effendi
Albert Howe Lybyer

This article, first published in 1917, takes us back to a time when study of Evliya Çelebi's *Seyahatname* was still in its infancy. In assessing the work, Lybyer relies on its two-volume English rendering by Joseph von Hammer. Lybyer brings together information on Evliya Çelebi's family background, education, and lifestyle in a biographical sketch. He then proceeds to assess Evliya's writings according to criteria such as historical accuracy and statistical precision. Lybyer concludes that while "Evliya's historical facts and his figures are unreliable" (236), the author has produced "a very human document", indicating that "[w]ith a different training, Evliya might have become a Balzac or an Arnold Bennett, a Prescott or a Macaulay" (231).

As a historian, Lybyer suggests collating Evliya's work with those of his Western contemporaries writing on the Orient, such as Sir Paul Rycaut, to gain a comprehensive understanding of the seventeenth-century Ottoman Empire. Today, such a comparative approach may also lend itself to literary assessments of the work. Lybyer himself had to deal with von Hammer's work "without a comparison with the original". But now, with critical editions of the *Seyahatname*'s various volumes finally becoming available (on this subject, see also Robert Dankoff's article in this issue) and von Hammer's work itself having become a time-honored classic, a critical comparison of original and "translation" should prove fascinating.

At the time of Lybyer's writing, at most four volumes of the *Seyahatname* were assumed to exist. It is this assumption that leads Lybyer to suppose that "[h]ad the Turkish writer carried out his plan to the full and narrated the experiences of his whole life, he might have produced a work unique in interest as well as in magnitude" (239). Today, with ten volumes of the *Seyahatname* known to us, Lybyer's supposition has become fact.

"The Travels of Evliya Effendi" was first published in vol. 37 of the *Journal of the American Oriental Society*, and is reproduced here with the kind permission of the American Oriental Society.

THE TRAVELS OF EVLIYA EFFENDI

ALBERT HOWE LYBYER

UNIVERSITY OF ILLINOIS

A comparatively small amount of material has been translated from Turkish into English and published. The Latin, German, and Italian, and even the Hungarian and Danish languages have all received considerable portions of the early Ottoman historical writings, of which English shares with French the defect of having received very little. A number of poems and humorous stories, and some longer stories, have been translated into English, often too freely to give a correct impression. E. J. W. Gibb has published an extensive anthology of Ottoman poetry.[1] But were it not for *The Travels of Evliya Effendi*, there would exist, I believe, no single sizable piece of Englished Turkish. This translation, furthermore, while probably corrected by an Englishman, was made by an Austrian German, the great Orientalist Joseph von Hammer.[2] Curiously enough, though doubly incomplete, it contains, I believe, in the 350,000 words of its 676 folio pages, the longest work that has been translated out of the Turkish, except possibly Fluegel's translation into Latin of Haji Khalfa's annotated bibliographical dictionary.[3] Evliya

---

[1] E. J. W. Gibb, *History of Ottoman Poetry*, ed. E. G. Browne, 6 vols., 1909—.

[2] *Narrative of Travels in Europe, Asia, and Africa in the Seventeenth Century*, by Evliya Efendi. Translated from the Turkish by the Ritter Joseph von Hammer (Oriental Translation Fund). Vol. 1, pt. 1, xviii + 186 pages; pt. 2, iv + 256 pages; vol. 2, v + 244 pages. London, 1846—1850.—The translator has provided an introduction, tables of contents, and about 50 notes, but no index. The 'Advertisement' bears the date Jan. 20, 1834, showing that the translation was completed before that date. It is not known what assistance, if any, von Hammer had in the preparation of his translation.—All subsequent references without titles are to the volumes and parts of this work.

[3] *Lexicon Bibliographicum et Encyclopedicum*, a Mustafa ben Abdallah Katib Chelebi dicto et nomine Haji Khalfa, edidit, latine vertit, et commentario indicibusque instruxit G. Fluegel, 7 vols., Leipzig, 1835-1858.

seems to have fallen far short, from the chronological point of view, of writing a narrative of all the travels and adventures of his forty or fifty active years, but he has largely compensated for this by including so great a part of all he knew or could learn about things in general. His work contains, besides its central motive, an autobiography of the author, a sort of guide-book to Constantinople and the Levant, a broken sketch of Ottoman history from the beginning to about 1676, no small quantity of unreliable statistics, a description of the administration of the Empire in the time of Suleiman, a lively enumeration of the 'thousand and one' trade-gilds of Constantinople, and a wealth of anecdotes, legends, and observations.

Evliya lived from 1611 until about 1680,[4] and thus witnessed most of the period of high and perilous equilibrium in Turkish history which stretched from the peace of Sitvatorok in 1606, when Austria ceased to pay tribute for her holdings in Hungary, until the year 1683, when the second failure of the Turks before Vienna initiated their long and incomplete retreat southeastward. All that is known of his life is to be found scattered piecemeal through his narrative. If his own story be accepted without question, he was descended from great men of the time of Sultan Orkhan and even of the Caliph Harun ar-Rashid.[5] His great-grandfather, Yawuz Ali Usbek, had been Mohammed II's stand-ard-bearer at the conquest of Constantinople.[6] Rewarded with an estate in the city, he built on it one hundred shops, and then by good Ottoman custom bestowed it upon a mosque as an endowment, in such a way that his descendants would always be

---

[4] 1. 1. 110: 'I, the humble writer of these pages . . . was born on the 10th of Moharrem, 1020 [A. H.].' Kara Mustafa is mentioned as grand vizir (1. 1. 156), which position he held from 1676 until his execution after failing to take Vienna, in 1683. If the number 51 be correct for the years of Evliya's active life (1. 1. 174), this would equal about 49 Christian years, and, added to 1631, would bring him to 1680.

[5] 1. 1. 35, 36. Evliya claims descent from Sheikh Ahmed Yesovi of Khorasan, who sent his disciple, the famous Hajji Bektash, to Sultan Orkhan; and from Mohammed Hanifi, whose son Sheikh Jafar Baba was sent as ambassador to Constantinople by Harun.

[6] 1. 2. 48. The burying-ground of Evliya's family was at Kasim Pasha, behind the Arsenal. Here lay his father, his grandfather Timurji Kara Ahmed, his great-grandfather, and many other relatives.

226   *Albert Howe Lybyer*

administrators and entitled to a share of the income.[7]   Evliya's
father, Dervish Mohammed Zilli, had been the great Suleiman's
standard-bearer, and was for an unbelievable number of years
head of the gild of goldsmiths of Constantinople.[8]   This very
numerous organization enjoyed special imperial favor, since
Selim I and Suleiman, following the practice by which every
prince of the Ottoman house must learn a trade, had been
apprenticed as goldsmiths (1. 2. 188).   Evliya's mother had been
a Circassian or, more strictly, an Abaza slave girl.[9]   Her brother
Malik Ahmed rose as slave-page in the palace through various
offices of government, until he became grand vizir of the empire
and was honored with the hand of the Sultan Murad IV's
daughter.[10]   The help and influence of this highly successful
adventurer accomplished much for his nephew, who was less
ambitious and important, but freer and happier.

The comprehensive character of Evliya's book is related to a
remarkable breadth of experience.   The offspring of a freeborn
man of ancient Moslem lineage and a slave woman from the
rough mountains of the Caucasus, he was educated according to
standard Moslem fashion along the road which led to the high
positions in religion and law, but he also had opportunities to
mount a certain distance in the government service, which was
gradually departing from the rule according to which its higher

---

[7] 1. 1. 31. Evliya's book gives many references to the numerous Ottoman
religious endowments; see for example, 2. 91. For a brief discussion of
the subject see my *Government of the Ottoman Empire in the Time of
Suleiman the Magnificent*, p. 200–203.

[8] 1. 1. 39, 141: 'Praise be to Allah, that my father was the chief of the
goldsmiths from the time of Sultan Soleiman to that of Sultan Ibrahim.'
The former died in 1566; the latter ascended the throne in 1640.

[9] 1. 1. 152. Her father, an Abaza, was the *Kiaya* of the *Kapujis* (superintendent of the gatekeepers) of the important man Ozdamir-Oghlu Osman
Pasha. She and her brother Malik Ahmed were sent to the home country
for what was considered a better bringing-up (1. 2. 61), and when the
brother was 15 years of age they were brought back and presented to
Sultan Ahmed, who took the boy into the page-school of the palace and
gave the girl in marriage to Evliya's father.

[10] 1. 1. 118, 152, 162; 1. 2. 13. This lady, whose name was Ismahan Kia,
died in childbirth in 1651, at the age of 27. Malik Ahmed served as
governor in a remarkable number of provincial capitals, including Diarbekir,
Buda-Pest, Cairo, and those of Bosnia and Rumelia, both before and after
his term as grand vizir.

positions were open only to those who had begun life as Christian slaves.[11]   In addition to this, Evliya was trained in his father's profession as a goldsmith, and so had a definite place in the economic organization of the empire (1. 2. 189).   Although he seems never to have been married, he was far from indifferent to the beauty of women, or, indeed, of boys.[12]   He became initiated as a dervish into one of the many mystical religious orders (1. 2. 93 ff.), but he also spent much time in the gay life of a well-to-do young man about town (1. 2. 246; 2. 28).   He passed through all of this as 'a poor, destitute traveler, but a friend of mankind' (1. 1. 2), and, as he himself says, being 'of a vagabond Dervish-like nature' (2. 28), he entered all doors but took up a fixed abode nowhere.

In his formal education he studied seven years in the Madressah of Mufti Hamid Effendi, one of the numerous endowed colleges of Constantinople (1. 2. 37).   Here he heard the general lectures of Akhfash Effendi, and he mentions gratefully the names of three of his teachers, and in particular that of Evliya Mohammed, after whom he was probably named.[13]   'Evliya' means 'saints,' and perhaps it was the accident of his name that led him to become a traveler, eager to visit the tombs of Moslem saints. He describes, however, a picturesque dream in which in the mosque of Akhi Chelebi he saw the Prophet Mohammed and was given a commission to travel through the world and visit the tombs of holy men.[14]   He was then just twenty-one years of age, and desired, he says, 'to escape from the power of my father, mother, and brethren' (1. 1. 1).   His first journey was confined, however, to a thorough and detailed inspection of his native city and its environs[15]; not for ten years did he venture a longer

---

[11] This rule is discussed in my *Government of the Ottoman Empire*, p. 45 ff.   The education for religion and law is described on p. 203 ff.

[12] See his descriptions of the inhabitants of various towns, 2. 128, 144, 149, 196, etc.   For example: 'The beautiful youth of both sexes at Meragha are everywhere renowned.'

[13] 1. 2. 83:   Sheikh Hedayi Mahamud Effendi 'adopted me as his spiritual child'.   In 1. 1. 32, 137 Evliya shows his reverence for the elder Evliya.

[14] 1. 1. 2—4.   Evliya's book mentions the tombs of hundreds of Moslem saints, whose final resting-places he sought out at every opportunity.

[15] The description of this, with much other material intermingled, occupies his first volume (which is also that of the translation, including parts 1 and 2).

228   *Albert Howe Lybyer*

flight for the sole purpose of travel. Meantime he accompanied his father on the military expedition to Tabriz in the year 1635 (1. 1. 129 ff.). His education had not ceased, and its last period, though the picturesque account is open to the suspicion of being overdrawn, was of exceptional character. Small of stature and of youthful appearance, he was possessed of an attractive voice, and had learned to sing, accompanying himself with various musical instruments; and to intone the Moslem call to prayer, read the Koran, and lead prayers in the most approved fashions.[16] In the same year 1635, on the Night of Power, when Santa Sofia was filled with reverent worshipers, and Sultan Murad IV himself was present in his private box, Evliya, by the advice of his father, and very probably with the collusion of his uncle, who then held the high office of sword-bearer, took a place on the seat of the muezzins, and at a suitable time, began to chant the Koran. The impression which he made on the Sultan resulted in a summons to the palace and an adoption into the corps of pages.[17] Though Evliya claims that he told the Sultan he knew seventy-two sciences and was acquainted with 'Persian, Arabic, Romaic, Hebrew, Syriac, Greek, and Turkish' (1. 1. 133), nevertheless he was given a series of text-books and assigned regular lessons (1. 1. 137). He claims to have 'enjoyed the greatest favor' of Murad (1. 1. 138), and certainly he showed through his life a special attachment and loyalty to him. Before the great expedition to Baghdad in 1638, which secured that city to the Turks 'unto this day,' Evliya had been graduated from the palace school, and made a *spāhī* or cavalryman, with a high salary.[18] It would seem, however, that he did not go on that

---

[16] His small size is revealed in 1. 1. 134, 139. He served for 3 years as reader in the mosque of Salim I (1. 2. 6) and frequently afterward as *Muazzīn.*

[17] A sprightly account of his life in the palace is given at 1. 1. 132—142. In previous times he would not have been allowed to remain more than a year, since pages were 'graduated' at twenty-five years of age. Hammer states erroneously that Evliya remained in the palace only a short time and then went on the expedition to Erivan (1. 1. iv). He went to Erivan first (1. 1. 129—131). The Sultan returned to Constantinople on the 19th of Rajab, and Evliya entered the palace in Ramazan, two months later. He remained about three years, it appears.

[18] 1. 1. 141—142: 'Previously to his Majesty's undertaking the expedition to Baghdad, I left the imperial Harem, and was appointed a Sipahi,

campaign, and that for some unstated reason he left the permanent public service before the year 1640.

Evliya's first independent trip for travel was made in the year last mentioned, to Brusa (2. 1 ff.). With this began his series of journeys out from Constantinople and back, by which in the course of half a century he saw most of the lands of the empire, and especially Asia Minor, the shores of the Black Sea, and the Balkan peninsula.[19] Nor did he omit the pilgrimage to Mecca, and he saw Egypt and Syria by the way.[20] He also passed the frontiers and visited northern Persia and Russia,[21] while his longest single journey was one of three and a half years in Western Europe, in the years 1664-1668.[22] It is particularly to be regretted that he left no account of this journey, for his view of the infidel countries written for the edification of the faithful would be both amusing and instructive. Some of his journeys were taken under military orders, as by sea to Crete in 1645[23] and to Dalmatia a little later.[24] Summing up his adventures, he says that in his life he was present at twenty-two battles (1. 2. 57), saw the countries of eighteen monarchs, and heard one hundred forty-seven languages.[25]

Evliya adorns his narrative with some book knowledge, includ-

---

with an allowance of forty aspers per day.' If this figure be correct, Evliya received a salary with which he was expected to bring into service, when needed, three or four cavalrymen besides himself.

[19] The second volume describes in detail his circuit of the Black Sea and his travels in many regions of Asia Minor and the adjacent portions of Persia. The first volume contains brief allusions to his journeys through most parts of European Turkey.

[20] The account of this journey is lost; see below, p. 239.

[21] 1. 1. 164. He traveled 70 days in Russia in the year 1668.

[22] 1. 1. 163. He visited Vienna, Dunkirk, Denmark, Holland, Sweden, and Poland. 'In the year 1668, on the night of the Prophet's ascension, I found myself on the Ottoman frontier, at the castle of Toghan-kechid, on the Dniester. Conducted by my guides, who were Kozaks [Cossacks], I saw lights in the minaret, and, for the first time, after so long an absence, I heard the sound of the Mohammedan call to prayer.'

[23] 2. 74 ff. Evliya is a valuable first-hand authority for the history of this expedition.

[24] 1. 1. 149. Evliya says that he was then in one of the Janissary companies, a statement not easily to be reconciled with his claim to have been in the superior position of *Spāhī* of the Porte seven years earlier.

[25] 1. 1. 174; 1. 2. 99. Evliya attempts, at 1. 1. 11—12, to give the name of Constantinople in 23 different languages. Some of the forms are cor-

230 *Albert Howe Lybyer*

ing allusions to the ancient literature of Arabia, Persia, Islam, and even Judaism and Christianity.[26] Yet from the fact that he went no farther in the religious school system, he does not seem to have possessed an exceptional order of intellectual excellence. It was probably a serious trial to his father that he failed to utilize any of the brilliant opportunities that were before him in business, the army, the government, the law, or the church. He did, however, finance many of his travels by utilizing portions of his training in these various directions.[27] He was evidently quick-witted, well-mannered, shrewd, and resourceful. Though so fond of good company, he insists strenuously and repeatedly that, like his father before him, he never tasted forbidden drinks. 'I, who spent so much time in coffee-houses, *buza*-houses, and wine-houses, can call God to witness, that I never drank anything during all my travels but this sweet *buza* of Constantinople preserved in boxes, that of Egypt made of rice-water, and that of the Crimea, called *makssáma*. Since I was born, I never tasted in my life of fermented beverages or prohibited things, neither tobacco, nor coffee, nor tea, . . . nor wine, . . . nor beer,' and so on to no less than sixty-eight items.[28] Can it be that he 'doth protest too much'? He recognized as prevalent and deplored other Oriental vices, but in this regard he made no affirmation of innocence, and indeed, laid himself distinctly open to suspicion.[29] At the same time, not only is there a religious ingredient in his work from beginning to end,

---

rect, as the German *Konstantinopel*, while others are clearly inaccurate; the 'African' name is said to be *Ghiranduviyyeh*, which seems to be a representation of the French *Grande Ville*.—In this connection may be mentioned the visitors to the Mosque of Suleiman (1. 1. 81), who in the picturesque account of their visit are related to have exclaimed 'Maryah, Maryah'; this may have been *merveilleux,* and if so, the visitors were presumably French.

[26] These allusions, too numérous for citation, are especially frequent in regard to literary, Biblical, and early Moslem personages.

[27] For example, he was *muazzïn* on the admiral's ship for the expedition to Azov in 1641 and for that to Crete in 1645; he went to Erzerum a little later as *muazzïn* of the Pasha and clerk of the custom-house, etc. (2. 59, 77, 78).

[28] 1. 2. 246. Evliya makes positive denial also at 1. 2. 54; 2. 139. The latter forms part of a most interesting description of his entertainment by a Persian governor.

[29] See the allusions at 1. 2. 34, 85; 2. 12; etc. The prostitutes in Constantinople in his time were boys, not women (1. 2. 53, 109).

but piety appears to be no extraneous and superadded feature of his character.[30]

For us of to-day who desire to learn from him about his people and his times, the questions of accuracy, veracity, and critical judgment are of great importance. In all of these respects credit can be given him for good intentions and sustained efforts, but in none can it be affirmed that he is unimpeachable. In general, he has the tendency frequent in Orientals, to substitute an exaggerated estimate for patient laborious calculation, he is not uninfluenced by a desire to exalt his own knowledge and achievement or to give point to a story, and he is credulous as regards such matters as the deeds of saints and the longevity and the adventures of ancient and garrulous campaigners. It is then not to be expected that his book would possess the calm, judicial, meticulously accurate, and designedly uninteresting character of the ideal work of a scientific historian. It is in fact a very human document. He called his city a 'mine of men' (1. 1. 23), and his book is primarily a mine of information about men. After all due criticism has been made, a great deal of illumination is thrown by it upon the social customs, habits of business, modes of thought, and life experiences of the seventeenth-century peoples whom he knew and visited, and particularly upon his fellow-Osmanlis. The persons whom he introduced in profusion, by masses, groups, or individuals, are all alive, active, and dynamic, whether officials high or low, townsmen or villagers, tradesmen or sailors, priests or soldiers. With a different training, Evliya might have become a Balzac or an Arnold Bennett, a Prescott or a Macaulay.

Evliya states that he began to write his travels in his twenty-second year, at the time when he first resolved to become a traveler (1. 1. 5). Nevertheless the work bears evidence that even the first and fullest portion, the elaborate description of Constantinople which occupies nearly two-thirds of the published translation, was composed in the later years of his life, probably in his seventh decade, after his travels had come to an end.[31]

---

[30] Such seems a fair inference, not merely from the frequent formulas and affirmations of a religious character, but also from Evliya's turning to prayer in times of danger and special rejoicing.

[31] References to many years of his experience are scattered through his first volume. See note 4.

232   *Albert Howe Lybyer*

It is likely, however, though positive proof is lacking except in a few instances, that he gathered materials in the form of notes of his own, and fragments and works of others, during all the active years of his life.[32] Unless he possessed an extraordinary memory, the precise statements which he makes presuppose extensive written support, for he has carried out well what he affirms to have been his original commission: 'Thou shalt travel through the whole world, and be a marvel among men. Of the countries through which thou shalt pass, of their castles, strong-holds, wonderful antiquities, products, eatables and drinkables, arts and manufactures, the extent of their provinces, and the length of the days there, draw up a description which shall be a monument worthy of thee' (1. 1. 4).

The historical narratives which are distributed through the book, associated often with the mosques and tombs of Sultans, are, apart from those of his own lifetime, a mixture of truth and error, in such a way as to indicate a combination of oral tradition and written record, modified occasionally by a native untrained criticism. An illustration of his historical offering may be condensed from his story of Constantinople, which he claims to have taken in part from the Ionian history (the 'history of Yanvan') read to him by his Greek friend, Simeon the Goldsmith.[33] King Solomon, who was a Moslem, was the first of nine builders of the city. Alexander the Great, the 'Two-horned,' was the fourth. He it was, furthermore, who cut the channel of the Bosphorus between the Black and the White (or Aegean) Seas (1. 1. 13, 14).[34] Puzantin, King of Hungary, evidently the eponymous

---

[32] He mentions: the historical work Tohfet (Tuhfat), 1. 1. 9; the 'history of Yanvan [Ionia?],' 1. 1. 27; the title deeds to his ancestral lands, 1. 1. 31; the statistical *Kanūn-nāmah* of Suleiman I, 1. 1. 88—105; a description of Constantinople in the time of Murad IV, from which he extracted a summary, 1. 2. 44, 100, 104; the constitutional laws of Sultan Suleiman, 1. 2. 89; the constitutions of the different orders of dervishes, 1. 2. 100; the description of Constantinople by Molla Zekeria Effendi, 1. 2. 102.

[33] 1. 1. 27. Either Simeon or Evliya introduced many things which could not have been found in a Greek history.

[34] 1. 2. 72: 'This is the canal which was cut by Iskender Zulkarnin to unite the Black and the White Seas. The traces of this work are even now to be seen on the rocks.'

Greek founder Byzas, instead of being the first founder was the
fifth. Constantine the Great instead of second was ninth. Evliya
is not quite clear as to the distinction between the first Constantine and the last, for he says that Constantine planted eleven
hundred cannon to defend the city, so that not a bird could fly
across without being struck, a statement which, aside from double
exaggeration, is of course anachronistic even for the thirteenth
Constantine. Having been besieged nine times by the Saracens,
half the city was surrendered to Sultan Bayazid I, and finally
the whole was taken by Mohammed II the Conqueror. At this
point is introduced an interesting and characteristic episode
(1. 1. 37—43). During the siege twenty relief ships came from
France and were captured by the Turks. On one of them was
a daughter of the King of France, who grew up to become the
cherished consort of Mohammed II and the mother of Bayazid
II. Now Evliya very clearly had doubts about this story, but
they were resolved in the following way. As a boy he knew an
aged friend of his father's, named Su-kemerli Koja Mustafa.
'He was,' says Evliya, 'a most faithful man, and one whose
word could be taken with perfect security' (1. 1. 39). Su-kemerli
related that he was himself a nephew of the French princess and
had been five years old at the time of the taking of Constantinople. Evliya quotes him again as having been 'when a youth
of twenty-five years of age, present at the conquest of Cairo by
Sultan Selim I.'[35] But if his former statement could have been
true, he would have been sixty-nine instead of twenty-five years
of age in 1517. Not only does Evliya overlook this discrepancy,
but he finds nothing difficult in the conclusion that in order to
tell these romances to him in about the year 1620, Su-kemerli
must have been about one hundred and seventy years of age!
Evliya can affirm that his own father was present in 1521 at the
capture of Belgrade, and yet lived until 1648![36] Such claims

---

[35] 1. 1. 39. See von Hammer's attempted correction of this, 1. 1. 184,
note 7, where he errs in his calculations by three years and is apparently
not at all surprised at the extraordinary age of Su-kemerli Mustafa.

[36] 1. 1. 39: 'My father . . . was with Sultan Suleiman at the sieges of
Rhodes, Belgrade, and Sigetvar.' Mohammed Zilla died in 1648 (2. 240).
The great architect Sinan is said to have lived to 170 years (1. 1. 171).
See also 1. 1. 46, 60, 152.

234   *Albert Howe Lybyer*

have not often been made since the days of the Biblical patri-
archs. One can imagine the ancient veterans swapping yarns,
which grow with the telling, while the young Evliya, reverently
repressing the tendency to doubt, stores all up in his retentive
memory. But such credulity impairs for us his value as a
historian, at least of times before his own. Still, judging from
his general tone and occasional affirmations, he endeavored to
state the truth as nearly as he could ascertain it. He wishes, he
explains, 'not to incur the tradition of liars, which says: ''A
liar is he who relates everything he hears'' ' (1. 1. 63; 1. 2. 21).

He corrects a historiographer's statement as to the place of
Selim II's death (1. 2. 10), and observes that whereas there is
shown in Santa Sofia the stone trough in which the newly born
Jesus was washed, he saw the real one at Bethlehem (1. 1. 65).
But he hastens to affirm as 'known to all the world,' that 'crooked
and sickly children, . . . when washed in the trough in Ayá
Sófiyah immediately become straight and healthy, as if revived
by the breath of Jesus.' In his travels generally he is scrupulous
in avoiding the attempt to describe what he himself had not
seen.[37] In his historical statements likewise he appears to have
applied such criticism as he was capable of[38] and in general to
have reproduced the standard view of the past as accepted by
the learned Turks of his time.[39] Neither the beliefs set forth
above as to Constantinople's early history nor the tradition about
the French princess is confined to Evliya's work alone.

He was an especial admirer of Sultan Murad IV, to whose
household he belonged for a time. Some of his anecdotes deline-

---

[37] 2. 67. At 1. 2. 132—133 there is a story of a man, a crocodile, and a
fish, which is evidently more than Evliya wishes to accept, though he was
confronted with witnesses; he likens the experience to that of Jonah. At
1. 1. 60—63 is another tale as to which it is well said, 'the proof of it rests
with the relator.'

[38] A curious use of criticism is found at 1. 2. 3, where the tradition that
Bayazid II died and was buried twice is *corrected* by the explanation that
his soul once yielded to the temptation to eat animal food and crept out
of his mouth in the form of a living creature; he prevented its re-entrance
and had it beaten to death; later, by decision of the Mufti, it was given
decent burial.

[39] Evliya was more credulous on the religious side than elsewhere. He
believed almost anything related of a saint; see, for example, 2. 70—72.

ate the peculiar character of this monarch, and reveal the child-like but dangerous impulsiveness that unlimited authority may develop. The Sultan possessed immense strength, even though one can not believe with Evliya that he once hurled a javelin a mile.[40] No wrestler could open his clenched fist. On one occasion Evliya advised him after vigorous exercise and a Turkish bath not to wrestle any more that day. Said the Sultan, 'Have I no strength left? Let us see,' and taking Evliya by the belt, he raised him above his head and swung him about for a long time, until he begged for release. Then the Sultan put him down, and gave him forty-eight pieces of gold for consolation (1. 1. 139). On another day Murad, sitting in the garden of Dolma-Baghcheh, was reading a new satirical work by the poet Nefii Effendi, 'when the lightning struck the ground near him; being terrified, he threw the book into the sea, and then gave orders to Bairam Pasha to strangle the author Nefii Effendi.'[41]

Evliya falls into a few anachronisms, as when he speaks of Prince Jem and Uzun Hasan as having flourished before the fall of Constantinople, instead of some time after (1. 1. 36). This is in spite of the fact that he expressly affirms his accurate knowledge of the dates of Mohammed II's reign, as obtained from the title deeds to his inheritance (1. 1. 31). Another anachronism illustrates also his credulity. At his father's suggestion a building that was believed to be a thousand years old, situated near Santa Sofia, was opened up in order to become the tomb of Sultan Mustafa I. Says Evliya: 'While the windows were being cut in the walls, a tobacco pipe was found among the stones, which smelt even then of smoke; an evident proof of the antiquity of the custom of smoking' (1. 2. 12). It is interesting to notice that Evliya understood the use of a telescope and had probably looked through one (1. 2. 50).

---

[40] 1. 1. 140. Evliya states that Murad, standing in the courtyard of the Old Palace, brought down a crow from the minaret of the Mosque of Bayazid II, one mile distant. He says that the spot where the crow fell was marked by a white marble column inscribed with a chronogram. Possibly the translator, having in mind the principal palace on Seraglio Point, inserted the words 'one mile distant' erroneously. The Eski Sarai of Mohammed III was much nearer than one mile to the mosque of Bayazid II.

[41] 1. 2. 63. See also the incident of the astronomer's well, 1. 2. 60. The pursuit of literature and science was hazardous in the time of Murad IV.

The Orient has seldom been inclined to count exactly and estimate accurately, and in its records enormous exaggerations are possible. Evliya's figures are subject to this tendency, even when quoted from documentary evidence said to have been obtained with great care. He had before him, he says, an enumeration with descriptions of all the buildings of Constantinople, made exactly and completely for Sultan Murad IV in the year 1638 (1. 2. 103). The summary contains the following figures: 'Great mosques of the Vezirs, 1985, small mosques of the wards, 6990, . . . primary schools, 1993, . . . caravansarais, 997, . . . baths, public and private, 14,536, . . . fountains, public and private, 9995.' Now it is clear that in many of these instances, a round number was guessed, ordinarily about ten times too large, as 2000, 7000, 1000, 10,000, and then a slight change was made to make the estimate seem to be the result of counting. Evliya says again that Suleiman's mosque cost 890,883 *yuks,* which von Hammer values at 74,242,500 piasters, equal to about as many dollars, an incredibly large sum.[42]

If Evliya's historical facts and his figures are unreliable, there yet remains much that is of importance and interest. After the description of the mosque of Suleiman is given a statistical survey of the empire in that Sultan's time, which was evidently copied from one or more written documents, with enlivening annotations from other sources (1. 1. 84—109). In this are included lists of great officials of the reign, the provinces and their *sanjaks,* the pay of the high officials, the number of feudal cavalrymen, and the conquests of Suleiman. A yet more extensive description, requiring some 80,000 words in the translation, is that of the procession of the gilds before the Sultan Murad IV (1. 2. 104—250). This is perhaps the outstanding feature of the book. Says Evliya: 'Nowhere else has such a procession been seen or shall be seen,' and he sighs with relief as he concludes: 'By the Lord of all the Prophets, God be praised that I have overcome the task of describing the gilds and corporations of Constantinople' (1. 2. 250). Participated in by two hundred

---

[42] 1. 1. 81. The statement at 2. 65 that the Tartar Khan had 800,000 horsemen is an error of copying or translation, since the number 80,000 is mentioned in the previous sentence; this also is very probably an overestimate. Likewise the statement at 1. 1. 145, that the Turkish fleet in 1695 had 11,700 vessels, is not Evliya's own, for his items add up to 1700.

thousand men, who were grouped into some seven hundred and thirty-five companies, this parade passed before the Alai Kiosk, where the Sultan sat, from dawn through the whole day until sunset. Its description gives an unexampled insight into the inner commercial life of Constantinople three hundred years ago. Evliya names the gilds in order, gives each its patron saint, tells the number of its members, and describes the exhibitions each presents. He also inserts many curious observations, as to the ordinary work of the gild members, related experiences of his own, notes from Moslem history, and occasional humorous remarks, anecdotes, and stories. An example may be taken from the account of the vinegar merchants: 'The number of men are one hundred and fifty. Their patron received the girdle from Ins Ben Malek, but I am ignorant of where his tomb is. . . . The oldest patron of the vinegar merchants is Jemshid, who having planted the vine at the advice of Satan, also made the first vinegar. Jemshid is said to be buried at Ephesus. They adorn their shops with large bottles, and roll along casks, crying, ''Good excellent English vinegar.'' They have old casks of from seventy to eighty years' standing, wherein they put neither raisins nor anything else, but hot water only, which in three days becomes the best vinegar. Such casks cost an hundred piasters: in this manner the vinegar makers as well as the sherbet makers sell each drop of water granted to them by heaven.'[43]

It is clear that Evliya possessed a very definite, if somewhat unpolished sense of humor. Elsewhere he says: 'Seven hours further on is the village of Karajalar, . . . three hundred houses of poor but very obstinate Turks: they will sell the trunk of a tree (for fire-wood) forty times over, putting it in the water every night, so that you may be compelled to lay out ten aspers in brushwood to set it on fire. A traveler marked one of these trunks by fixing a nail in it, and when he returned three years afterwards from the siege of Erivan they gave him the very same trunk.'[44]

---

[43] 1. 2. 150. Among many other examples of humorous or picturesque description of gilds are those of the executioners, 1. 2. 108; the schoolboys, 115; the bakers, 120, 121, 126; the captains of the White Sea, 134—135; the dispute of the butchers and the merchants, 136—138.

[44] 2. 94. At 1. 2. 85 Evliya says: 'So famous are these meadows of Kiathaneh, that, if the leanest horse feed in them ten days, he will resemble in

238   *Albert Howe Lybyer*

Now and then he manifests a naïve and delightful, if not profound philosophy, as for example in his explanation of why there are so many sheep in the world: 'Although a sheep brings forth but one a year, yet are all mountains covered with them. Meanwhile it is a strange thing that dogs and swine have every year many young, so that one would believe that the world must be filled with them, yet God blesses the sheep because it gets up early and breathes the wind of divine mercy. The swine on the contrary turns up the earth with its snout the whole night, and sleeps during the day. The dog likewise barks the whole night, and in the morning with its tail between its feet lies down to sleep. Therefore the young of swine and dogs never reach a long life. This is a wonderful effect of the wisdom of God' (1. 2. 147—148).

Evliya's descriptions of travel are uniformly sprightly and lively. He narrates the experiences of his journeys, and in connection with each place of sojourn tells something of its appearance, size, history, the characteristics of its inhabitants, its fruits and products, gardens, defenses, buildings, its officers, their incomes, and the saints who are buried near.[45] Not infrequently he repeats conversations and addresses, and he never hesitates to speak in the first person, yet always in a natural and inoffensive way. His style is regularly characteristic and individual.

It would be too much to ask of Evliya that he should provide serious and adequate reflections upon the institutions and the probable future of his country, for he is no political or social philosopher. The contemporary English observer Paul Rycaut, who could not equal Evliya in inside knowledge, possessed from the advantage of foreign birth a far superior objectivity of view.[46] By combining the information given by the two with the

---

size and fatness one of the large elephants of Shah Mahmud [of Ghazni].' At the siege of Constantinople there were 40 ships 'filled with some thousand scarlet scull-capped Arabs, burning as brandy, and sharp as hawks' (1. 1. 37). After a battle near the Iron Gates 'the white bodies of the infidels were strewed upon the white snow' (1. 1. 159). Does it reveal humor, credulity, or mere stupidity when he says (1. 1. 56) that the doors of St. Sofia 'are all so bewitched by talismans that if you count them ever so many times, there always appears to be one more than there was before'?

[45] Cf. the description of the town of Kopri, 2. 218.

[46] Sir Paul Rycaut, *The History of the Present State of the Ottoman Empire*, London, 1668.

testimonies of other travelers, as the Frenchmen Du Vignau and Tavernier,[47] it is possible to reconstruct with much vividness, depth, and truth the vanished Ottoman society of the seventeenth century.

The translation, so far as it may be judged without a comparison with the original, is careful and generally accurate. The English used is occasionally a little foreign,[48] but on the whole it is smooth, clear, and lively. The introduction contains a number of errors, due perhaps to von Hammer's reliance upon memory for Evliya's statements about his career.[49] The translation reaches the end of the second of four volumes written by Evliya, at the year 1648 (2. 243). Immediately afterward he went on his pilgrimage to Mecca, on which he passed through Palestine and Egypt. Von Hammer once saw the third volume, containing the travels in Egypt, in the library of Sultan Abdul Hamid I, but could never again find it there or discover another copy anywhere (1. 2. 200, 255 n. 23). Nor could he find any evidence that Evliya had continued the account of his travels beyond the year 1655 (1. 1. xii). Had the Turkish writer carried out his plan to the full and narrated the experiences of his whole life, he might have produced a work unique in interest as well as in magnitude. As it is, one cannot perhaps dissent seriously from the summary opinion of the translator, who says: 'Evliya must be considered as but an indifferent poet and historian. But in the description of the countries he visited he is most faithful, and his work must be allowed to be unequaled by any other hitherto known Oriental travels' (1. 1. xiv). At any rate he deserves to be placed in the group with such famous wanderers as Masudi, Benjamin of Tudela, Ibn Jubair, and Ibn Batutah.

---

[47] J. B. Tavernier, *Nouvelle relation de l'intérieur du Serrail du Grand Seigneur*, Paris, 1681; Sieur Du Vignau, *L'État présent de la puissance Ottomane*, Paris, 1687.

[48] For instance, the use of 'chapel' (*Kapelle*) for 'band', of 'scorch' (*écorcher*) for 'flay', etc.

[49] See notes 17 and 35. Von Hammer says also that Evliya's uncle Malik Ahmed went to Constantinople to be married to a second princess (1. 1. xii), whereas the text states that he went to be present at the marriage of a princess. He says that Evliya traveled 41 years (1. 1. vi), while the text gives the number as 51 (1. 1. 174).

Annemarie Schimmel (1922-2003)

Engin Sezer
Associate Professor, Bilkent University

The world of the academic studies of Islam and Sufism has lost one of its most prolific and able scholars. Annemarie Schimmel passed away on January 27, 2003, at the age of eighty after a life devoted to studying the Islamic world, particularly its mystical dimensions.

Born on April 7, 1922, in Erfurt, Germany, her first encounter with the Orient was through fairy tales. At fifteen she discovered the poetry of Friedrich Rückert (1788-1866), a professor of Oriental languages at Berlin University who was well known for his graceful translations of Arabic and Persian poetry into German as well as for his own lyric poetry in German in the mystical tradition of the Middle East. Schimmel acknowledged a substantial debt to him and later remarked in her autobiography *Morgenland und Abendland: Mein west-östliches Leben* (East and West: My Western and Eastern Life; München: C. H. Beck, 2002) that Rückert's translations, still unsurpassed, took her breath away at first reading and were one of the voices of her youth. Immediately she had a desire to learn an Oriental language, and she was introduced to a teacher of Arabic. With the full support of her family behind her, she started learning her first Oriental language.

In the fall of 1939, upon graduating from high school at seventeen, she enrolled in the University of Berlin, where she began studying Persian and Turkish in addition to Arabic. Her favorite course, however, was Islamic art, given by Ernst Kühnel. She also took Islamic history and geography from Richard Hartmann (1881-1965), author of some eighteen books on the Islamic world in the early twentieth century. He too had visited Turkey, and had published a book in 1922 entitled *Im neuen Anatolien: Reiseeindrücke* (In the New Anatolia: Travel Notes). She broadened her Turkish studies to include comparative Turkic languages and peoples under Annemarie von Gabain (1901-1993), one of the most prominent Turkologists of the twentieth century.

Her initial study of Turkish led to the translation of a novel by Yakup Kadri Karaosmanoğlu (1889-1974) into German. Called *Nur Baba* (The Sheik of Divine Light) in Turkish and *Flamme und Falter* (The Flame and the Butterfly) in Schimmel's German translation, this is a novel about a handsome urban cleric who has some following among people seeking emotional comfort. He is actually an avid womanizer and uses religion as a cover. The heroine is the wife of a Turkish diplomat left behind with her children in Istanbul. Desperately lonely, she seeks help from the Sheik of Light, but soon yields to his charm, only to be relinquished by him soon after, and finally ends up in an asylum. What attracted Schimmel to this novel was, as she later remarked, the conflation of the themes of religion and eroticism. She was curious to see how the two could coexist.

In October 1940, upon first reading Jalāl al-Dīn al-Rūmī's divan in Persian, Schimmel set to translating it into German. She kept much of this rendering unaltered to the end of her career. She later recounted that she had felt as if "struck by lightning" upon that first reading.

In 1941, Schimmel received her first doctorate and continued her studies toward a second doctorate, which she completed in 1945. The same year she joined the University of Marburg, teaching Arabic and Persian and studying under Friedrich Heiler (1892-1967), a well-known historian of comparative religion. This culminated in 1946 in a postdoctoral thesis, a requirement for promotion to associate professorship.

An important chapter in Schimmel's life and career opened in 1954, when she accepted a visiting professorship of the history of world religions at the newly established Divinity School of Ankara University. This position brought her into close contact with Turkish scholars of Islamic studies, Islamic calligraphers, and Islamic art, not to mention the rich archival material there at her disposal. What was most important perhaps was the opportunity to observe the Islamic religious experience of the faithful individually and collectively. A marriage in this period did not last long.

The position at Ankara University ended in 1959, and in 1961 she received a professorship at the University of Bonn, where she taught until 1969. Here she published a semiannual journal of Islamic studies by the name of *Fikrun wa Fann* (Ideas and Knowledge). In 1969 she was appointed to the chair of Indo-Muslim Studies at Harvard University's Department of Near Eastern Languages and Civilizations. Upon her retirement in 1992, she returned to Bonn, where she lived out her last decade. Her autobiography was her last work.

Schimmel was in many ways a typical product of the German academic tradition of the pre-World War II period, which was highly selective of promising minds and rigorous in its expectations of excellence. First of all, scholars were expected to acquire a perfect command of the basic language skills relevant to their fields of study, and academic courses of extraordinary rigor were routinely provided by able scholars. The system was also keen on granting scholars the free time they needed to carry out pure research. Promising and persevering minds were not inconvenienced by demanding teaching assignments or academic chores. A true meritocracy took pains to select the crème de la crème.

Second, neither Europe nor Germany in particular were foreign to Islamic studies, to Sufism, or to the fundamental linguistic training required for pursuing an academic career in these areas. F. A. D. Tholuck's studies on Islamic Sufism in the 1820s proved quite influential in academic circles, and a scholarly tradition of the study of Islamic mysticism became established in the nineteenth century, particularly in England and Germany. Schimmel's own teacher in Marburg, Friedrich Heiler, was a proponent of the phenomenological and comparative methods in the study of religion. He attempted to develop an understanding of the common element of all religions by concentrating on praying. The above-mentioned Friedrich Rückert, a professor of Oriental languages at the University of Berlin between 1841 and 1849, was one whose works initially sparked a fire in young Schimmel for Oriental poetry.

Possibly, though, the biggest influence on Schimmel's work was Evelyn Underhill's (1875-1941) famous book *Mysticism: The Nature and Development of Spiritual Consciousness*, published in 1911. An English poet, a novelist, and a researcher of mysticism, Underhill offered an extensive study of the typology of spiritual thought and practice. Schimmel acknowledged Underhill's work in her *As Through a Veil: Mystical Poetry in Islam* (1982) with unusual acclaim: according to Schimmel, Underhill approached mysticism as "a practical life process" and specifically pointed out its vitalistic, psychological, theological, and magical aspects. Particularly emphasized by Underhill was the symbolism used in the expression of mysticism. Schimmel welcomed Underhill's *Mysticism* as "still outstanding because of her clear and sympathetic understanding and classification of the mystical experience" (2-3).

Schimmel created a new scholarly dimension, an epistemological framework for the study of Islam in general and Sufism in particular. She notes in her *Deciphering the Signs of God: A Phenomenological Approach to Islam* (1994) how, when she was teaching at the Divinity School of Ankara University in the 1950s, she "worked to introduce young Muslim theologians to the techniques of modern critical scholarship and European thought systems to enlarge their horizons" (244-45). This effort precisely sums up Schimmel's specific contribution to understanding the Islamic experience particularly in its mystical form.

Schimmel set out from the basic principle of Sufism expressed in sura 41 "Adoration", verse 53 of the Koran:

> We will show Our signs to them
> in the horizons of the external world
> and within themselves,
> until it becomes clear to them that it's the truth.
> Is your Lord not sufficient? He is a witness over all things.
>
> (Ahmed Ali, *Al-Qur'an* [1993], 411)

A Sufi, following this verse, is constantly in search of the signs of God in the universe, in nature, in his daily mundane life, in folklore and tradition, in himself, and in the religious texts themselves, as signposts in his quest toward his reunion with God. His religious experience and his ultimate mission crucially depend on the proper identification and decipherment of such signs. This also makes Sufism a way of life, as Evelyn Underhill so aptly observed, and the scholar of Sufism has to study the expression of this experience, which comes out in the form of artistic calligraphy, miniatures, tile decorations, textiles, and particularly as mystical poetry. Schimmel believed that while all these forms of expression had their formal differences, they complemented one another into an organic whole that had to be understood and appreciated by the scholar. Her many books were serious attempts to inquire into the diverse aspects of these phenomena, and she did not have much respect for the Western scholars of Islam who did not show the proper understanding or appreciation for this aspect of Sufism.

As the Sufi follows a symbolic universe for signs, his artistic expression also comes in terms of symbols. So a proper understanding of religious expression in its numerous forms requires dealing with symbols, metaphors, word plays, and other artistic means that extend the expressive power of the artistic medium including the language itself. This is where the theoretical significance of the "techniques of modern critical scholarship and European thought systems" come into play. Therefore, according to Schimmel, Islamic scholarship involves unraveling one puzzle after another, and not an encyclopedic description of the general principles of Sufism as one tends to encounter.

Sufism as religious experience is embedded in daily life, something Schimmel was so perceptively aware of. In her *Calligraphy and Islamic Culture*, for example, she describes in detail the trying life of the calligrapher, made to work unrelentingly by the patrons, the poor pay at times, how they would lose their jobs when their eyesights deteriorated, and so on. How the individual survives in this world of mystical experience, and how this information is to be recovered from all sorts of religious and secular texts, was Schimmel's scholarly quest.

Along these lines, she performed extensive research on all aspects of the representation of Islam and Sufism in the Indo-Muslim world. Next to Rūmī, Muhammed Iqbal was her favorite poet with a key to understanding Islamic cultures.

In all of her research, Schimmel's methodology was built on an excellent command of Arabic, Persian, Turkish, and Urdu as well as more or less all Western European languages, which she also spoke fluently; her incredible, in fact sometimes eerie, power of memory; an in-depth knowledge of Western philosophy, literature, and religious scholarship; and lots and lots of common sense. She had this firm conviction that truth was simple rather than complicated, and that it could be, and had to be, expressed that way. She also believed in the expressive power and beauty of everyday language for handling even the most intricate thoughts. To her, the purpose of scholarship was to make subjects ever more transparent, not more opaque, than they already were.

In her studies Schimmel persistently kept away from the political dimension of Islam, which she probably did not consider a part of the positive religious experience. Her reluctance to criticize radical Islam is usually taken to be due to her apologetic attitude towards it. She drew much criticism on this score but did not take time to reply to such critics. In an interview on a Dutch television station in 1995, she was put on the spot by an unseen moderator when her opinion was asked about the book *The Satanic Verses* by Salman Rushdie. She replied that Rushdie offended the sentiments of Muslims. This drew severe criticism from the German novelist Günter Grass and the philosopher Jürgen Habermas, among others. The reason was more likely her abhorrence of politics and all things political, considering that she did not have much to say about Nazi Germany either.

As a person, Schimmel was very friendly and always full of joy. She loved her subject with a childlike enthusiasm and was always ready to engage in interchange on some intellectual topic, always taking the other person very seriously. She never took herself as seriously as she did her work but had a genuine, in fact sometimes self-effacing, humility about her. This is probably why her autobiography is very superficial.

In her retirement party at Harvard University, after colleagues and students had sung her praises, she thanked everyone shyly and said that with all that acclaim she felt like the peacock in Sa'dī's poem. She said, "You praise the beauty and the nice colors of my tail, but what I do is to look down and only see my ugly feet".

James Stewart-Robinson (1928-2003)
John Crofoot

James Stewart-Robinson, Professor Emeritus of Turkish Studies at the University of Michigan-Ann Arbor, was a scholar of Turkish civilization equally comfortable in Ottoman and Modern Turkish. His life was closely wrought with that of twentieth-century Turkey. He was born in 1928 in Edinburgh, Scotland, to a Scottish father and a French mother and was raised in Turkey. French was the language of his childhood home, English was the language of his secondary schooling, and Turkish was the language both of his earliest schooling and his earliest friendships. In 1946, Stewart-Robinson returned to Scotland to complete his military service and pursue his university studies. While he was completing his doctoral dissertation on the Ottoman *tezkire* genre, he moved to the United States where he taught Turkish language and literature until he retired.

Stewart-Robinson returned to Turkey only on rare, brief occasions as an adult; however, the record of his professional career attests to the depth of his personal commitment to Turks, Turkish culture, and Turkish language. His scholarship spans the pre-modern and modern ages, poetry and prose, Ottoman court literature and Turkish folk literature. He obtained his doctorate from the University of Edinburgh in 1959 with a dissertation entitled "Ottoman *Tezkire-i shuara* Literature: Its Development and its Value as Literary Criticism". Parts of this work were published in a series of articles: "The Tezkere Genre in Islam" (*Journal of Near Eastern Studies* XXIII, 1964), "The Ottoman Biographies of Poets" (*Journal of Near Eastern Studies* XXIV, 1965), "Ahdi and his Biographies of Poets" (*Iran and Islam*, 1971), and "The Ottoman Biographies of Poets and Mustafa Mucib" (*Michigan Oriental Studies in Honor of George G. Cameron*, 1976). Later in his career, he turned his interest to Namık Kemal and Yunus Emre.

Stewart-Robinson also wrote and spoke on the legacy of Mustafa Kemal Atatürk. In his reflections on Atatürk and Turkey's transition from empire to republic, Stewart-Robinson drew both on his academic knowledge of Ottoman society and on his own childhood and youth in Ankara and Istanbul. His appreciation of both Ottoman and modern Turkish culture created a unique understanding of Turkey's achievement as a republic. Many are fortunate to have heard his formal and informal discussions of Atatürk's legacy, but it is a tragedy that a full record of Stewart-Robinson's deep knowledge of Turkish history and letters does not occupy more space on library shelves.

Professor Stewart-Robinson, known among his students as "James Bey", favored service over publication. He worked tirelessly to ensure that students at the University of Michigan were able to advance their studies in Turkish language and literature. In addition to training and supervising teaching assistants who taught elementary and intermediate Turkish language, James Bey frequently overloaded his own teaching schedule in order to accommodate students seeking instruction in Ottoman language or modern Turkish literature. In addition to training specialists in Turkish studies, he also introduced hundreds—even thousands—of students to Turkish and other Middle Eastern literatures through survey courses for undergraduates and graduate students alike.

James Bey was a courteous, gentle, and generous guide. He encouraged students to articulate their views, nudging them to refine their arguments and alerting them to mistakes in translation or interpretation. He was also a "team player" and eagerly fulfilled his part in support of collective efforts. On numerous occasions he acted as chair of his department and other administrative units at the university. In addition to his service to the American Research Institute in Turkey, he participated in the efforts of the American Association of Teachers of Turkish to develop new materials for Turkish language instruction in the United States.

One of the things that his students and teaching assistants remember most vividly about James Bey is that he was personable and accessible. He recognized that each individual had interests and obligations that extended beyond academia. He respected these interests and enjoyed learning about them. James Bey was particularly supportive of the Turkish student groups at the University of Michigan and the local Turkish-American cultural association, and he advised several Turkish students in a wide variety of disciplines.

James Stewart-Robinson was also devoted to his wife, Elizabeth, and their three daughters, Milena, Angelique, and Yvette. In addition to the service he rendered to his profession, he took great pleasure in his role as husband and father.

The legacy of Professor Stewart-Robinson includes scholars of various disciplines who are highly regarded in Turkey as well as in the United States. In 2001, a number of his former students in Turkish literature compiled a festschrift in his honor (*Intersections in Turkish Literature: Essays in Honor of James Stewart-Robinson*). The volume was edited by Walter Andrews (University of Washington), and includes essays by Sarah Moment Atiş (University of Wisconsin) and Frances Trix (Wayne State University), as well as Rose-Marie Varga, Jennifer Noyon, and John Crofoot.

TURKISH ABSTRACTS

The Poet and the Patron:
A Sociological Treatise Upon the Patrimonial State and the Arts
Halil İnalcık

Hükümdarın lütfunu ve bunun getirdiği itibarı elde etmeye yönelik bir rekabet mekanizması olarak patronaj, Semerkant'tan Delhi'ye kadar birçok merkezde olduğu gibi Osmanlı payitahtında da önemli rol oynamış, şiir, inşa ve diğer sanat biçimlerinin gelişmesini büyük ölçüde etkilemiştir. Bu makalede, yüksek saray kültürü hakkında bilgi verilerek, şiirlerin yayılma, değerlendirilme ve ödüllendirilme biçimleri tartışılmıştır. Çalışmada daha sonra, patronajın, Fuzûlî'nin yaşamı ve yapıtları üzerindeki etkisi araştırılmış; bu amaçla çeşitli tezkireler ve in'âm defterleri ile bazı Türkçe ve Farsça divanlar incelenmiştir.

The *Seyahatname* of Evliya Çelebi as a Literary Monument
Robert Dankoff

Seyahatname'nin bugüne kadar edebî bir başyapıt olarak incelenmemiş olduğu söylenebilir. Bu çalışmada *Seyahatname*, tür, biçim ve üslûp konularına odaklanılarak incelenecektir. Eserin bir gezi edebiyatı örneği olduğunu söylemek, gerek içeriksel gerek yapısal bakımdan eksik bir tanım olacaktır. En doğru türsel betimlemeyle, *Seyahatname*, "gezi anlatısı ve kişisel anı defteri olarak kurgulanmış Osmanlı coğrafî ansiklopedisi"dir. Evliya, yolculuğu boyunca gördüğü yerleri ve yaşadığı maceraları, birinci tekil kişi anlatımıyla sunduğu bir çerçeve oluşturmuş ve metnin, betimlemelerden oluşan ana yapısını bu çerçevenin içinde kurmuştur. Evliya'nın, aliterasyon, akılda kalıcı cümleler, kelime oyunları ve benzetmelerin çokça yer aldığı, dolayısıyla sapmalar içeren betimlemeleri, aynı zamanda sıcak ve bereketli bir üslup oluşturmuştur. Tüm bu öğelerin kattığı cazibe olmasaydı, açıkçası metin çok sıkıcı olurdu. Evliya'nın edebî yeteneğini, yazarın usta bir düzyazı üslupçusu olduğunu gösteren anlatı bölümleri ortaya koyar; az sayıdaki şiir denemeleri ise, daha zayıf kalır.

Images of the Woman in Turkish Drama as Illustrated by the Plays of Adalet Ağaoğlu
Sevda Şener

Türk tiyatrosunun kadınları ele alış tarzı, karmaşık ve sıklıkla gözardı edilen bir araştırma alanıdır. İlk olarak bir konferans bildirisi biçiminde sunulmuş olan bu makale, bu konuya bir giriş niteliğini taşımaktadır. Makalenin birinci kısmı, genel hatlarıyla tarihsel bir yaklaşım izleyerek, Türk tiyatrosundaki yaygın kadın imgelerini ve bunlardaki gelişim ve değişimleri 1920'li yıllardan başlayarak yirminci yüzyıl boyunca takip etmektedir. Bu imgelerin birçoğunun arketipsel niteliği üzerinde durulurken, aynı zamanda oluşum ve gelişim süreçleri de belli bir toplumsal ve tarihsel bağlama oturtulur. Böylece, "modern yeni zengin orta sınıfın günahkâr kadını" ve "saygıdeğer, bilge yaşlı köylü anne" gibi farklı imgelerin ortaya çıkışı, hem savaşlar ve anayasal değişim gibi Türk toplumunu yeniden şekillendiren önemli olaylarla, hem de Avrupa politik tiyatrosu gibi yeni benimsenen tiyatro akımlarıyla bağlantılandırılır. Makalenin ikinci kısmı, yukarıda sayılan en önemli imgelerden bazılarının izini başarılı Türk oyun yazarı Adalet Ağaoğlu'nun yapıtlarında sürer. Ağaoğlu, oyunlarının çoğunluğunu 1960'lı yıllarda yazdıktan sonra ağırlıklı olarak romana ve kısa öyküye yönelmiştir. Makalenin genel gözlemleri ve bunların Ağaoğlu'nun yapıtlarıyla ilişkilendirilmesi sayesinde ortaya çıkan tablo, Türk tiyatrosundaki kadın portrelerinin, özellikle kadın oyun yazarlarının 1960'lı yıllardan sonra artan katkılarıyla, toplum tarafından koşullandırılmış basmakalıp örneklerden bireysel, karmaşık ve tartışmalı kimliklere doğru geliştiğine işaret etmektedir.

The Travels of Evliya Effendi
Albert Howe Lybyer

İlk olarak 1917'de yayımlanan bu makale, bizi Evliya Çelebi'nin *Seyahatname*'siyle ilgili çalışmaların henüz emekleme çağında olduğu bir döneme geri götürmektedir. Lybyer, yapıtı değerlendirirken Joseph von Hammer tarafından yazılmış iki ciltlik İngilizce versiyondan yararlanır. Lybyer, Evliya Çelebi'nin aile geçmişi, eğitimi ve yaşam tarzıyla ilgili bilgilerden yararlanarak, özet bir yaşamöyküsü sunar. Bunun ardından yazar, *Seyahatname*'yi tarihsel ve istatistiksel doğruluk gibi ölçütlere göre değerlendirir ve "Evliya'nın, tarihsel olgularına ve rakamlarına güvenilemez"se de (236), "çok insancıl bir belge" (231) üretmiş olduğu sonucuna varır. Lybyer'a göre Evliya, "başka bir eğitim" almış olsa, "bir Balzac ya da bir Arnold Bennett, bir Prescott ya da bir Macaulay olabilecek" yetenektedir (231).

Lybyer, bir tarihçi olarak, on yedinci yüzyıl Osmanlı İmparatorluğu hakkında daha kapsamlı bir anlayışa varmak için Evliya'nın yapıtını, Sir Paul Rycaut gibi, Şark hakkında yazmış olan Batılı zamandaşlarıyla bir arada ele almayı önerir. Bu tarz bir karşılaştırmalı yaklaşım, günümüzde yapıtın edebî değerlendirmelerinde de yararlı olabilir. Lybyer, "orijinal metinle karşılaştırma [olanağı] olmaksızın" von Hammer'in yapıtını esas almak zorundaydı. Ancak, farklı *Seyahatname* ciltlerinin edisyon kritikleri nihayet yayımlanmıştır (bu konu için, Robert Dankoff'un bu sayıdaki makalesine de bakınız). Von Hammer'in yapıtı da zamanla saygınlık kazanmış bir klasiğe dönüşmüştür. Dolayısıyla bugün, orijinal ile "çeviri"nin eleştirel bir karşılaştırmasının yapılması ilginç sonuçlar verecektir.

Lybyer'ın yazdığı dönemde, *Seyahatname*'nin en çok dört ciltten oluştuğu tahmin ediliyordu. Lybyer, bu düşüncenin ışığında, "eğer Türk yazar planını tümüyle uygulayıp bütün ömrünün deneyimlerini anlatmış olsaydı, ilginçlik ve büyüklük açısından eşsiz bir yapıt vermiş olabilirdi" varsayımında bulunur. *Seyahatname*'nin on cildinin varlığından haberdar olduğumuz günümüzde, Lybyer'ın varsayımı gerçeğe dönüşmüştür.

"The Travels of Evliya Effendi" (Evliya Efendi'nin Yolculukları), ilk kez *Journal of the American Oriental Society* (Amerikan Şarkiyat Derneği Dergisi)'nin 37. cildinde yayımlanmış ve burada, American Oriental Society'nin izniyle yeniden basılmıştır.

A Multicultural Biography of an Era in *The Other Side of the Mountain*
Yasemin Alptekin

Dağın Öteki Yüzü, Türkiye Cumhuriyeti'nin 20. yüzyıl başından günümüze kadar olan tarihinin, üç kuşak aracılığıyla yeniden canlandırılmasıdır. Şu farkla ki, *Dağın Öteki Yüzü*'nde tarihin canlandırılışı, bir tarih kitabında olacağı gibi kronolojik bir sırayla değil, insanlık durumu ve (aşk-nefret, umut-umutsuzluk, üzüntü-beklenti, tutku-tatminsizlik, başarı-başarısızlık, dinamizm-bitkinlik, mutluluk ve gözyaşı gibi) tüm insani evrensel karşıtlıklar aracılığıyla sunulur. Romanın dekoru, Avrupa ve Balkanları da içeren geniş bir coğrafyayı kuşatır. Romanın bu geniş coğrafyasının da yansıttığı gibi, roman kişilerinin insanlık durumları yerel olmaktan çok evrensel niteliktedir.

Making History, Fiction, and Theory Reconcile:
An "Aesthetic Reading" of *The Other Side of the Mountain*
Dilek Doltaş

Linda Hutcheon, "historiographic metafiction" terimi yoluyla hem modernist okumalara bir eleştiri getirmek, hem de tarih, kurgu ve kuram kavramlarını postmodern bir yaklaşımla birleştirerek bu alanların çevresinde dolaşan anlatıları yorumlamak ister. Ancak Hutcheon yazısında, postmodernizmin temel savı olan, tarih, kurgu ve kuram gibi kavramsal ayrımların kabul edilemezliğini görmezden gelir. Murray Krieger'ın "reading aesthetically" yöntemi ise bize bu tür kavramların çevresinde dolaşan anlatıların kavramsal çelişkilere neden olmadan nasıl yorumlanabileceğini gösterir. Erendiz Atasü'nün *Dağın Öteki Yüzü* adlı anlatısını Krieger'ın yöntemiyle okuyarak bunun nasıl gerçekleştiğini anlayabiliriz.

CONTRIBUTORS

YASEMİN ALPTEKİN, Ph.D., teaches at the Department of English Language Teaching at Yeditepe University in Istanbul, Turkey. Her research interests are ELT teacher training with global perspectives via literature in English, cross-cultural awareness in teaching western literature, and socio-linguistics in translated literary works. She translated *Nine African Stories* by Doris Lessing into Turkish.

ROBERT DANKOFF grew up in Rochester, New York. After graduating from Columbia University (1964) he spent two years in Sinop, Turkey, teaching English. He received his Ph.D. from Harvard University (1971) and has taught at Brandeis University, the University of Arizona, and since 1979 at the University of Chicago, where he is Professor of Turkish. His research has concentrated on linguistic and literary topics relating to Central Asian and Ottoman Turkish texts. He has published several text editions and translations, including: *Wisdom of Royal Glory (Kutadgu Bilig): A Turko-Islamic Mirror for Princes* (1983) and *The Intimate Life of an Ottoman Statesman: Melek Ahmed Pasha (1588-1662)* (1991). His most recent books are *An Ottoman Mentality: The World of Evliya Çelebi* (2004) and *Evliya Çelebi Seyahatnamesi Okuma Sözlüğü* (2004, with Semih Tezcan).

DİLEK DOLTAŞ received her B.A. with honors in English from Smith College in 1967. Her Ph.D. (Hacettepe University, 1971) was in Medieval English Literature. She then concentrated on the fields of English literature, contemporary literary theory, and Turkish literature. She has published various books and articles in these fields. Doltaş taught literary criticism, English, and comparative literature at Hacettepe and Boğaziçi (Bosphorus) Universities. She now teaches part-time at Boğaziçi University and is Dean of the Faculty of Arts and Sciences at Doğuş University, Istanbul.

HALİL İNALCIK, a veteran scholar of Ottoman history, was born in Istanbul in 1916. Between 1942 and 1972, he taught Ottoman and European history at Ankara University's Faculty of Language, History, and Geography. From 1956 to 1972, he offered courses at the same university's Faculty of Political Science in the History of Administrative Organization and the History of Revolution. In the years 1972-1986, he was a professor in the University of Chicago's Department of History. Between 1953 and 1993, he served as a visiting professor in the United States at Columbia, Princeton, Penn, and Harvard. İnalcık is an honorary member of numerous Turkish and foreign institutions, including the American Academy of Arts and Sciences, the British

Academy, the Turkish Academy of Sciences, the Royal Historical Society, and the Royal Asiatic Society. He has received honorary doctorates from seven universities in Turkey and abroad. To date, he has published seventeen books and nearly three hundred scholarly articles.

ALBERT HOWE LYBYER (1876-1949) was an influential scholar and political adviser specializing in the Balkans and the Middle East. After receiving his bachelor's (1896) and master's (1899) degrees from Princeton University, Lybyer was ordained an Evangelist in the Presbyterian Church in 1900. Serving as a mathematics instructor at Robert College in Istanbul from 1900 to 1906, Lybyer went on to receive his Ph.D. from Harvard University in 1909, after which he taught medieval and modern European history at Oberlin College until 1913. In that year, he became Professor of History at the University of Illinois, a post he was to hold until 1944, when he became Professor Emeritus. His regional expertise was called upon by his country in the years 1918 and 1919, when Lybyer served as a member of both the Inquiry into Peace Terms and the American Comission to Negotiate Peace, and as a technical adviser to the Interallied Commission on Mandates in Turkey.

Lybyer's scholarly publications include *The Government of the Ottoman Empire in the Time of Suleiman the Magnificent* (1913) and *The Influence of the Rise of the Ottoman Turks Upon the Routes of Oriental Trade* (1916). From 1923 to 1930, Lybyer served as associate editor of *Current History*, where he wrote a monthly article on the Near East. His unpublished papers, preserved at the University of Illinois, contain items of particular interest such as his correspondence with Halide Edib-Adıvar (1884-1964), a major novelist of the Turkish Republic.

SEVDA ŞENER was born in Istanbul on April 25, 1928, and attended primary school in various towns of Anatolia. In Ankara, she continued on to TED High School and in 1950 graduated from the English Department of Ankara University's Faculty of Letters (Dil ve Tarih-Coğrafya Fakültesi). Her academic career began in 1958 at Ankara University's nascent Drama Department, which opened the very same year. After additional coursework in drama at both Bristol University and the University of Vienna, Şener received her doctorate in 1962 and Ph.D. in 1972. She served as Head of the Drama Department for several years until her retirement in 1995. She has been a member of ITI (the International Theater Institute) of Turkish Center as well as of ACIT (the International Association of Theater Critics) of Turkish Center. She has also been the recipient of several prizes, including the International Adelaide Ristori Prize and the National Muhsin Ertuğrul Prize.

Her publications include: *Musahipzade Celâl ve Tiyatrosu* (Musahipzade Celâl and His Theater; 1963); *Çağdaş Türk Tiyatrosunda Ahlak, Ekonomi, Kültür Sorunları* (Ethical, Economic, Cultural Themes in Contemporary Turkish Drama; 1971); *Çağdaş Türk Tiyatrosunda İnsan* (Human Character in Contemporary Turkish Drama; 1972); *Dünden Bugüne Tiyatro Düşüncesi* (Theory of Drama from the Beginning to the Present Day; 1982); *Oyundan Düşünceye* (From Play to Thought; 1993); *Yaşamın Kırılma Noktasında Dram Sanatı* (The Art of Drama, at the Breaking Point of Life; 1997); *Cumhuriyetin 75. Yılında Türk Tiyatrosu* (Turkish Theater on the 75th Anniversary of Turkish Republic; 1999); *Nâzım Hikmet'in Oyun Yazarlığı* (Nâzım Hikmet as Playwright; 2002); *İnsanı Geçitlerde Sınayan Sanat, Dram Sanatı* (The Art of Drama, at the Crossroads of Life; 2003); *Gelişim Sürecinde Türk Tiyatrosu* (Turkish Theater During the Period of Evolution; 2003).

SUBSCRIPTIONS

The *Journal of Turkish Literature* (JTL) is marketed as a book, price per copy: USD 25.
Please send remittances to:

> Syracuse University Press
> 1600 Jamesville Avenue
> Syracuse, NY 13244-5160
> United States of America.

Alternatively, for purchases within Turkey, remittances are accepted at:

> Account 940000-3
> Yapı Kredi Bankası
> Bilkent Şubesi
> 06800 Bilkent, Ankara.

Postage is included for mailings to addresses in Turkey.

The first issue of JTL is also available from the same sources for USD 25, postage free.

ERRATUM

In *JTL*'s issue number 1 (p. 146), the obituary of Andreas Tietze erroneously stated that "he was appointed Professor of Turkish at the University of California at Berkeley". Andreas Tietze was appointed to the post at the University of California at Los Angeles.

INFORMATION FOR AUTHORS

SUBMISSIONS

JTL invites articles on any aspect or period of Turkish literature, mainly on Seljuk, Ottoman, and modern literature, as well as Central Asian literature.

All submissions must conform to the "Style Guidelines" on pages 158-60 of the first issue of *JTL* (2004) and will be subject to review by international peer referees through a blind review process.

JTL welcomes English-language submissions in any form (electronic, typewritten, legibly handwritten). Please direct electronic submissions to *jtl@bilkent.edu.tr* in a format compatible with Microsoft® Word. All other submissions should be mailed to:

> Journal of Turkish Literature
> Bilkent University Center for Turkish Literature
> Faculty of Humanities and Letters
> 06800 Bilkent, Ankara, Turkey.

Along with each article, submit a 250-word abstract as well as a 150-word autobiographical note providing background about you as the article's author.

For book review submissions, although abstracts and autobiographical notes are not necessary, be sure to provide your institutional affiliation (if applicable) and professional title. Also, please consult the editors in advance about the book or books you would like to review for *JTL*.

ACCURACY

Although the *JTL* staff makes every effort to ensure the accuracy of *JTL* content, ultimate responsibility for accuracy lies solely with authors. In particular, this burden includes, but is not limited to, the faithful quotation and meticulous citation of published sources. The act of submission for publication in *JTL* implies complete understanding, and constitutes tacit acceptance, of this burden of responsibility for accuracy of content.